MANAGING
NEW PRODUCTS

Thomas D. Kuczmarski ——————

MANAGING
—————— # NEW PRODUCTS
Competing
Through Excellence

PRENTICE HALL, *Englewood Cliffs, New Jersey*

Library of Congress Cataloging-in-Publication Data

KUCZMARSKI, THOMAS D.
    Managing new products / Thomas D. Kuczmarski.
        p.   cm.
    Includes index.
    ISBN 0-13-550716-2
    1. New products. 2. Product management. 3. Marketing.
    I. Title.
    HF5415.153.K83   1988
    658.5'75—dc19

Editorial/production supervision
    and interior design: Sonia Meyer
Cover design: Ben Santora
Manufacturing buyer: Barbara Kelly Kittle

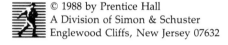 © 1988 by Prentice Hall
A Division of Simon & Schuster
Englewood Cliffs, New Jersey 07632

Printed in the United States of America
10 9 8 7 6 5 4 3

ISBN   0-13-550716-2   01

Prentice-Hall International (UK) Limited, *London*
Prentice-Hall of Australia Pty. Limited, *Sydney*
Prentice-Hall Canada, Inc., *Toronto*
Prentice-Hall Hispanoamericana, S.A., *Mexico*
Prentice-Hall of India Private Limited, *New Delhi*
Prentice-Hall of Japan, Inc., *Tokyo*
Simon & Schuster Asia Pte. Ltd., *Singapore*
Editora Prentice-Hall do Brasil, Ltda., *Rio de Janeiro*

To Susan Smith Kuczmarski,
Educator, Innovator, and Partner,
and to my parents, Mildred and Alex Kuczmarski

CONTENTS

Part II
Igniting New Product
Champions _____

PREFACE

Twelve years ago, when I was a new areas brand manager at the Quaker Oats Company, I searched for guidelines on what it took to be successful at developing new products. While a few text-books outlined a development process, I could not find anything that really described HOW to increase the success rate of internally developed new products. Most of the literature talked about statistical models and quantitative tests that were aimed at reducing the risks of commercialization. Simulated market tests seemed to be "in" as research firms conveyed an ability to predict first-year sales for a new product with a high degree of accuracy.

These financially oriented and process-driven approaches for managing a new product program left me cold. What were the real success factors that separated the winners from the losers? During my five years at Booz·Allen & Hamilton, I began to address this issue. I worked with several companies to assist them in improving their success rates in new products. I also directed the firm's study on best practices in new product management. As part of that study, I conducted personal interviews at over one hundred companies to discern the underlying factors that drove new product performance. The study surveyed the new product management practices of over seven hundred companies that introduced thirteen thousand new products during a five-year period. The study represented the largest data base ever established on how companies manage new products. The Booz·Allen publication *New Products Management for the 1980s* received widespread interest and publicity. More than ten thousand requests poured in for copies of this publication. Why? Because the study uncovered key qualitative factors that are instrumental to new product success.

During the past four years, Kuczmarski & Associates, a management consulting firm specializing in new product management and marketing strategy, has afforded me the opportunity to understand, in further depth, the success formula for new product management. The majority of our clients have had successful results in new products within a relatively short period of time. However, much of my thinking since I was at Booz·Allen has changed. Managing my own business—a new product in and of itself—offers a perspective on the subject that a large corporation could never provide. Profound similarities exist between successful entrepreneurship and successful new product management in large corporations. Infusing entrepreneurship into a corporation's new product culture is one essential ingredient for success.

I have written several articles on the subject of managing new products and have learned a great deal from students and faculty in teaching International Marketing, Distribution Channel Management, and Marketing Policy at Northwestern University's Kellogg Graduate School of Management. I have had many requests from business executives as well as business school professors to compile the writings and consulting experiences into a book. The basis for this book therefore stems from my experience in working directly with over two hundred companies on ways to improve innovation and new products management. I have identified the factors that influence new product success by observing the common patterns and threads that cut across companies most successful at commercializing new products. While manufacturers such as 3M, Apple Computer, and Kellogg may be representative examples of successful new product companies, *no* company is always successful with every new product. Part of the success formula is an acceptance that at least one-third of all new products launched are doomed to fail. However, similar characteristics do emerge across companies that have had consistently strong results in new products. These success patterns are presented in this book.

In short, with the assistance of many dedicated and insightful new product practitioners, *Managing New Products: Competing Through Excellence* will, we hope, assist managers in building innovation into their new product programs and breathe entrepreneurship back into the corporate bureaucracy.

The reader will not find this book to be light, casual reading. The elements for successful new product management are complex, intertwined, and closely interrelated. Therefore, I have broken down this continuous and iterative process into several segments. Understanding each component of the management process will require careful study.

I would like to thank the many business executives and academicians who have offered their insights on successful new product practices. The most important person, however, has been Dr. Susan Smith Kuczmarski, who consistently provided guidance, encouragement, and insight. Two associates of my consulting firm, Anne Gray and Dorothy Aloma, provided editing assistance that was integral to the completion of the manuscript. Richard Koff and Mel Ingalls were invaluable in the development of the software program, The New Products Diagnostic Audit. Martha Donovan, Michael Cappy, and Ingrid Verhulst deserve special thanks for their continued support.

In addition, several partners and associates at Booz·Allen & Hamilton provided me the opportunity to understand new product management better. Since 1955, Booz·Allen & Hamilton Inc. has conducted five major studies on the management of new products. That research has resulted in several often cited concepts, including the product life cycle, the six-step product and development process and the new product idea "mortality curve." I am grateful to Booz·Allen for allowing me to refer to their pioneering work in the field of new product management throughout the book.

I would like also to thank the members of my advisory board, who have demonstrated their continued support and assistance. Finally, I would like to thank Lynn Bace, Group Director of marketing, KFC Corporation, and John Dixon, vice-president of technology, Pillsbury Co., both of whom provided substantive and constructive reviews of an early draft of the manuscript.

I wish to also thank the Prentice Hall staff for their contributions and cooperation. In particular, Whitney Blake, Sonia Meyer, and Shirley Stone, have been most helpful throughout the process.

FOREWORD

In today's intensely competitive business climate, new products are not just desirable for a company. They are mandatory. All companies face this reality, whether they are in consumer products, heavy manufacturing, or services. Successful new products constitute the lifeblood of industry. Sooner or later, almost every manager will have to be involved in the process of identifying innovative concepts, making them work, and bringing them to market.

Unfortunately, very few of us have the opportunity to study how this process should be managed to maximize the chances for success until we are forced to learn by trial and error. *Managing New Products* can save managers a lot of trouble. It is a primer in the new product management process.

A primer is exactly what is needed because success with new products requires a very disciplined approach. To paraphrase Thomas Edison, successful new products are the result of one percent inspiration and ninety-nine percent perspiration. Successful new products do not result from a brain storm of ideas by gurus. Rather they require the disciplined orchestration of an entire business organization and the development of a detailed marketing strategy.

What I consider the basic principles for new product success do not constitute a magic formula. There is no mystery about them. But, while they may be easy to understand, they are difficult to execute successfully.

First, you need effective market research to supply the best understanding of changing consumer needs. Following that, market research must identify new product opportunities on which you can capitalize. You minimize the chances for success if you fail to do effective market research. Effective market research does not necessarily mean the most sophisticated research. When I meet with the head of our market research department, I am much more interested in the new growth opportunities his department has uncovered than I am in new research techniques.

Next, there must be innovative product development addressing the needs and opportunities identified by market research. I emphasize innovation. To be successful, new products must have a clear, significant, point of difference—a true reason for being—that is related to a need in the marketplace. A product with no significant distinction from others in a category will probably not prove successful.

But even the most effective market research and product development efforts will be seriously undercut, in today's highly competitive environment, without the formulation and implementation of the most aggressive marketing strategy, directed to the right consumer audience, with the right messages. To execute this step well, you have to be committed to supporting new product introductions with a major marketing investment, both in quantity and quality.

Such investment is only worthwhile if your efforts in research, development, and marketing prove financially successful. That may seem an obvious point, but we have all been in situations where financial success was assumed to go hand-in-hand with the name recognition produced by an aggressive marketing strategy. Buying market share for its own sake can often fail to deliver the necessary financial success. Another accepted philosophy is that of "building a business," a philosophy by which you could miss your financial targets year after year with promises of steady returns somewhere in the distant future.

In today's American business environment, however, one can only invest for a relatively short period of time in products that do not translate into improved value for your stockholders. In short, you cannot have marketing success without financial success. You may get marketing achievement without financial success but that is a very different and lesser type of accomplishment. A product manager who does not recognize the difference between the two will face serious problems.

Effective execution of these basic principles requires commitment to creativity and innovation. A common pitfall in the consumer products industry is institutionalized competence. While our marketing-oriented society has created a high degree of sophistication and competence, it has also created a high degree of sameness in marketing methods. As a result, innovation suffers. By innovation, I do not mean the generation of one breakthrough idea. Rather I mean a frame of mind that seeks new ways of doing things in all the areas that lead to success in the marketplace. It is a bias that continually seeks and evaluates alternative solutions and their consequences.

Innovation naturally implies risk. A manager unwilling to experiment and take risks cannot innovate. If you decide not to take risks, then you are, in fact, taking the biggest risk of all: doing nothing. It is not enough to do what predecessors did, even if that track record was excellent. Managers must also be generating new ideas for future growth.

Of course, taking risks means failing once in a while. But you cannot fear failure. Recognize that you cannot have innovation unless you are willing to tolerate a certain degree of failure. The analogy I like to draw is with skiing. If you are not falling down, then you are not learning how to ski. Clearly, your net input as a manager must be positive but, realizing that failure is part of the new product process, learn to spot shortcomings quickly and make recommendations for change. That is not always easy to do because new projects tend to gather a series of advocates at each step of the process. But an effective marketing manager will develop this insight and flexibility.

Managing new products successfully requires planning, discipline, innovation, risk taking, and plain hard work. Achievement will not come from mere inspiration. I am grateful to Tom Kuczmarski for providing us with this detailed guide to all that the process entails.

William D. Smithburg
Chairman and Chief Executive Officer
The Quaker Oats Company

It is a rare company that can escape the impact of today's rapidly shifting markets and expanding technology. Existing products can be expected in the course of time, either to be preempted by new and improved products or to degenerate into profitless price competition. Only through continually bringing forth new products can most manufacturing companies sustain their long-run growth and profitability.

1

INTRODUCTION

CORPORATIONS NEED INNOVATION

New product development takes guts. It can be a risky business. It calls for having the gumption to stand behind something unknown, untested, and unproven. It takes commitment to believe in a product concept that management is neutral about. Success requires tenacious follow-through, risk taking, and perseverance.

U.S. corporations need to change their approach to managing growth. They need to see the role that innovation and new products can play in improving the future earnings stream and resultant return on equity of the corporation. Acquisitions alone will not guarantee the returns required by shareholders. Licensing agreements with foreign competitors will only forestall the creeping encroachment. Gradual market-share advances from existing product lines will not provide the revenues and profits needed to survive in our increasingly competitive and shareholder-sensitive marketplace.

Innovative new products can represent the lifeblood of corporate growth. New products have the power to propel a corporation with a mediocre performance record into a high-growth star. New products have the power to turn a team of managers into a motivated, committed, and dedicated corporate resource. New products carry the power to catapult a small division into the big leagues. New products also have the power to change the perception of the financial community and positively affect stock price.

U.S. corporations face a major challenge—how to breathe entrepreneurship and innovation back into the mindset of the risk-averse manager, introduce truly innovative new products, and expand into new markets. More time-efficient, cost-effective, and people-motivating ways to launch new products must be established. During recent years, management attention has focused on margin maintenance, cost containment, and the perceived cure-all—head-count reduction. Capital restraints, decreases in R&D spending, and management ineffectiveness have limited new product introductions and business diversification. Only by reversing this trend and bringing forth new products can U.S. companies achieve a sustainable competitive edge.

Corporations must consider growth through internally developed new products a critical component of their business strategy. New products can play a dramatic and instrumental role in shaping a company's future performance and increasing shareholder wealth. If properly managed, new products offer spurts of growth that cannot usually be matched by existing products.

Innovation is the functional skill that's required to get a successful new product program under way. Innovation is a skill that can be taught, learned, and assimilated. It is not a mysterious process, rather a disciplined technique requiring trained managers who are confident in their ability to manage innovation. Just as the manufacturing department makes products, and the sales department sells products, the "innovation department" develops new products. Yet the term *innovation* continues to get squeamish reactions and misinterpreted responses by corporate top management.

It is difficult to understand why so much confusion surrounds the term *innovation*. The definition of *innovation* is "that which is newly introduced; a change." A company that introduces something new is offering innovation. Granted, the development of this skill is not accomplished overnight. Innovation and change require time, patience, and long-term commitment. The tangible results of innovation may be invisible for several months or even years. The threads of innovation may require years of sewing before the king's quilt is complete. Yet at the same time, innovation should not be perceived as something attainable only by the anointed few. If a company wants to begin or introduce something new, it can. It must ensure that a new product blueprint exists that describes the path to take. Also, top management must be committed to providing the funds, talent, and culture needed to nurture innovation and entrepreneurially oriented product champions. The formula is not all that complex; the results can be managed in the same way that any functional department plans for and manages its activities and performance.

A more elaborate way to define innovation is "invention plus application." This suggests that innovation is not just a new idea but a way of transforming a new idea into a commercialized product. Furthermore, innovation is not a creative brainstorming activity where folks jump up from the conference table shouting, "I've got it." Although new ideas can surface from that approach, the method is too haphazard and unreliable and therefore too costly for corporations to take it seriously—nor should they. Instead, companies must look upon innovation as a multidisciplinary and focused management process.

Top management often equates new products with high risk. Of course new products are risky. If one begins or introduces something new, there is bound to be a degree of uncertainty in its outcome and acceptance by consumers. But the relative degree of risk can be managed and balanced. Scarred by past failures, management is often inclined to run scared and drop the new product ball when the team has hardly had time to practice. The team is just learning the ground rules, and the coach calls the game. New products often do absorb corporate funds and management time that result in no clear-cut product winners. Top management begins to ask, "What's the return that we can expect from this new product investment? Why should we continue to funnel dollars into this high-risk, bottomless pit?" So it is understandable that corporations are often reluctant to dedicate an adequate portion of their scarce financial and human resources to new products. Consequently, managers seem more and more inclined to focus on "me-too" products rather than taking the risks to develop truly innovative ones. While hundreds of reasons exist, some of the more common ones that have impeded risk taking include:

□ No road map to frame new product concept development
□ Inadequate funding behind new products
□ Management focusing on *projects* rather than setting up a new product strategy and process
□ Rigid management structures and policies
□ Reward and incentive systems geared to quarterly earnings and near-term profitability rather than new product performance
□ Risk-averse settings where failure in new products is unaccepted and entrepreneurial product champions are not recognized or encouraged

In addition, adequate homework and research early on in the process are usually woefully lacking in many companies. They don't see the value of investing the time up front; impatience reigns, and failures result. Thus, management, with its eye ever on short-term profits, has cut off its nose to spite its face. Not only do cuts in today's R&D spending mean difficulties down the road and perhaps the withering of a great idea already cooking in the lab, the short-sightedness has discouraged the bright thinkers from staying—or entering—big business. On the other hand, several successful companies understand how to manage the new product process in a way that minimizes the risk, maximizes the results, and increases the shareholder value of the corporation. How do they do it? Why are they willing to take the risk? They do it and are willing to take the risk because they see the power that can be generated from new products if the process is managed in a systematic and disciplined way—with a blueprint in place to guide entrepreneurial product champions.

New products will continue to be difficult, trying, and yet, essential. The key to successful new product development is understanding what drives innovation—how it works, what it takes, and how to motivate managers to be creative, analytical, and committed. The ingredients for success rest upon top management support, a new product strategy, and product champions.

But top management in large U.S. corporations still tends to veer away from this perceived risky business—new product development. Frequently, the need for innovation is not readily apparent to top executives. After a couple of failures, they have the rationale that they've been looking for from the beginning—to cut the new product budget and pursue acquisitions. Moreover, they further rationalize that keeping the ship afloat today is more important than sailing to parts unknown tomorrow. Firefighting will always be part of business management—the key is to strike a balance between managing today's business and tomorrow's new products. However, the power of new products *is* understood by many successful companies. So the obvious question emerges, How can corporations exploit the positive power of new products while limiting the degree of risk and potential loss? The answer: by having the guts to take the risks and demonstrate the commitment to provide the resources—the rest can be learned.

ACQUISITIONS ARE RISKY, TOO

During the late 1960s and early 1970s and then again in the first half of the 1980s, many corporations opted for heavy doses of acquisitions as their route to growth. Management across many industries has perceived acquisitive growth as a safer and lower-risk approach than developing new products internally. "You know what you are getting for your dollars when you buy an ongoing business. When you channel funds into new products, who knows what will come out?" states the president of a three-billion-dollar food company. But in fact, acquisitions offer no less risk than new products.

Why didn't the Dart & Kraft merger work? Why did they decide to split back up into two companies? How is it possible that Beatrice's acquisition strategy didn't work after having bought so many companies? The list of acquisition failures is endless. Yet for some strange reason, the majority of top managers in this country are naively enamoured with acquisition as the best route to growth. It is an immediate gratification. Perhaps acquisitions act as a pacifier for some corporate leaders. Yet while buying up other companies may offer an instant power excursion and ego trip, in the long run acquisitions carry a different kind of risk from internally developed new products, although the risk is on a similar level.

Short of a change in government policy or attitude toward acquisitions, major corporations will continue to seek out the "hot" growth companies. They will be forced to buy other companies for growth if they don't give innovation a shot. As corporations grow older and larger, they tend to gain weight, become sluggish, and show signs of arthritis in their decisionmaking. They prefer to stick to products they are comfortable with and concentrate on "yeah, buts" rather than "what ifs." Unless companies are willing to commit to developing new products internally, no major growth options exist other than acquisition or joint venture.

As small entrepreneurial businesses continue to sprout, large corporations will have a future source of supply for acquisitions. However, at some point, it will be recognized that in order to maintain the entrepreneurship in these companies and their corresponding success, the acquiring company must yield to innovation. Placing an entrepreneurial, fast-growing company into the shroud of corporate bureaucracy is usually a sure-fire way of stifling the growth patterns previously enjoyed. Moreover, the acquisition price for small companies will likely increase as entrepreneurs come to understand that they have something that many corporations are unlikely to achieve internally.

Acquisitions have proven repeatedly to have no built-in success formula. Companies take risks and win and lose at acquisitions and new products. Acquisition is not the be-all-and-end-all solution to growth and diversification. Yet acquisitions are indeed viable growth alternatives. However, a corporation's long-range strategy must factor in a role for new products internally if the company really wants to be a growth leader in the 1990s.

THE NEW COMPETITOR—THE LITTLE GUY NEXT DOOR

Without dramatic attitudinal and fundamental structural change, U.S. corporations will eventually succumb to, or continue to "suck up," the impressive growth of small entrepreneurial companies. While acquiring high-potential start-ups may provide legitimate sources for growth, the ability to launch new products that are internally developed will provide more control over a corporation's desired growth. Internal new product development enables a company to be in the driver's seat—setting the direction offensively for growth that a company wants to take. With acquisitions, one has to choose from available candidates, which may or may not fit the company. Some companies wait for years before the right acquisition candidate comes along.

The often-spoken-of competitors in the late 1970s and the early 1980s were the Japanese and other *foreign* manufacturers. The unrecognized competitor of the late 1980s and early 1990s will be *domestic* competition—the uprising competitive forces represented by small U.S. businesses. Many large corporations are going to find themselves sitting on their fat duffs and losing their competitive edge and market-share position before they can pick themselves back up again. "No way," shouts the naysayer. "Large corporations have the financial power, asset power, and people power to tower above and compete effectively against small upstarts." If that were true, then how did Apple Computer, Dove-Bars, California Coolers, and Edward Lowe Industries end up competing effectively and superiorly to the omnipotent giants of IBM, Sara Lee, Seagram's, and Clorox? Answer: guts, commitment, and a relentless entrepreneurial drive to succeed.

While examples abound of big corporations that have demonstrated a successful track record in developing new products, most need to examine some of the exemplary approaches, styles, and directions taken by small companies. Corporations need to rebuild the entrepreneurial pilings that often become splintered and decayed over time. Corporate hierarchical management layers and a flurry of memos will not cure the problem. If the "model" for U.S. companies to follow in the recent past was Japanese companies, the "model" to follow today is the small company down the street from the sprawling corporate office.

Companies complain about loss of market share, yet they seem reluctant to compete head to head by developing truly new products that will provide a sustainable competitive edge. Rather, they often choose "safe" approaches: increase trade deals and advertising support, drop the price, and expand the distribution channels. How long does it take for competition to respond to or duplicate these types of moves? Not long. And worse, what they do in the short term is often counterproductive in the long term. It's not as though the Japanese have a secret formula for innovation or technological invention. They have merely enjoyed the same kind of phenomenal growth that the U.S. experienced at the beginning of our industrial age. In the few years surrounding the turn of the last century, the U.S. produced a remarkable number of inventions, ranging from the light bulb and automobile to the telephone and radio—innovations that totally changed people's lives.

While the small entrepreneurial company today might be compared to emerging companies during the late 1800s, the environment in many large corporations today might be compared to the feudal system in the 1600s. Back then, the feudal lords kept the serfs satisfied with all of the physical necessities of life—clothing, food, shelter, and work. For the most part, a serf was compensated for the work completed, life was reasonably comfortable and secure, and he was protected from the risks of those cast out to fend for themselves—away from the security of the feudal system. However, the serfs began to leave the feudal grounds, depart for the towns, become apprentices, learn a trade, and establish their own businesses as tradesmen. Some similar patterns exist today. The corporate "lifer" appears to be dwindling away. Enduring loyalty to one corporation is no longer a common phenomenon; in fact, today it's a rarity. New graduates from business schools are viewing small companies with the same esteem as large corporations. A few are even leaving business school to start their own companies.

Within many corporations, management blindly believes that employees are content with the food, clothing, and shelter that their weekly or monthly paycheck provides. Wrong. Many of the "corporate serfs" of today are leaving the feudal offices and starting their own entrepreneurial businesses. One challenge of corporate management, then, is to provide a new and motivating environment that will curtail the exodus of apprenticing entrepreneurs. This book will present approaches that successful companies have used to capture the talent and rekindle the mindset of these entrepreneurial innovators. By keeping a talent bank of motivated product champions, companies can innovate within the confines of their existing corporate fences. In order to make successful new products happen, U.S. corporations have to be willing to take more risks and treat managers as entrepreneurs.

WHY READ THIS BOOK?

This book is intended for top management and new product managers. Regardless of the size of the organization, these two players represent the nucleus of any new product development program. One cannot succeed without the support of the other. Therefore, this book is directed at two levels of management within a company: top management, who have the power to make change occur, and the managers who are involved in and responsible for new product development results. Both levels of management need to be on board. A dedicated team of new product managers cannot be successful without top management's commitment and support, nor can top management execute a successful new product program without a dedicated and talented team of new product people. The two work hand in hand with each other.

Thus, this book is aimed at identifying for top management the critical factors that shape a successful new product development program. For new product managers, this manuscript is intended to serve as a handbook that describes how to develop new products successfully. A new product blueprint, a strategy, and a development process are the basic tools needed to set the stage for innovation. The new product blueprint outlines the direction to take; the new product strategy is the cornerstone for a successful process since it identifies the game plan for knowing how to get there; and the development process represents the road map, which is followed by a multidisciplinary mix of product champions and functional managers. This book describes how to blend creativity with analytics to identify new product concepts. The approaches suggested in the book will breathe creativity and spark more innovation into many of the bureaucratic corridors of U.S. corporations.

If you see no growth role for new products in your own company, then you need to read this book even more carefully than the company that recognizes new products as a key source of future growth. For while acquisitions can be a very appropriate growth mode to augment new products, companies that tend to focus all of their growth funds and management talent on acquisitions are usually poor new product developers. So you can either continue to buy companies, wait for the potential of existing product lines to materialize, hope internal management will discover some new growth finds, or make some major changes in the way your company manages innovation and new product development.

If you should decide that your corporation's best interests lie in launching new products, this book will provide a framework in which to focus new product activities. Within this framework, we present an effective step-by-step process—a process that begins with a diagnostic self-assessment and a new product strategy. In addition, the book will make suggestions about the atmosphere and attributes that are most likely to aid a corporation in its quest for successful new products.

Innovation will fuel the future strength of the U.S. economy. It is tantamount to corporate survival. Those corporations that do not innovate between now and the turn of the century may not survive. The decline of our country's global competitive advantage has been labeled the most important consequence of the decline in technological innovation. If you're not socially inclined—if you feel that the economy of the U.S. is too big an entity to be affected by your actions—then turn to the health and well-being of your own corporation. Study upon study relates the ills of corporations in their inability to innovate. Other studies suggest that the corporations that are making it are those that are able to accommodate *change*, that strive to create an entrepreneurial culture for their employees—in short, corporations that can and do innovate. Successful new product management requires that top management and internal product champions maintain a consistent level of commitment to the new product effort. In light of the financial, performance, and time demands on management, maintaining new product commitment does take guts.

Don't Be Afraid To Fail

You've failed
many times,
although you may not
remember.
You fell down
the first time
you tried to walk.
You almost drowned
the first time
you tried to
swim, didn't you?
Did you hit the
ball the first time
you swung a bat?
Heavy hitters,
the ones who hit the
most home runs,
also strike
out a lot.
R. H. Macy
failed seven
times before his
store in New York
caught on.
English novelist
John Creasey got
753 rejection slips
before he published
564 books.
Babe Ruth struck out
1,330 times,
but he also hit
714 home runs.
Don't worry about
failure.
Worry about the
chances you miss
when you don't
even try.

United Technologies Corporation
1986

2

APPLAUDING THE TEN KEY SUCCESS FACTORS

Regardless of company size, competition, or industry, similar patterns emerge among companies that are successful at managing new products. In this chapter, I list the ten most common factors found in those companies and discuss the first factor—developing a new product blueprint. The remaining success factors are touched upon to provide a complete picture of what it takes to be successful at new products. These factors will be discussed further in subsequent chapters.

RISK IS THE BACKBONE

Companies successful in new product development always share two common elements: a blueprint and entrepreneurs, that is, a plan of action and committed people willing to take risks. Top management must lead the risk taking and accept the uncertainty of profit generation from new products. The real corporate winners can swallow the risk and digest the uncertainty to fuel the lifeblood of future growth—successful new products. Companies need to set new product objectives, develop a blueprint, and create a team of motivated managers across functions to increase the success rate of commercialized new products.

Management's reluctance to accept the risk of failure is evident in the consistently conservative mix of new product types most frequently introduced—mere modifications and improvements to existing products. With truly innovative new products, there *is* greater variability of return and outcome. How well the product will be accepted by consumers is always uncertain. Yet the higher-risk new product opportunities are often the ones that provide the highest returns. New-to-the-world products and new product lines usually account for companies' most successful new products, even though they usually represent a small percentage of all new product types launched. The lopsided emphasis on me-too new products is somewhat troubling. Companies that avoid the "long shot" in favor of the low-return, "sure bet" are sacrificing the longer-term growth and profit opportunities that will keep them in the race and ahead of the pack.

Risk is the backbone of new product development. It is the central core, the spinal cord, the brainstem. Risk can be defined as the probability of success or failure. Companies are in the business of reducing risk and maximizing returns. But it is easy to forget that both need to be in balance. Concurrently, return potential drives management to develop and launch new products but an aversion to risk impedes it from doing so. Ask yourself how many new product concepts have been killed not by the results of careful analysis or research but rather because of management's risk posture. On the other hand, don't be misled into believing that companies take a less creative approach to new products if they build upon their existing strengths. There are limited capital and human resources in any company. As a result, those limited resources have to be utilized in a way that will decrease risk and increase payout. Structuring innovation enables a company to optimize these two scarce resources rather than minimizing and diluting their impact. Building innovation should be a predictable and manageable endeavor—not a dice game dependent on luck.

So what can management do? First, companies need to strike a better balance between the uphill battle for consistent quarterly earnings and the longer-term return expected from investments in high-risk categories. At present, management's focus on near-term profitability is its major obstacle to new product success. Second, management needs to create a corporate environment that encourages risk taking and reinforces entrepreneurship.

Successful companies start by first understanding their internal strengths and weaknesses to establish clearly which pillars to build upon in developing new products. The chances for failure grow exponentially as a company introduces a product that doesn't play off its existing strengths. This does not mean that companies should develop only lots of line extensions and additions that are nothing more than feature or flavor changes to existing products. Rather, it implies that to some extent, the existing competitive advantages of a company should be exploited when developing a new product. Brand-name equity, a low-cost manufacturing process, a proprietary technology, channel clout, and category market-share leadership all represent examples of strengths upon which new products can draw. Yet many companies go after new products that have no relationship to their *existing* strengths. That's not to say those products can't be acquired or developed, but it *always* increases the risk.

Consequently, management must be able to accept uncertainty and cope with risk. New product failures are unavoidable. They are a part of the success formula. The key is for management to recognize and feel reasonably comfortable that certain approaches can help to diminish the risk—but they can never eliminate it.

KEY SUCCESS FACTORS

Innovation is not merely a creative, unstructured brainstorming activity. It is a multifunctional and disciplined management process that fuses analytics to creativity. Most companies cannot afford the luxury of sitting around a conference table to "blue sky" hundreds of ideas, which, in turn, are funneled through a costly screening-and-development process. Rather, company-specific new product objectives and the growth roles that new products are intended to satisfy should focus idea generation and concept development. Statistical models and quantitative theories, for the most part, are only tools to be used in developing successful new products. Vision building and association making are the essential beginning points that are often overlooked by new product decision makers. Both require the ability to see beyond the existing data base; they require leap-frogging, that is, drawing a conclusion from three or four often different and unrelated bits of information. Companies also need to encourage managers to *use* intuition, not avoid it. Call it business judgment or gut feel if you wish. The key is to make managers feel that success is bolstered by blending business analysis and knowledge with intuition and creativity.

Success factors are relatively common across innovative companies. The following attributes (Exhibit 2-1) depict the underlying requirements for a successful new product program. While all ten factors are critical to success, the new product blueprint, strategy, execution process, and commitment are the most vital.

1. *New Product Blueprint*—Defines the overall direction for and role of new products relative to a company's growth objectives and strategy. Describes the importance and purpose of new products within the context of other sources for growth, e.g., acquisitions, existing business expansion, joint ventures.

2. *New Product Strategy*—Identifies the game plan, that is, how a company plans to achieve the blueprint. Defines new product financial goals, strategic roles, new product types, product/market categories, performance benchmarks, and screening criteria.

3. *Consistent Execution Process*—Pinpoints the development stages that a new product concept passes through to reach commercialization. Offers a commonly understood and consistently applied approach for all participants in the new product

EXHIBIT 2-1 Success Factors for Effectively Managing New Products

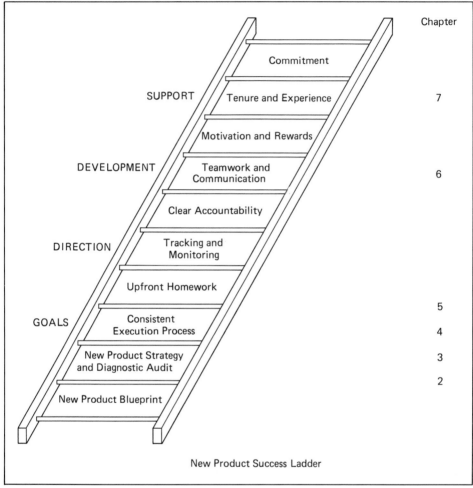

New Product Success Ladder

process. Ensures that the same approach for new product development is executed over time.

4. *Enough Up-Front Homework*—Provides market, competitive, and consumer information on target categories, consumer needs, and business analysis on new product concepts.

5. *Tracking System*—Measures progress and performance of new products. Identifies development costs, new product performance relative to original objectives, and competitive responses after launch.

6. *Clear Accountability*—One person should be responsible for managing and executing the new product strategy and process, and the roles of all new product participants must be clear.

7. *Teamwork and Communication*—How will the organization be structured, what formal and informal communication mechanisms will there be, and what approaches will be taken to facilitate teamwork across functions?

8. *Motivation and Rewards*—What are the appropriate financial compensation and incentive programs as well as nonfinancial rewards to use in building a risk-taking and innovative environment?

9. *Tenure and Experience*—The right people have to be motivated to stay involved in the new product development process for three to five years or more.

10. *Commitment*—Top management must provide a supportive environment, risk-taking culture, and appropriate human and financial resources needed to execute the new product program on a consistent basis.

DEVELOPING A NEW PRODUCT BLUEPRINT

A new product blueprint describes the role of new products relative to a company's growth objectives and strategy. (Exhibit 2-2.) Driven by the risk posture of top management, long-term financial objectives of the corporation, and the growth strategy defining how the financial goals will be met, the blueprint states the intended role of new products in satisfying the corporate strategy. Growth targets may be reached by merely investing in and expanding the existing business or by acquiring companies, by launching internally developed new products, or through a combination of various growth modes. The essential purpose of the new products blueprint is to articulate, in writing, and place dimensions around, the role that new products are expected to play in fulfilling corporate growth objectives.

Moreover, management's vision for new products must be a part of the blueprint. The vision should include the size, type, and number of new products desired, and it should be clear whether management envisions new businesses or product lines or just product improvements coming out of the effort. For any com-

EXHIBIT 2-2 A New Product Blueprint—The Link Between Corporate and New Products Strategy

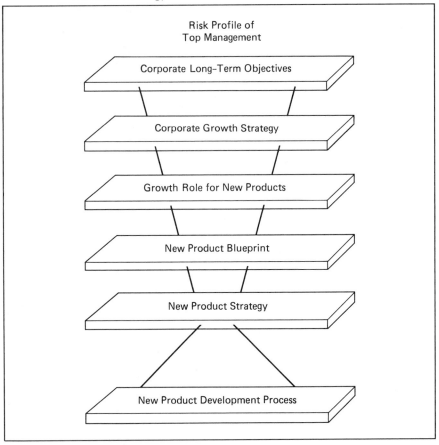

pany, the growth expectation for new products typically falls under one of the following five categories.

Zero Role

For some companies, new products are not expected to play a role in the revenue or profit growth of the company. For them, acquisitions, licensing agreements, geographic expansion of existing products or services, and the like, are the chosen growth routes. As a result, any new product that surfaces internally, by accident or fluke, is evaluated on an opportunistic basis.

Update Role

For others, new products take a modest role in the growth process, typically exemplified through line extensions, additions, and revisions to existing products. With this role for new products, companies for the most part view them as the way to keep their existing product lines alive and competitively positioned. New products become tools to enhance the core business. Usually, new products contribute less than 10 percent of annual revenue growth in this type of company. Emphasis is placed on taking a proactive approach to new products but within a fairly narrow scope and framework.

Modest New-Growth Role

This type of company clearly sees the role of new products as a growth mode integral to the success of the corporate strategy. A deliberate portion of the new product effort is directed at truly innovative new products, not only new to the company but often even new to the world. However, line extensions, flankers, and other new product types are also part of the new product portfolio. New products typically account for 10 to 20 percent of this type of company's revenue stream.

High New-Growth Role

The place to be in this type of company is in the new product area. Top management is involved, committed, and dedicated to this activity. Beyond developing a mix of new product types, this kind of company will pursue the development of new categories and lines of products that will afford the opportunity to enter totally new businesses. Often, the financial contribution of new products to revenue growth will exceed 20 percent annually.

Survival Role

These companies are indeed active in new products but tend to react to competition by launching only me-too products that have slight improvements, lower cost, or different whistles and bells. Contribution to revenues may represent up to 5 to 10 percent from competitive-response new products. The major difference from the update-role companies is the reactionary approach rather than an offensive, proactive approach.

Any one of these new product growth roles may be appropriate for a company at any given time. Moreover, there may be a combination of roles within a corporation since different divisions may have diverse new product needs and objectives. The role of new products does change in most companies over time. This is an important issue that is often overlooked. Usually, a company's planning cycle occurs every twelve months. External market forces, competition, consumer preferences, and financial requirements change, and consequently, the role for new products may be altered. The paradox is that once the growth role for new products has been determined, it *cannot* change every year. Constant change is one of the major impediments to successful new product development. A company cannot keep stopping and starting the new product effort and still expect tangible results. Consistency is required since the development cycle for new products extends well beyond the twelve-month planning cycle. As a company's new product role gradually changes, information about that role must be communicated throughout the organization. Herein lies a frequent void between top management and middle management. The guy at the top has forgotten to tell the rest of the troops that the role of new products has shifted.

Implicit in each growth role for new products is the risk posture of top management and its relative commitment to new products. As a result, companies that have a modest or high new-growth role tend to exhibit more of a charged up, entrepreneurial, and dynamic new product culture. There is a certain domino effect and interaction that occur among the growth role selected for new products, environment created, the commitment made, and the attitudes toward new products. Selection of a high growth role may be more apt to generate a team of highly motivated managers; an update role may stimulate a few sparks but certainly no blazing fires.

But the new product blueprint needs to contain more than just the relationship of new products to corporate growth goals. The blueprint must map out the evolution of roles over at least a five-year period. It must include information on the resource requirements that will be needed to accomplish the defined role for new products. An estimate of available capital and development dollars that will be devoted to new products is a key component of the blueprint. A new product budget must be established. But how can a company possibly know what its resource needs will be prior to even identifying specific new products?

That's the whole point. Successful companies establish broad benchmarks that begin to frame the order of magnitude of the new product efforts. They establish the process to guide the development of products rather than letting a series of new product projects gradually define the process.

For example, one food company with roughly $100 million in sales had been experiencing market-share losses resulting from a competitor's new product inroads. This encroachment made them turn to new products as a solution. Three years ago they developed a new product blueprint and estimated an expenditure of $6 million in development costs during the next five years and an additional $2 million in plant and equipment capital. Moreover, they even outlined the requirement for five new product people within the next two years and four additional R&D technicians. New products were viewed as playing a high growth role for the company.(See Exhibit 2-3.)

While members of top management gulped when first presented with an expenditure level that represented 8 percent of current revenues, they also recognized that the new product objective was to add an incremental $20 million to $25 million in revenues, which would generate, on average, 40 to 45 percent gross margins. After only three years since the initial development of a new product blueprint and strategy, the company has launched fourteen new products—two new to the world, six new to the company, and six line extensions—that today represent over $18 million in revenues and $7.3 million in incremental gross profits.

A sound new product blueprint, as shown in Exhibit 2-4, must address the following issues:

☐ A description of the *role* that new products will play in the overall growth plan of the company.

☐ An estimated five-year budget that indicates the level of *development expenditures and investment capital* for the entire new product effort.

☐ A profile of the *human-resource requirements* needed.

☐ A broad financial objective and *revenue target* for the composite of all new products launched during the planned period. This would include either a total revenue number or percentage of sales.

☐ A description of how the role of new products will *mesh with other growth modes* that will be pursued, e.g., acquisitions, licensing, strategic alliances, contract arrangements, and so on.

EXHIBIT 2-3 Guidelines for a Food Company's New Product Blueprint

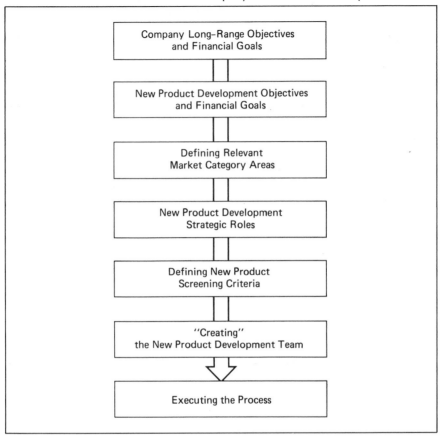

□ An articulation of *top management's expectations for new products and its intended level of involvement,* i.e., guidelines and performance benchmarks that define a successful new product development program and management's activities and type of participation in the process.

EXHIBIT 2-4 Example of a New Product Blueprint

Role: High New Growth

Internally developed new products are expected to represent 50 to 60 percent of new revenue growth; 20 percent to come from acquisitions, and 20 to 25 percent from existing businesses.

Revenue Target

Corporate growth targets are to generate $150 million in incremental revenues during the next four years.

The target for new product revenue is $90 million by the beginning of year 5.

Budget

The new product development expense budget for the next two years will approximate $5 million for salaries, market research, prototype development, and market-testing costs.

Capital available for plant and equipment investments needed for new products cannot exceed $7.5 million.

Commercialization launch costs cannot exceed 40 percent of year 2 revenue projections per new product.

Human Resource Requirements by Year 2

New product director
Four new product managers
Two business analysts
One market researcher
Three laboratory technicians

Interface with Other Growth Modes

Acquisitions will be aimed at acquiring product lines that will support or be complementary to the thrust of internally developed new products.

Licensing agreements will be limited to personalities that can be used in concert with new products developed.

Top Management's Expectations/Involvement

By year 3, top management expects at least ten new products launched, representing cumulative revenue potential of over $50 million within one to two years.

Management also expects a steady pipeline flow of new product concepts to be established by the end of the first year.

Top management will attend all monthly new product steering committee meetings and will approve/disapprove the new product strategy, all concepts prior to prototype development, and any capital expenditures over $100,000.

The worst type of new product blueprint is a list of new product projects. If your company has a list of projects currently under way that serves as a proxy for a new product blueprint, you should burn it at once. It is totally meaningless, distorts the objectives, focus, and level of commitment to new products and accomplishes nothing more than generating a lot of aggravation. Many top executives proudly show off their list of new product projects. However, when the time comes to commit $1.5 million behind one new product launch, the enthusiasm suddenly dissipates.

The new product blueprint is a concrete and tangible form of top-management commitment. It reinforces the need for top management to lay itself on the line relative to the future role of new products. It also shakes out many clandestine skeletons that hide in top management's closets like, "Well, it looks like a great opportunity, but we just don't have the funds to support it this quarter—or next." Then why has some ambitious manager been working day and night to develop a prototype?

The blueprint also enables the people working on new products to have some faith that all of their frustrations and anxieties are worth it. It is a form of security, offers long-term perspective, and establishes a common set of expectations. More concretely, it is a written document that indicates the importance of new products to the company and the role new products represent in shaping the company's future.

A final note on the key elements of a new product blueprint: management should provide guidelines that define a successful new product development program—the minimum standards. In other words, in three to five years from now, what will it take for management to be able to say that they have been pleased with the way new products have been managed—that the effort was a success?

Success guidelines can be defined along a number of dimensions. Keep in mind that we are talking not about specific new product success criteria but, rather, about guidelines for judging the overall success of the new product development program.

The purpose of success guidelines is to get some feel for what top management wants to accomplish for the company with new products—the type of comment that the CEO would like to make at an annual shareholders or board meeting. CEOs who have been asked what it would take to rate their new product development programs a success three to five years from now, have made comments like the following:

To exceed the target of achieving 10 percent revenue growth from new products.

To drop $2 million in incremental profits to the bottom line from new products regardless of the type, category, or revenue size.

To demonstrate to the investment community that the company is committed to growth from new products.

To launch, on average, four to five new-to-the-company products each year.

To beat out our major competitor with enough new products that his head begins to spin.

To get new products that will strengthen our position in the European market.

To be able to commercialize just a couple of big hits to reinforce to all managers that new products must be a way of life for us.

Thus, identifying the one dimension most important to top management for new products to satisfy is an integral component of the new product blueprint. Another benefit is that the blueprint sharpens and clarifies management's expectations for new products, and those expectations can then be better communicated throughout an organization.

The new product blueprint is usually drafted by the new product manager in concert with top management. Senior management must be included in the approval process in order to build a feeling of ownership and commitment throughout the company. While the blueprint sets the direction for all new product activities and relates the role of new products in satisfying corporate objectives, the new product strategy is the management tool that describes how the blueprint will be implemented. Thus, the new product strategy serves as the game plan to guide the management of new products.(See Exhibit 2-5.)

DEVELOPING A NEW PRODUCT STRATEGY

Once the blueprint has been developed and approved, the next step is to begin determining how new products will be managed to satisfy the growth role. Developing a new product strategy serves as a management rudder to steer new product resources along a chartered course. In effect, the strategy helps to determine how best to allocate human and financial re-

EXHIBIT 2-5 Two Big Questions about New Product Development

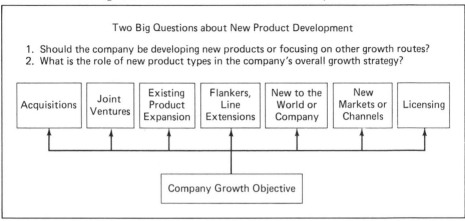

sources to meet the business objectives that new products are trying to satisfy. The three key components of a new products strategy are (1) information about the financial-growth gap, (2) strategic roles, and (3) screening criteria.(See Exhibit 2-6.) The best way to start is by identifying the underlying factors that have contributed to a company's past new product performance. That can be accomplished by conducting a self-assessment, or diagnostic audit, on the company's past performance, as described in Chapter 3.

Growth Gap

The growth gap can best be determined after examining how previous goals were established for new products. The diagnostic audit provides a perspective on past performance that should be factored into future projections. How realistic were new product goals given the resources, direction, and funding that supported previous new product efforts? Understanding how financial objectives were developed is often valuable in setting new goals.

The new product growth gap itself is the difference between total expected corporate revenues and forecast revenues from other growth modes, e.g., acquisitions, joint ventures, and existing business expansion. The growth gap calibrates the total revenue growth and dollars expected during a five-year period that will be generated from new products.

EXHIBIT 2-6 The Benefits of a New Product Strategy

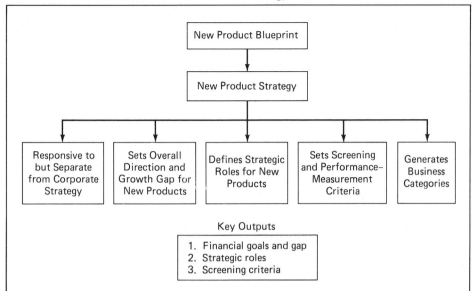

Strategic Roles

The growth gap provides linkage between the blueprint, which sets future new product objectives, and the diagnostic audit, which examines achievement of past objectives. Once the growth gap has been determined, the next task in designing a new product strategy is to define the strategic roles that new products will satisfy. This step is vitally important to success. Without it, the only role that new products are perceived to play is revenue and profit generation. Granted, that is the objective of all new products, but that role by itself provides little direction for new product activities. Strategic roles enable managers to see the purpose of a new product, in terms of defending or expanding an existing business, or creating new businesses.

Moreover, defining strategic roles for new products takes the planning process one level deeper. It gives *shape* to the game plan and *direction* to the players. Strategic roles provide a dimension to new products that relates directly to the business requirements of the company. They can be classified into two groups: requisite roles and opportunistic roles. New products that satisfy requisite roles typically defend or expand the existing business. Opportunistic roles that new products fulfill usually move a company into a new market, category, or business.

Some strategic roles are clearly market, consumer, or competitor driven. Others capitalize on internal strengths or shore up internal company weaknesses; still others are expansion driven. Following are some of the strategic roles that companies use to guide new products.

Requisite Roles

Requisite roles may be market or competitor driven. For example, the role for a new product may be to defend a market share position in a specific category, or to establish a niche in lawn and garden care products. Other roles might include developing products geared to the elderly or achieving a position in a nutritional health food category.

Driven by internal company strengths, other requisite roles could range from capitalizing on a proprietary technology to applying a patented process to a new product. Internal weaknesses may also guide new product roles: utilize excess capacity, use by-products and waste materials, offset seasonal slumps, or develop a cost-reduced product to compete with foreign imports.

Opportunistic Roles

Opportunistic new product roles are usually expansion-oriented, thereby moving a company into a new business area. Possible roles might be to gain a position in a foreign country, develop products geared to latch-key children, or increase market share in a specific U.S. region. Other examples of roles include: gaining entry into a new market that can then be further penetrated with existing products, broadening distribution channels by entering hardware stores, or expanding a presence in Third World countries.

While hundreds of other examples exist, the aforementioned roles illustrate ways in which new products can be focused to serve a variety of business requirements and needs. Usually a company will have a portfolio of strategic roles that new products are intended to fulfill. Sometimes one role may address multiple business needs. Capitalizing on a proprietary technology may provide geographic-expansion opportunities, preempt a new category before competition can enter it, and defend market-share position within a category.

Moreover, at times, a single new product may satisfy more than one strategic role. A new computer product may exploit a brand-name franchise, prevent a competitor from entering a niche category, and maintain market position as category leader. A new home appliance, e.g., Sunbeam's Oskar, might have enabled the company to counteract a foreign competitor's cost advantage, develop a line of products using a proprietary manufacturing process, and offset seasonality—thereby cutting across all three types of strategic roles.

Selecting the "right" set of strategic roles for a company requires an understanding of its internal strengths and weaknesses as well as an accurate portrayal of the competitive advantages and vulnerabilities of each existing business. Developing strategic roles for new products requires an identification of the key competitive and growth challenges facing the existing business. Once this list of issues has been developed, managers can assess whether a new product could play a role in addressing or resolving each issue. We address this matter in Chapter 3 when we describe how to conduct a diagnostic audit, which offers an approach for identifying internal strengths and weaknesses, competitive advantages and threats, and business requirements. However, for the moment, suffice it to say that strategic roles play an important directional and focusing part in the new product strategy. Even if a new product satisfies a strategic role, further performance criteria are needed to choose among new product concepts. Screening criteria provide a filter through which to pass category and concept opportunities.

Screening Criteria

Screening criteria should be driven, in part, by the blueprint, growth gap, and strategic roles. If $100 million is expected from new products within five years, a revenue screen of $100,000 per new product would be silly. Screening criteria should be used to determine the relative attractiveness of each new product concept and category under consideration. New product screening criteria must be both qualitative and quantitative. Furthermore, screening criteria may be differentiated by strategic role and new product type.

Criteria for qualitative new product screens often include market, risk, strategic-role, internal-strengths, and competition. In contrast, the quantitative screens may include a minimal revenue threshold, gross margin minimum, payback period, return on invested capital, or a return on assets requirement for any new-to-the-company product. But screens need to reflect the relative degree of risk, which differs by new product types and the strategic role they intend to satisfy. As the risk increases from line extensions to new-to-the-world products, the expected returns need to be higher to accommodate the risk. The important point about screening criteria is the way they are used. They should help filter out ideas early on in the process to enable managers to focus on fewer, better concepts.

The worst mistake that companies make regarding screens is to set up a *single* criterion against which all new products must be judged. Does it make any sense to have a $10 million revenue threshold and a 45 percent gross margin target by the third year for *all* new products? No. It does not account for the varying degrees of risks associated with different strategic roles and new product types. Yet companies often set an across-the-board hurdle rate, which is used to kill off many good new product concepts. If the criteria are set too high, creativity and motivation may come to an abrupt halt. If the only kind of new products the management is willing to accept are the "big-hitters," they will need to be extremely patient and able to commit a healthy stream of development dollars to the cause. However, a great deal of applicable experience accumulates by also developing a series of "little winners."

Unless a company perceives a zero role for new products, the objectives set will most likely be satisfied through a combination of new products—large and small—that are not just from one or two big-hitters.

A consumer packaged goods company that has not launched a successful new product during the past five years believes it must set a $25 million minimum revenue criterion for any single new product. The argument is that anything less would not provide the marketing dollars required to advertise the product nationally. No wonder management is still scratching its head trying to figure out why people just don't seem committed to new products.

Take the example of the company that sets a 20 percent return on invested capital for all new products. What happens to those new products that are intended to fill other strategic roles, for instance, to utilize excess capacity or offset seasonal downturns? In practice, if a new product were to contribute to overhead absorption and increase plant utilization but needed new tooling and a new set of die cuts, a 12 percent return on invested capital might well make sense. The point is that successful companies do not establish one set of screening criteria that are applied to all new products under consideration.

Let's be sure to communicate one critical aspect of screening criteria. New product screens can be used either as a club or a tool. If management chooses to use screening criteria as a club, low-ball projections in business analysis and second guessing in financial forecasts will negate the value of any set of criteria. Management will find a way *around* the screens to kill off any new product that just doesn't seem to fit its arbitrary comfort zone.

So the objective is to develop guidelines that can assist the decision-making process and serve as a tool in setting new product priorities and allocating resources.

A company that manufactures and markets computer paper, wanting to counteract a low-margin and cyclical business, developed screening criteria that were both qualitative and financially oriented. The strategic or qualitative criteria that any new product concept had to meet included:

□ Product must be sold to existing target-customer base.

□ Does not require post-sale maintenance or service by company.

□ Can be distributed via current channels.

□ Product performance must be as good as or better than competition.

□ Have limited product liability.

□ Products must be based on low technology.

□ Requires virtually no advertising support.

Thus, this company was clearly saying that while new products were an important component of their growth plans, they were not willing to venture out into new channels or seek out totally new customers. In addition, recognizing their internal strengths, they knew that advertising and high tech were not their fortes. Therefore, they decided to stay away from these areas and develop new products that would build on existing strengths rather than indulging in wishful thinking. Besides these qualitative criteria, the company established a set of financial criteria, differentiated by new product type. (See Table 2-1.)

Given the increased risk associated with new-to-the-world products, this company saw the appropriate need to accelerate the performance standards of these types of products. The criteria for pretax margin did not change much across types. Man-

TABLE 2-1

Minimums	New to the Company	Line Extensions	Flankers
Year 2 revenues	$1,000,000	$500,000	$200,000
Cumulative revenues			
by year 3	$3,000,000	$1,500,000	$700,000
Gross profit margin	25%	20%	15%
Pretax margin	6%	5%	5%
Breakeven	3 years	2 years	1 year
ROIC	5-year payback	3-year payback	3-year payback

agement recognized that even though the new-to-the-company products would generate higher gross margins, more investment spending would be required to launch and steadily build those products. Flankers and line extensions would, for the most part, sell themselves through brand-name pull and the direct sales force's ability to get displays. Incremental marketing support for the majority of these types of new products would not be required.

Another example of the screening criteria set by a consumer durables company is shown in Table 2-2.

The value of screens to this company was demonstrated to management and the new product team by the fact that previous new products launched by the company had averaged $350,000 in year 2 revenues. The time and money that had been poured into new products were yielding "revenue mice"; the company was now after fewer but more powerful "revenue lions."

Screens can also be developed according to strategic roles rather than by new product type, as illustrated by the beverage-company example in Exhibit 2-7. However, implicit in the strategic roles were different types of new products.

Choosing screening criteria for strategic roles or new product types depends upon the financial benchmarks that management is most interested in measuring. Some companies set criteria by both strategic role and new product type to gain further precision in the priority-setting process. The important point is to set criteria that are differentiated across some dimension.

A final note on screening criteria. Don't totally dump concepts that don't make it through the screen. A major missed opportunity is losing track of concepts that are not right for a given period of time but are wildly successful at some point in the future. Sara Lee launched gourmet ice cream well before the palates of the American Yuppie were prepared for it. Had they repositioned it and relaunched a few years later, they might have been able to ride

TABLE 2-2

	Revenue Threshold by Year 2	Gross Margin	ROCE
New to the world	$10 million	45%	25%
New to the company	$ 5 million	40	20
Extensions and additions	$ 2 million	30	15
Cost reductions	$250,000	Higher than existing product	

EXHIBIT 2-7 Strategic Roles for a Beverage Company

Entering the category of products for minorities
Revenue target: $1 million by year 3
Gross margins: 40%
Payback by year 4
Capital investment under $500,000

Utilizing byproducts and waste materials
Revenue target: $250,000
Gross margins: 30%
Payback by year 2
Capital investment under $200,000

Preempt competition in a new category
Revenue target: $5 million by year 2
Gross margins: 45%
Payback by year 4
Capital investment under $750,000

on the wave of DoveBar, Früsen Gladjé, and Häagen-Daz success. So, keep "unused" new product concepts in an active file that is reviewed periodically. Better yet, all new product concepts should be segmented into three or four priority groups. In this way, there is a backlog of ideas that can be used to keep the new product development pipeline full. The following four categories can be used to set priorities for new product concepts.

☐ *Top 10:* New product concepts that are currently under development and approved by management.

☐ *Backburner:* Concepts that pass the screens but are lower priority; most will likely be worked on after the top 10 have either made it to commercialization or been screened out. This group of concepts should be reviewed as frequently as the top 10 to ensure that an adequate core of potential new products exists.

□ *Refrigerator:* "Unused" concepts that may warrant examination and consideration in the next few months but do not appear to represent near-term opportunities.

□ *Freezer:* "Unused" concepts that clearly do not pass the current screens but are worthy to be kept in cold storage; some day to be thawed out and reexamined.

Screening criteria help managers prioritize new product opportunities and thereby allocate resources more cost effectively. As an R&D manager at Kraft, Inc., said, "Nothing burns me up more than to have spent nine months developing a product that suddenly gets killed because marketing says that the revenue potential is too low. Why didn't they figure that out before I had three lab technicians working full time on it?" Thus, screening criteria bring further clarity to the objectives and direction of the new product process, offer a consistent way to set priorities and better allocate resources, and force concepts to be more thoughtfully flushed out before valuable resources spend time against them.

MAINTAINING A CONSISTENT EXECUTION PROCESS

Companies most successful at new products have had the same development process in place for four to five years or even longer. They haven't changed the approach; the steps from idea generation to commercialization remain the same. The key benefit of this consistency is the learning economies that accrue by doing something the same way time and again.

The key to any new product development process is making it understandable and actionable to everyone in the organization involved in new products. Consistency in the way the process is interpreted and followed is vital. The process should be structured, with a sequence of steps that define the stages a new product concept will pass through on its way to market launch. But it also has to be simple, straightforward, and systematic. The difficult part is making sure that people adhere to the steps in the process while, at the same time, recognizing that a certain degree of flexibility is critical for getting new products to the marketplace.

An industrial-tool manufacturer that we worked with in developing a new product strategy had a well-detailed new product development process. There were fifty-four steps in their process. Can you imagine? Fifty-four separate and distinct steps that a new product concept had to pass through before finally making it to commercialization. It's not difficult to figure out why no new products were getting out to the marketplace.

Any step-by-step process that can be effectively executed by a company most likely needs to have more than four steps and probably fewer than twelve. Any more or less will probably leave too much variance in the way new products are managed or begin to stifle and suffocate the development process. Again, there is no hard-and-fast process for every company. Each needs to be tailored to the specific differences and new product needs of a company. At times, the process steps should be skipped. If competition has a product in a test market that will compete with your new product, you may have to circumvent the test-market stage of development; but be careful if you do. And be aware of the increased risk that may result. Commercialization may be necessary, however, to preempt a competitor's national roll out. For example, in 1983 Puss N' Boots had developed a cat treat product called Pounce. Beatrice had a cat treat product called Bonkers in test market. Pounce was rolled out nationally four months later, to beat Beatrice to the draw. Pounce today enjoys a 60 percent share of the cat treat category.

For the most part, any new product development process can be defined broadly by two major steps, as shown in Exhibit 2-8.

☐ Identifying and evaluating new product concepts
☐ Developing prototypes and launch plans

Most of the material written on new product development tends to describe a six- or seven-step process, including:

☐ Idea generation
☐ Concept development
☐ Business analysis
☐ Screening
☐ Prototype development
☐ Test market
☐ Commercialization

EXHIBIT 2-8 Building Blocks That Most Companies Use in New Product Development

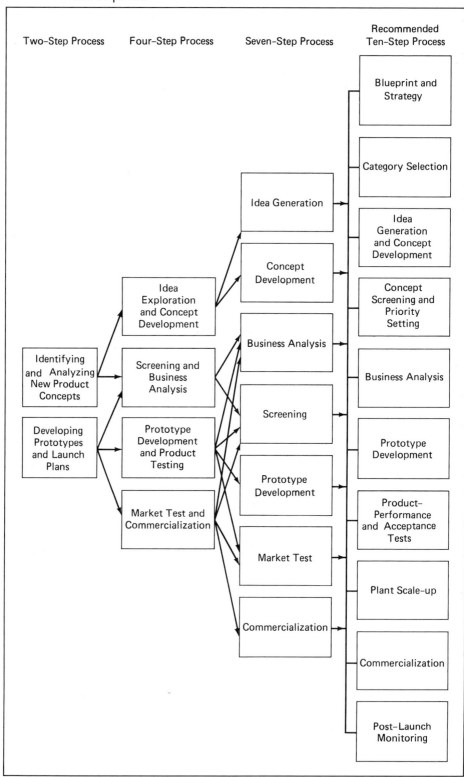

It is necessary to break down these steps into more detail in order to provide managers with enough guidance to monitor the progress of a concept to the point of market launch. More clearly delineated steps in the process also provide go/no go points for management. Developing a company-specific process will vary greatly by industry, types of new products to be developed, and the role of new products in the company. However, the key is to develop one single process that is used, adhered to, and understood throughout the company. A general framework should accomplish, in one form or another, the following sequential tasks:

1. Develop a new product blueprint and strategy.
2. Analyze and rank potentially attractive categories.
3. Generate ideas and develop concepts within categories selected.
4. Screen concepts and set priorities.
5. Conduct business analyses of selected concepts.
6. Develop prototypes.
7. Run product-performance, customer-acceptance, and market tests.
8. Initiate plant scale-up.
9. Develop launch plans and commercialize the new product.
10. Monitor performance regularly against the original plan.

The next challenge is to define the components of each of these steps so that managers understand the specific tasks that are required at each stage. In chapter 5, we will address in detail each process used and describe the steps in the process.

"Hiding" games do not work. Trying to cover up new product performance is, in the long run, a no-win proposition. Even when top management does not understand the risky nature of new products, it makes no sense to make a new product appear rosier than it is. Someone in the organization should keep track of how each new product performs for at least three years relative to the original forecasts. This actual-to-forecast new product information should provide insights on how well each new product has performed and why, and the variance in forecast versus actual performance. Moreover, the information should cite revenue and profit patterns during a three-year period, financial impact of competition on new products, and guidelines for forecasting new products in the future. In summary, the new product development process must be tailored to the specific needs of a company. But there are common stages across all companies that need to be systematically applied to any new concept. At the same time, while managers should impose discipline in adhering to the stages of the process, the process should be flexible and adaptive enough to bend slightly when competitive pressures call for it. The development process, like all aspects of new product management, blends a structured, analytical, planning approach with creative, responsive, risk taking. There is no getting away from the dual "analytics and guts" success factors.

DOING YOUR UP-FRONT HOMEWORK

You have entered the danger zone when two consumer focus groups have been completed and all twenty consumers are wild about the new product concept that has been presented to them. Frequently, after this has happened, I have seen a new product concept suddenly jump in priority, get moved to the "fast track," and receive oodles of top-management support, especially if top management was sitting behind the one-way mirror listening to consumers rave about this new concept.

I've also seen the majority of these products fail. They fail because managers become so infatuated with a positive reaction from consumers that they lose perspective on how competition will respond to this product, the cost structure, the optimal positioning and packaging, and the like. Anticipating how competition will respond with a me-too product is part of the homework assignment. Once consumers have a positive reaction to a new idea, concept development begins—it doesn't end. And the beginning includes extensive up-front homework that will provide the information required to launch a competitive product into the market place successfully.

But the up-front homework really starts even before idea generation or concept development. As discussed earlier, it actually begins during the category identification stage of the process. How can a company select a category to pursue new product ideas in if there is no understanding of the dynamics, competitive makeup, key success factors, and risks associated with that category.

Regardless of the new product type, even for a truly new-to-the-world product that indeed may have no direct competition, there are three key reasons why homework is valuable. First, there are most likely existing alternative products that consumers can still substitute in lieu of this new-to-the-world one. Secondly, competition will arrive someday. There may be preemptive measures that could be taken and built into the product that may forestall the inevitable. Third, consumers may need heavy doses of education to know why to buy and how to use the product; thus, information on positioning and consumer communications becomes integral to the success of the product.

Consequently, some preliminary business analysis needs to be conducted on a category basis. There should be more in-depth analysis of each concept that makes it to the business-analysis stage of the process after initial screening has taken place. The "homework" category includes taking a look at the relative strengths and weaknesses of the company and at how the category that a new product would be competing in offers opportunities for the company to play off its strengths. Take, for example, the decision by J. C. Penney to invest in the expanding Alcott & Andrews specialty stores. J. C. Penney's decision to invest in the corporate women's apparel business was most likely based on the following factors:

☐ Rapid growth of that segment among specialty apparel stores

☐ Fragmented and relatively few competitors positioned as specialty apparel stores for businesswomen

☐ Centralized buying capability providing cost economies

☐ Existing direct-mail catalog business geared to professional women

☐ High-traffic target-audience locations

☐ Market research conducted on apparel needs of businesswomen

The actual development of the stores resulted in far more specific analysis of where, what and how best to position and launch the store openings. Enough homework had been done to determine that entering the professional businesswomen's apparel market was attractive. The next level of homework was the market-by-market analysis needed for each store location, merchandise mix, advertising campaign, and so on.

Product champions often try to avoid homework. Once a great new idea has been generated, they want to "hustle" the concept through the process. While tenacious commitment to moving a concept through the development stages is commendable, information and analysis that will improve the chances for success or identify major impediments to success should not be short circuited.

TRACKING AND MONITORING

Performance of new products needs to be regularly monitored to compare actual results with original forecasts. Variance in performance needs to be identified, and causal factors that influenced a new product's performance need to be uncovered. The primary purposes of a formalized tracking system are to identify development costs, new product performance relative to original objectives, and competitive responses after launch. The major benefits of a tracking system are to establish a data base to improve future forecasting and develop a rationale for each new product's success or failure. Such a system also offers insights into ways to change future new products and provides a mechanism to monitor overall performance in managing new products.

Top management and new product management need a report card that defines how well the process is working and how new products have performed. Often, once a new product is launched, it becomes part of the annual budget of an existing business; however, the new product's financial projections must be examined relative to the original forecasts.

Another part of documenting new product performance is to track the competitive response to a launch. Competitors' retaliatory actions against a new product will frequently negatively affect the original forecasts, but management must know *how* performance was affected by competition to identify unrealistic forecasts that may have been set at the outset.

Moreover, development costs need to be carefully tracked to determine the overall payout of the new product program. More must be calculated than just invested capital. The people costs and research time must be integrated into the new product budgets. There should be a separate budget established for all related new product development costs. Of course, a separate budget means that management will be able to clearly identify whether the investment is generating an adequate return. That's the point. Hiding new product failures under the carpet only perpetuates a risk-averse and me-too approach to new products. Thus, tracking new product performance is a key step in identifying a company's internal strengths and weaknesses—an underlying principle in successful new product development.

ASSIGNING CLEAR ACCOUNTABILITY

Management must decide who is responsible for managing new products and let everyone in the company know. Responsibility may fall to one full-time person, a team of six, or even a marketing manager who is involved with new products 50 percent of the time. The key is to delineate the roles and priorities of all participants in the new product process. The more successful companies specify who is accountable for attaining the results desired from new products. The following are responses frequently made by managers when asked, "Who is responsible for new product development in your organization?"

Well, there are a number of people responsible for new products; the lab focuses on prototype development and marketing develops the launch plans.

We have a new product committee that reviews all of the working concepts.

I don't know who is responsible for new products. Well, ultimately, it's the president.

The VP of marketing.
The VP of engineering.
The VP of planning and diversification. (Comments made by managers in the same company.)

In any successful new product organization, there is usually *one* person who is held accountable for managing the entire new product process. Obviously, the president of a division, sector, group, or company is ultimately responsible for having successful new products meet the financial goals established. But who is accountable on a day-to-day basis for managing new product concepts through the process to commercialization? Who coordinates and facilitates the new product team or venture group? Who recommends that the priority of product A gets moved up to surpass product B? Who organizes the market research that is under way on four concepts? Who deals with manufacturing and research and development when they continue to talk different languages? Who explains to top management why the development of projects C and D are taking longer than he had anticipated? Who recommends how best to allocate the resources?

All of these activities cannot be done by a committee, team, or multidisciplinary task force without a leader. A *team* is indeed most appropriate to use in marshaling requisite resources to develop new products. However, one single individual needs to be held accountable for managing the new products process. Someone who has no firefighting or existing business crises to attend to. Someone who does not have to cut the new product budget to fund interim-plan profit shortfalls on the core business. Someone who is directly responsible for the day-to-day activities involved in developing new products, and someone whose compensation at the end of the year will be decidedly affected by new product performance. Someone who cannot easily pass the buck, and one who also knows that he or she alone will be held responsible for managing the new product process.

Moreover, the person in charge of new products should serve as a coordinator, facilitator, and shepherd. Titles range from new product manager or growth developer to vice-president of diversification or director of new-business expansion. The title doesn't really matter that much, clear responsibility *does*.

TEAMWORK AND COMMUNICATION

Teamwork requires a leader; effective communication requires frequent dialogue. One way that teamwork can be fostered is by having a leader in place who provides an environment where open communication is the norm. New products is not a function that allows people to work independently for a month and then regroup and report on progress made. Regular weekly dialogue, at a minimum, is a must among the key new product players.

One way to solidify the leadership position is by having a full-time person assigned to manage the process. If new products have been cast into an update, modest, or high-growth role, e.g., expected to contribute 5 to 10 percent or more to revenues, the new product leader must report directly to the CEO or president.

That's the rule—no exceptions. The most common argument against it heard from the CEO or president is the span-of-control issue. "I already have seven direct reports; I can't have another one. I'll have the new product manager report to marketing." Or, "I have a strong operating management team: the VP of sales and marketing, the VP of manufacturing, the VP of finance, and the VP of research and development. The new product manager should report to the VP of R&D since most of the resources will come from the lab." Additionally, "I don't really know much about new product development. I'd feel more comfortable if the new product manager reported to the director of engineering. I'll meet with him frequently, though."

When new products are expected to play an important role in the organization, management must take responsibility for having that function report directly to the top. The new product effort demands top-management visibility and exposure. Elevating the position and status of the new product manager signals several things to employees:

☐ New products are as important to the organization as other functional and operating entities.

☐ Top management is committed to and involved with new products.

☐ The new products effort has a clearly defined leader and group of dedicated resources.

☐ Funding for new products will be considered in concert with existing business investments rather than subordinate to them.

☐ New products is an ongoing function of the organization, not an ad hoc task force or temporary committee.

The list of benefits continues. But the real issue remains: How can top management afford not to be actively involved in new products? Answer: only those top managers who truly do not care whether new products succeed can afford inactivity.

For those of you who do not have the new product organization reporting directly to top management, a rationale may exist. But change it tomorrow. Identify a person who can be held accountable for new products and add one more direct report to an already heavy span of control. Alternatively, collapse two existing direct reports into one, e.g., move the VP of research and development under the VP of manufacturing, and move the VP of sales under the VP of marketing. Now even though a new product manager has been added, the span of control has been *reduced* by one.

Whatever it takes—get the new product function reporting to the top decision-making layer of management within the organization. Top-management support and commitment, as I continue to stress, must be clearly demonstrated to the organization.

Furthermore, many companies argue that it would be too expensive to set up a separate new product department or organization. "I can't afford to add more people to establish a new product department. I'll just assign someone in marketing," is often the common plea. Again, it does depend upon the growth role that new products are expected to play.

Keep in mind, the new product organization may represent only one or two start-up people. It does not mean building a new wing to the office complex. Top management can be committed and supportive of new products, provide the people and funds required, and set the mission and charter of new products without requiring the new product organization to report directly to the top. But it is far more difficult to communicate the importance of new products when the new product manager has a temporary cubicle that is set up in one of the large corridors of the lab, with the industrial design manager as her boss.

In short, establishing a separate new product organization, with one person clearly accountable for new products, who reports to top management, will greatly enhance the probabilities of new product success and greatly enhance communications. There is a focal point, a leader of the team. Moreover, instilling a sense of teamwork and establishing formal communication mechanisms are integral to the success formula.

MOTIVATING AND REWARDING NEW PRODUCT PEOPLE

"We endorse your new products strategy, we're forming a new organization, we're hiring a new product manager, and we've already started using the process. But change our compensation system? Impossible." This is a common reaction by companies. They can buy into all aspects of formalizing new product development except for the one major and common missing link—motivation and rewards. Compensation and financial incentives must be viewed as an integral ingredient of the motivation-and-reward game plan. However, dollars and cents are not the only vehicles to use in motivating a team of new product developers. Psychic, emotional, and career-advancement rewards are also powerful motivators. Money does talk, though. Companies that want an entrepreneurial environment need to have compensation programs that simulate those of a start-up business. Unfortunately, most large companies relentlessly resist any changes in compensation practices.

Comments of the president of a major consumer durables company typify the attitudes toward compensation by most managers.

President: "We can't pay a bonus to our new product managers that would exceed that of the president of the division. Out of the question."

Consultant: "But what if the new product manager launches three new products that bring in $10 million in incremental revenues and $800,000 in additional profits? What's wrong in giving him an $80,000 bonus based upon new product performance?"

President: "Ridiculous. There were several people involved in the successful performance of that product; especially the lab and manufacturing people."

Consultant: "All the better! Why not give each of the ten-member team—the team responsible for the new product—an $8,000 bonus?"

President: "This is foolishness. Two of those team members only get $30,000 in annual base salary. That would mean their bonus represents 27 percent of base. Our maximum is 15 percent of base in bonus. Besides, people get paychecks for doing their job. If I eliminate the paycheck, I'll be glad to institute a bonus."

And so it goes. For every suggestion to change the compensation-and-reward structure for people involved in new products there is a probable negative response. On the other hand, listen to top management talk about the entrepreneurial and intrepreneurial environment they are tying to foster. For some reason, hundreds of thousands of dollars can be spent on a new corporate jet, but $75,000 in bonus monies, allocated to a new product development team, is perceived as detrimental to the "integrity" of the compensation system.

Come on. If you want people to act like risk-taking entrepreneurs, then treat them that way. Provide enough economic incentive so that new product team members are willing to commit themselves to get successful new products out the door. Make the incentive contingent upon the actual performance of new products in the marketplace. If the product launches fizzle out, then the bonus is $0, not the normal 10 percent of base. On the other hand, if new products add $1 million in profits, then why shouldn't the new product manager receive a $50,000 or $60,000 bonus?

Or to stimulate an entrepreneurial culture, for example, let new product team members "invest" in the new products that they launch. Let them buy three year "options." Assume five individuals invest $5,000 of their own money for 1 percent of the product profits, and the product drops $800,000 to the bottom line by year 3. This would mean that they could cash in $8,000 or get a 60 percent return on their investment for three years. In contrast, if the new product generated only $100,000 in profit, they would have lost $4,000.

The key is tying some portion of compensation to new product performance. Whatever the benchmarks or rewards are, something different is needed to stimulate, motivate, and reinforce risk taking on the part of new product development managers.

RECOGNIZING THE VALUE OF TENURE AND EXPERIENCE

A myth that continues to permeate most of corporate America is the perception that one cannot have a "career" in new products. However, some smart companies are recognizing the tremendous leverage that comes in having "old-timers" in this function. The reason is that accumulated experience does breed success. As a result, the new people that come to the new product area have a trained mentor who can expedite the learning process for all of them.

Successful companies understand the benefits and value of tenure—longevity in the new product area usually leads to a seasoned understanding of how the process works. Moreover, product champions do not spring up overnight. A person needs time in new products to feel comfortable with the process before emotionally committing to and standing behind a concept. Enlightened companies have fully dedicated new product people, who receive bonuses, vacations, and promotions—just like real live business managers.

Constantly infusing new people into the new product process is not the key to creativity. If anything, churning managers through this complex management process stifles creativity. How can you be creative until you know what you're doing? It is far better to develop and nurture a group of managers who have been through "the wringer," understand how new products are developed, and maintain a consistent and systematic approach. Consistency breeds creativity and effective results. It is the attitude and energy level underlying the experience base that breeds success.

The major problem that a new product manager of a consumer packaged goods company had was getting the team to find time to work on new products rather than on their day-today business activities. The company had never had a formalized new product team, and the team members did not really understand how the process worked. Even though the new product manager had a great deal of experience at other companies and had introduced three to four products that had generated over $50 million in cumulative revenues, he was not getting support from his newly formed team. The lack of cooperation was not so much due to existing business pressures as it was due to a discomfort level by team members, who had not done this kind of work before.

A creative and unique house can often be designed by an architect who has been designing houses for years. Brand new architects are not the creative masters of this art form; the old-timers are. Likewise, the contractor building the house who has a cadre of experienced and skilled workers will perform a better job of constructing the house than the newly opened construction shop will. The new product strategy can be compared to the blueprint, the new product team to the seasoned construction company, the new product manager to the head architect and job foreman.

A new product team needs time to crystallize and solidify into a harmonious and cohesive group. PRACTICE is essential to new product success.

Yet with all the advancements made in sophisticated market-research techniques, computerized modeling, and software forecasting, why hasn't there been greater progress in managing new product development? The answer is that only humans can sprinkle doses of creativity into logical analysis. Left-brain and right-brain thinking must come together for success with new products. Thus, the typical management approaches for running an existing business are dramatically different from those required to nurture and encourage creative risk taking. As a result, experience with this difficult process is essential for consistent results.

If successful results are desired, management has to deal with new product people differently. This is by no means meant to imply that new product managers should be given free reign to "do their own thing." It does suggest that the motivation factors, compensation, and incentive structures, in concert with the managerial style used, must be different from those of managers of existing business. The question, therefore, becomes how to put into a structured analytical process, people who are encouraged to think and act in ways that do not deliberately conform to the corporate mindset.

DEMONSTRATING TOP-MANAGEMENT COMMITMENT

Ultimately, top management either makes or breaks the success of new-product-development programs. Commitment to new products stems from the top. Without it, the most creative, dynamic, and gung-ho manager will most likely fail in commercializing new products successfully.

So the first message that must be communicated throughout a company is that top management has a great degree of commitment to internally developed new products and considers them very important. The role of new products within a company must be commonly understood and believed in by all levels of management across functional and operating divisions.

But what does top-management commitment look like? How can you tell when a company has it? Top management must demonstrate commitment—not just talk about the need for it. Commitment can be demonstrated by assigning the best managers to new products, by rewarding new product participants with incentives consistent with long-term goals, by treating new products as an investment center rather than an expense, and by providing leadership that pulls all functional managers together in backing the new product effort.

The following are other tangible signs of top-management commitment to new products.

☐ Having lunch monthly with the new product group

☐ Dropping down to the laboratory and donning a white coat for a day

☐ Attending a new-products focus group to hear what problems consumers are citing

☐ Writing personal memos to new-product personnel—to people directly and indirectly involved in the process, commending their contributions

☐ Holding an annual awards dinner that rewards the top five new product "contributors" in the company

The point is that beyond consistently providing the people and funds needed to manage new products, top management must act in ways that illustrate to managers an interest, involvement, and willingness to participate in the process. And not only does this demonstration of top-management commitment signal the importance of new products, it also generates psychic rewards that link directly back to our discussion of motivation and rewards.

After talking with a few managers, one can form a fairly accurate picture as to whether new product commitment exists—before ever seeing the actual new product track record.

In a winning company, managers' comments will include:

> You see, the president advanced his career when he was in the new product area. He's a real believer and knows that failure is part of the new product game.
>
> The president helps write our new product strategy, which includes a description of the overall mission of new products, financial targets, and screening criteria.
>
> Our division vice-president comes down to the laboratory at least once a month and spends the day walking around and asking us questions.
>
> Top management sits on the new product steering committee and is actively involved in setting priorities and allocating resources. But they don't get in our hair. They let us manage the process.
>
> We have a separate new product department with five people who focus on new product opportunities outside the scope of our existing business.
>
> All of our divisions are expected to generate 20 percent of their revenues each year from new products. We have monthly review meetings with our new product manager to ensure that all activities are focused on one common objective.

In companies less successful in new products, the comments that surface include:

> I know that new products are essential to the growth of the division, but I have to concentrate on the profit performance of the existing business. I can't have the new product manager report directly to me—my span of control would become too broad.
>
> We have a list of new product projects and each operating manager is accountable for getting certain ones done.
>
> He's very supportive of new products. The only problem is that he says we can't afford failures.

We've tried a number of different approaches and designed several processes for developing new products. Each of the last three presidents has changed the process.

You really have to get your feet wet in the new product area in order to advance in the company. But you don't want to stay there too long since you're really out of the mainstream. Your career is affected.

"Out of the mainstream" is often the perspective of companies that have not appropriately elevated the status of new products in a company. Why? Because management may feel more comfortable with acquisitions, focus more attention on them and set a more well-defined strategy for them.

Making a commitment to growth through internally developed new products calls for a "can-do" attitude on the part of top management. The less confident and risk-averse executive may be far more willing to spend capital and allocate human resources against ongoing businesses than on unfamiliar and unproven new product ventures.

Thus, the overall starting point for successful new product development must be a belief by top management that new products is the key to future success for the company. And consequently, top management must ensure that the best people will take risks and be recognized for it. It takes guts for top management to make new product commitments to its boards, shareholders, and other executives. It's difficult to swallow failures and recognize that failure is part of the new-products game. It takes stamina not to cut the new product budget when quarterly earnings pressures continue to mount.

To determine whether top-management commitment exists at your company, answer the following questions. If the answers are, for the most part, in the negative, send a completed copy, unsigned, to your own top management.

1. Is there one person in the organization who is clearly responsible and held accountable for new product development?

2. Does this person report directly to top management?

3. Is top management involved in the new product process on a monthly basis?

4. Does top management participate in decisions that relate to allocating financial and human resources for new products?

5. Do you ever see top management in the labs, plants, or job shop?

6. Are new products prominently displayed in the annual report?

The key is getting top management on board the risky new product roller coaster. They need to appreciate the dips and turns along the way and be willing to get back on, even after they fall off once or twice.

IN SUMMARY

Ten key success factors provide the framework for a successful new product program. With clear goals (blueprint) and a game plan (new product strategy), a consistent execution process will set the stage for innovation. Adequate homework, tracking, and clear accountability will enhance the development process. And support through teamwork, communication, experienced managers, rewards, and top-management commitment will help to foster an environment conducive to risk-taking and product champion building.

New product development is a multidisciplinary process that blends analytics with creativity. A variety of functional and operating managers is needed to develop and launch a new product successfully. Consequently, no one individual within a company can single-handedly launch a new product.

Conversely, one individual, a new product champion, who is emotionally committed to a new product, often represents the internal catalyst behind a new product's success. The challenge for new product champions is how best to keep a wide range of internal and external resources focused and committed. This challenge becomes intensified as often the new product being developed is outside of the champion's direct responsibility, and it provides little enhancement to his or her career and offers a high degree of risk.

What drives successful new product development? Analytics or creativity? Knowledge or intuition? The answer is both—matched with practical application and pragmatic insight. Statistical models and quantitative theories, for the most part, are only tools to use in developing successful new products. Vision building is the essential beginning point. New products is one business discipline in which people rather than computers are the essential key to success. Computers can only assist in logic and analytics; people have the capacity to link analytics and creativity together.

New product development is the same as playing any team sport—it requires commitment, training, game plans, dedicated resources, vision, an intense desire to win, a coach, and intuition.

However, unlike the football team, which is concentrating all of its efforts and resources against developing one sport, a new product team is often heading in several directions with different competitors, in pursuit of various "sports" or new product types, with scattered resources. No wonder acquisitions are the end run for many companies—developing new products internally is a difficult game.

Successful new product development is not unstructured brainstorming that germinates from a flurry of idea-generating sessions, although that may be one part of the process. Rather, success in new products comes from hard work, steady, consistent commitment, dedicated resources, proper homework, and execution of the process. The reason why managing new products is so difficult is that it is a multidisciplinary activity. Few new products have been developed that did not involve marketing, manufacturing, sales, finance, research and development, engineering, and purchasing. As a result, a new product manager usually has the awesome task of coordinating these multiple functions to get a new product out the door. However, normally the people don't report to him, and they get no special incentives for helping out with new products, nor do they even receive recognition for their contributions from their bosses. So why bother?

The patterns of success don't seem to change. They center on the attributes presented in this chapter. Each success factor is important for fostering an effective new product program.

This chapter has described the ten key attributes of successful new product development. A company that can truly execute a program that embodies these characteristics is virtually guaranteed attractive returns from its new products efforts.

The next chapter will focus on how to examine a company's strengths and weaknesses and how these should relate to the development of a new product program.

Few organizations would feel comfortable assuming that their markets are not changing, yet their continuing emphasis on the development of line extensions often assumes that the underlying technical and market environments will not shift to alternate forms, new technologies, different competitive environments, and new ways to satisfy needs.

C. Merle Crawford and Thomas P. Hustad
"From the Editors,"
Journal of Product Innovation Management,
March 1987

3_____

CONDUCTING A DIAGNOSTIC AUDIT

KNOWING YOURSELF

One important characteristic of companies that manage new products successfully is the ability to learn from past mistakes and build upon previous successes. Learning from past performance requires capitalizing on the things that were done right and correcting the things that were done wrong. A new product diagnostic audit identifies both. Corporate plans that outline the role of new products in creating growth are just not enough. An audit is tailored to the needs of a company's new product program and serves as a report card on how well the company has been performing in new products.

The audit pinpoints what to fix from the past and how to develop the blueprint to guide the future. It is a tool that a company can use to forge a successful new product program, laying the groundwork for specific changes to improve the success rate of commercialized new products. Thus, the purpose of the audit is to identify the internal "assets" upon which to build a new product program. It isolates problem areas and provides a foundation for developing a new product strategy.

The audit examines: (1) historical new product performance, (2) internal strengths and weaknesses relative to key competitors, (3) whether the best common new product practices are in place, (4) top-management commitment. It entails looking at a company, *as it is*, from an internal perspective. Not what it thinks it is, hopes to be, plans to be, or dreams of becoming. It is a hard look at the existing strengths of a company that can be exploited in developing new products.

The diagnostic audit identifies the mix of skills and "assets" that are available to enable a company to (1) increase the success rate of new products, (2) enhance the effectiveness of management time spent on developing new products, and (3) allocate required capital and human resources more effectively.

The diagnostic audit sets the stage for formulating a new product strategy. The strategy must ultimately provide management with a way to mesh existing business growth with new product diversification. In short, the new product strategy, guided by the diagnostic audit, should enable a company to optimize its allocation of resources, match its new product activities to growth objectives, and focus management attention on important areas of new product emphasis.

The most successful companies are those that build upon their strengths; however, do not misinterpret this to mean that they don't take risks. Companies that understand that any organization has limited resources are those that tend to generate a higher return on new products. The new product diagnostic audit helps to assess your firm's successes, failures, strong points, areas of opportunity, weaknesses, and changes required to be more successful.

Besides the number crunching that is necessary to evaluate past new product performance, it is useful to determine, qualitatively, just how much synergy exists among functional areas, how creative managers are in generating solutions to everyday problems, and how easy it is to break the mold in your organization. Thus, there is both a quantitative and a qualitative side to the audit. The quantitative side examines past new product performance, success rates, returns and paybacks, variances from original forecasts, and screening criteria. The qualitative side examines internal strengths, top-management commitment, the process, organization structure, communication vehicles, and reward systems.

The diagnostic audit offers an understanding of what it is that a company has to draw and build upon in developing new products. However, few companies want to examine themselves. It is much easier to continue to live in a myopic dreamworld that provides a "pseudosphere" of false comfort. Some companies perpetuate an unrealistic belief that "we can achieve anything we set out to accomplish." While certainly an admirable philosophy, the reality of new product development is that companies cannot afford to spend the money or take the risk to go after just anything. So the diagnostic audit is aimed at calibrating the strengths of a company that may serve as levers in developing new products.

KNOW YOUR LIMITATIONS

How many top managers assume that their companies are highly successful in new products because they launch truckloads of flankers and line extensions each year? Developing new products is a multidisciplinary and focused process, which *fuses* external market needs with internal functional and technological strengths. The challenge is to first identify the internal levers that will have the largest impact on the commercialization of new products.

One common indicator of a company's new product attitude is a question often raised by new product managers, "Why do they always cut the new product budget before anything else?" One reason frequently cited by top management is that they are not willing to accept the risk of failure inherent in the new product game. This aversion to failure often translates into a proliferation of line extensions, flankers, and me-too products that are relatively low-risk new product candidates. Often, it is much easier to simply hide new product activity in existing-business budgets.

Recognizing the internal barriers or obstacles to new products success is an important part of the diagnostic audit. A company must appreciate its limitations and cultural impediments to be better able to build upon its strengths. To come up with an effective plan, a company must conduct a careful examination of the internal tools that it has to work with in cultivating its growth garden. The new product diagnostic audit provides the launching pad from which to fire new products off into the marketplace. In effect, it's like the coach who has to watch his new players in practice before he can call the shots on who should play which positions. A company has to know its internal strengths and short-falls before it knows how best to map out the "right" approach. The first step in managing growth is to discern the internal strengths and weaknesses that represent the "asset" base. This will identify the weak seams in the fabric that need mending.

WHO CONDUCTS AN AUDIT?

Who should conduct a diagnostic audit? Usually, it is the new product manager or whoever is most responsible for coor-dinating and moving new products from idea generation to com-mercialization. This could be the R&D director, the VP of diversifi-cation, the VP of marketing, or the manager of planning. Top management should be involved in the audit, along with the new product people and other functional managers who will participate in the development process.

Using an outside consultant can also be beneficial. For one thing, you can let the consulting team worry about internal "political mines." The outside consultant will probably be more objective and less emotional when it comes to analyzing past per-formance and future expectations. A consultant may be more willing to cite weaknesses that need to be corrected and can recom-mend changes with no vested interest. Strengths and weaknesses are very often more honestly portrayed by outsiders who come in with a fresh perspective. Further, the outside consultant may serve as a sounding board—someone who can discuss necessary changes with management. However, a company can most definitely conduct a new product diagnostic audit itself.

Whoever is responsible and accountable for new product development must be willing to have this "preventive medicine" examination. In addition, top management must be willing to listen to the results of the audit and integrate the findings into the new product strategy and design of the development process. Finally, the diagnostic audit requires a high degree of objectivity and willingness to "dig" for hard-to-find data. It takes time to conduct and yet needs to be perceived as a valuable part of developing a systematic and effective new product process.

WHY CONDUCT A DIAGNOSTIC AUDIT?

The audit enables a company to exploit and capitalize on what it does best, thereby reducing its relative risk and increasing its chances for new product success in the marketplace. But so few companies actually take the time or are willing to conduct a self-appraisal. An internal look can, at times, uncover "underwear" that ends up looking dirty on the corporate clothesline. Thus, a willingness to see things as they actually are is a key requirement before going forth with this endeavor.

After completing a diagnostic audit for a consumer goods manufacturer, the president asked, "How is it possible that we achieved our revenue goals set for new products but only reached breakeven in profitability?" The answer was easy—once a new product had been booted out the door and launched into an autopilot trajectory, the company never bothered to look back. They never once compared the financial performance of the new product to the original objectives set when the new product was given birth in the marketplace. Rather, the annual operating budget and annual forecasts masked all historical perspective on these "growing children."

Nearly two-thirds of survey respondents in a study conducted on new product practices stated that the fit of a new product with internal strengths was the second most important success factor in developing new products. While matching a product to external customer needs was obviously cited as the most important criterion, the winners of today already recognize the need to develop new products on existing strengths—not on wishful thinking. As the chairman of Norcross Companies has stated,

"Buy assets and sell potential." That is certainly true for the company involved in new products.

The new product diagnostic audit reports on the state of health of a company's new product program. In short, it

☐ Quantifies past new product revenue and profit performance.

☐ Isolates underlying causes and rationale for each new product success or failure.

☐ Helps to classify by relative risk level the types of products introduced.

☐ Compares actual performance to original product forecasts.

☐ Identifies development costs for new products, according to development expenses, capital investment, and launch costs.

☐ Determines the usefulness of the screening criteria in place.

☐ Identifies and assesses internal functional strengths and competitive advantages.

☐ Identifies shortfalls and problem areas in the development process, organization, and compensation structure.

☐ Assesses top management's commitment to new products and the resultant culture that emerges.

☐ Measures the success factors that a company has within the organization.

Thus, the purpose of the audit is to pinpoint specific changes that can improve the success rate of commercialized new products. It will also establish the foundation for creating a well-defined new product strategy. Understanding where a company has been in the past will increase the chances of developing a realistic road map for the future.

HOW TO CONDUCT AN AUDIT

Keep in mind that much of the historical new product data will most likely need to be reconstructed. Historical new product information often migrates to the dark corners of corporate inactive files. However, by interviewing management and digging through old files and surveys, a fairly good data base can be constructed. When dealing with any former new product people, be sure to build their egos before asking for historical new product information, especially if the product was a bomb. They may be sensitive to the past if the variance between expected performance and actual results was fairly large.

Stages of an Audit

Each of the stages of the diagnostic audit will be described in detail in the remainder of this chapter. In addition, the software program, *The New Products Diagnostic Audit* by Thomas Kuczmarski and Richard Koff, is a useful tool for accumulating the data required to perform the audit and analyzing its significance. It also provides an easy way to catalog performance from one year to another.

The four stages of a new product diagnostic audit include:

1. *Historical New Product Performance and Growth Gap.* Examining the company's new product past-performance record and future financial targets and comparing them.

2. *Strengths-and-Weaknesses Assessment.* Analyzing the internal functional strengths and identifying the major assets upon which to build a new product strategy.

3. *Best-Practice Scoreboard.* Determining which key success factors for new product development are in place.

4. *Top-Management Commitment.* Evaluating the degree of top-management commitment to the new product effort.

As part of the audit, companies should identify the ways they plan to grow. There are several growth modes that a company can pursue—not just new product development. How a company wants to grow is often an indication of the overall risk profile for the organization. Increasing market share of existing products through line extensions and flankers is certainly lower risk than entering new markets and categories with new-to-the-company products. It is helpful to think about these approaches to growth and determine which ones will be considered and most likely used by your own company. Examples include:

☐ Expanding market share of existing products through changes in marketing mix
☐ Introducing existing products into new geographic markets and distribution channels
☐ Expanding the overall market by developing new uses for existing products

☐ Licensing existing technology or products over to other manufacturers or receiving licenses from others

☐ Developing new products internally

☐ Entering into joint-venture agreements with another manufacturer

☐ Acquiring companies or products to get into new businesses or to expand and bolster existing product lines

Once the growth modes have been examined, the following questions can serve as a backdrop—a preliminary discussion guide that will bring out many of the issues addressed in the diagnostic audit. The overall objective is to determine how your company has performed in new products. The answers to these questions should provide a snapshot of some of the challenges facing your company in the new product arena.

DIAGNOSTIC WARM-UP CHECKLIST

☐ What have been the major internal factors influencing the company's new product performance during the past three to five years?

☐ What new products have competitors introduced within the past five years? How have their new products performed in comparison to yours? Why?

☐ Which current functional strengths have had the greatest and most frequent impact on successfully commercialized new products? What specific shortfalls need to be corrected in the following areas?

  Sales and marketing
  Manufacturing
  Research and development
  Engineering
  Finance
  Market research

☐ What strategic roles have new products satisfied for the company, and how has performance contributed to the company's financial objectives?

☐ On what types of new products has the company focused, e.g., totally new to the world, new lines to the company, line extensions and adaptations, new additions to existing lines, cost reductions?

☐ What screening criteria have been used to evaluate new products that have been under development? Under what circumstances did the criteria change? What were go/no go decisions really based on?

☐ How effective are the communication and coordination between the sales/marketing, manufacturing, and engineering functions? How does the current process address the need for multidisciplinary integration of various functional areas?

☐ What formal and informal communication mechanisms exist that foster team interaction in the development process?

☐ How does the current organization structure enhance the management of the new product process? What are the major weaknesses?

☐ How can the current process, approval procedures, and development time be streamlined to decrease the gestation time of new products?

☐ Who has been held accountable for new products, and how have the performances of new product managers been measured? Where in the organization should the new product effort report?

☐ What type of compensation incentives or reward systems have been used to support the objectives, structure, and process?

☐ What role has top management played in the new product program?

In answering these questions, a company will begin to understand some of the underlying reasons behind its new product performance. Moreover, the answers will provide indications of the types of objectives and roles that new products will play in meeting the overall growth objectives of the company.

While the diagnostic audit is a vital tool for setting up a new product program, the key to new product success remains with top management and the degree to which they provide "carrots" for inspiring entrepreneurial managers in the company. Too often, managers go unrewarded for the risks that they take in the new product arena. Just as bad, however, are rewards for introducing unsuccessful products—rewards given just because managers were able to get something out the door. Management must meet the new product challenge directly and work vigorously at the implementation of the strategy. Without proper execution and full management support, the best plans become worthless—indeed, they become dangerously expensive.

If a diagnostic audit is performed thoroughly, this tool will serve as a lever in moving top management out of the storm's eye and into the turbulent whirlwind of new product activity. Tooling up for new product success must begin with identifying the hammers and nails that can be used in establishing the new product framework. With the framework built and resources in place, a successful outcome will result.

The first stage of the diagnostic audit looks at the financial and strategic performance of the company's new product portfolio as well as the performance of each new product introduced during the past five years. Beyond examining the company's new product past performance record, this first stage also looks at the aspects of the development process, resource-allocation mix, and competitive new product activity. In stage I there are six steps that examine performance:

1. Identify historical new product revenue and profit performance.

2. Determine the new product survival rate.

3. Assess new product performance against original objectives—the success rate.

4. Determine the underlying causes behind new product success or failure.

5. Pinpoint new product development time and costs—the payback.

6. Identify strengths of top new product competitors.

Each step will add insight into the company's new product strengths. The first involves taking an in-depth look at the historical revenue-and-profit performance of new products.

STAGE I. HISTORICAL NEW PRODUCT PERFORMANCE AND GROWTH GAP

Step 1. Identify historical revenue and profit performance of commercialized new products—determine the bang from your buck

Let's begin with a simple evaluation of how much money was generated from all of the new products introduced over the past five years.

First, list by year the names of all of the new products introduced in the past five years. Second, categorize each new product according to one of the following seven new product types. Some of the following new product definitions are reprinted with the permission of Booz, Allen & Hamilton Inc.

1. *New to the world.* Products that create a totally new category or market.

2. *New product/line to the company.* Products that may already exist in one form or another but not in your company.

3. *Line extension/flanker.* Products that are closely related to an existing line and provide a way to expand the number of products offered to customers, e.g., new flavors, new sizes.

4. *Revision or improvement to an existing product line.* Products that offer improved performance or greater price/value to customers. These frequently replace an existing line item.

5. *Cost reduction.* Products that have a lower manufacturing unit cost than formerly. These may or may not be perceived by consumers as also having a product improvement.

6. *Repositioning.* Existing products that are reformulated, repackaged, or remarketed to attract new customers or pursue a new market.

7. *Licensed, joint ventured, or acquired new product.* New products that are generated through licensing agreements, a majority or minority joint venture with another company, or products that are acquired from another company.

Thus, a company that has launched ten new products in the past five years might categorize its new product types as follows:

New to the world	1	10%
New to the company	2	20
Line extensions	5	50
Repositionings	2	20
	10	100%

In this case, the company appears to have taken a relatively moderate-risk profile toward new products. With 70 percent of all new products launched falling into the broad category of "me too" or "better than," relatively little risk may have been assumed. However, 30 percent of their new products did fall into the higher risk category of new-to-the-world and new-to-the-company types.

The next step is to take this list of new products and

calculate annual and cumulative revenues and profits for each during the past five years. The most important number will be the cumulative profit for each. Cumulative calculations are important because management often forgets that the gestation period for a new product does not necessarily correlate to quarterly earnings reports. Thus, profits cannot be expected to be attractive until a new product has reached the growth stage of its life cycle. Obviously, this stage will be different for each new product.

The cumulative profit must eventually be reviewed in light of the original start-up and investment costs involved in developing the new product. Most important, this review may provide management with some insights for allocating future dollars against those types of investments that have been most fruitful in the past. The start-up costs will have to include the initial capital that was used not only for plant scale-up but also for testing equipment required in the initial laboratory stages. However, at this point, the only items under consideration are the revenues and profits generated from each new product. So for each new product launched during the past five years, list annual revenues and profits by year and add them up to determine cumulative revenues and profits during that time period.

As an illustration, let's take a look at the new product scoreboard for a $20 million company (Table 3-1).

This $20 million company introduced new products that increased its revenue size by 13 percent—from $20 million to $22.6 million. Moreover, since the company grew to $25 million in total revenues, new products represented roughly 50 percent of the growth with the remainder coming from market-share gains made by existing products. With cumulative revenues of $2.6 million coming from new products and a cumulative operating profit of nearly $500,000—almost a 20 percent profit margin—it appears as if the new product effort is relatively successful.

However, management had wanted an incremental $4 million in revenues from new products and expected to add an additional $800,000 to the bottom line. Furthermore, total development costs during that five-year period came to $650,000; capital investments of $275,000 were made in plant modifications and equipment. In short, the company invested $925,000 and generated a net return of $493,000. Now the performance looks a bit different, doesn't it? However, three of the four new products appear to be growing rapidly and will most likely hit the profit target within the next two years.

Depending upon who interprets the data, new product performance can be evaluated in various ways. Technically, the

TABLE 3-1 A NEW PRODUCT SCOREBOARD FOR A $20 MILLION COMPANY

	Year 1	Year 2	Year 3	Year 4	Year 5
Revenues					
Product A	$ 35,000	$ 60,000	$ 76,000	$ 110,000	$ 165,000
Product B	25,000	20,000	18,000	19,000	29,500
Product C	250,000	350,000	375,000	421,500	478,000
Product D	20,000	22,000	26,000	28,000	35,000
Annual revenues	$ 330,000	$ 452,000	$ 495,000	$ 578,500	$ 707,500
Cumulative revenues	$ 330,000	$ 782,000	$1,277,000	$1,855,500	$2,563,000
Operating Profits					
Product A	$ 2,000	$ 3,500	$ 6,000	$ 7,500	$ 15,000
Product B	2,500	2,600	3,600	3,800	3,900
Product C	25,000	60,000	70,000	120,000	155,000
Product D	2,000	2,200	2,600	2,800	3,000
Annual profit	$ 31,500	$ 68,300	$ 82,200	$ 134,100	$ 176,900
Cumulative profit	$ 31,500	$ 99,800	$ 182,000	$ 316,100	$ 493,000

original new product goals were not met. A corporate officer could actually claim that the new product effort resulted in a negative return on dollars invested. On the other hand, the new product program resulted in incremental revenue and dollar growth, sizable enough to be meaningful, and apparently will reach break-even shortly. Moreover, the goals established were missed only by a small amount, so we would evaluate this company's new product performance as reasonably good.

As previously stated, however, examining revenues and profits alone is not enough. Profits generated from new products must be compared to the development and investment expenditures made to get the product into the marketplace.

Let's look at another company that introduced more than 125 new products during the past five years. While the bulk of the new products launched were line extensions and flankers, each one required financial development and management time. During a five-year period, new products added $11.7 million in incremental revenues to this $110 million food company. Management had set a target of $10 million in revenues and $1 million in operating profit. The revenue target was clearly met, and the profit target fell short by only $75,000. From a financial standpoint, this company obviously made its new product targets. Annual and cumulative revenues and profits are presented in Table 3-2.

The objective is to separate the profit generators from the profit losers relative to the amount of dollars spent in developing each. The key is to keep this analysis simple—no internal rates of return, net present values, capital asset pricing models, or the like. But studying *only* the revenues may provide a false picture of new product performance. As we all know, bigger is not necessarily better. However, now you should have a snapshot of total revenues and profits generated from new products. The next step is to look at the types of new products developed.

Therefore, we need to examine the types of new products introduced. As mentioned, there are seven categories in which to group new products: new to the world, new product/line to the company, line extensions/flankers, revisions, or improvements to, an existing line, cost reductions, repositionings, and licensed, joint ventured, or acquired new products. In keeping with the same example above, we see that the 125 products introduced segment into the three categories as shown in Table 3-3.

Nearly two-thirds of the new products introduced by this company were line extensions and flankers to existing product lines. One of the primary strategic roles for new products was to defend market-share position against competitive inroads. Another

TABLE 3-3 BREAKDOWN BY NEW PRODUCT TYPE

Category	Number of New Products	Percent of Total Number
New to the world	8	6.4%
New to the company	41	32.8
Line extensions and flankers	76	60.8
	125	100.0%

was to gradually increase share of shelf space. Therefore, in this case the large proportion of line extensions and flankers seems appropriate.

The ultimate determination of success and failure is the degree to which new products meet the internal objectives established. But often these objectives become hazy, and they are rarely really determined until after the product is launched. There is a need to examine how well each new product as well as the portfolio of new products has performed, particularly by type. If a company has a 50 percent success rate overall for new products but has a 90 percent failure rate in the new-to-the-company category, a major problem area begins to surface.

Determining the success rate of new products is a function of how well they perform in the marketplace and how well they perform relative to the original objectives set for each new product—the *external* survival rate and the *internal* success rate are the next two measures that the audit will examine.

Step 2. Determine the survival rate—market acceptance, the harsh reality

Next the acid test begins. How many of the identified new products have already been taken off the shelf, dropped by the distributor, are scheduled for discontinuation, or are under consideration to be "canned" shortly? Determining the survival rate means identifying what percentage of all new products launched during the past five years are (1) still in the market; (2) already discontinued, (3) scheduled for discontinuation.

Determining the survival rate by new product type often reveals some initial indicators, flashing warning signals, and corrective guideposts for future new product planning. For example, if all of the discontinued or soon-to-be-canned products are new to the company, perhaps there was not enough testing done in areas in which the company had little understanding or in which requirements to compete were so foreign that it was just easier to disregard early signals. Knowing what has actually gone on in the past is the best data base for building up the number of successes in the future. One consumer packaged goods company's survival record for forty-three new products is shown in Table 3-4.

For the most part, this company did better than average in its overall survival rate—achieving a 62 percent hit rate with twenty-seven of the forty-three launched still on the market. Only 38 percent of all new products introduced during the last five years were market failures.

However, the real message is that this company was able to achieve only a 25 percent hit rate on new product lines to the company. With new-to-the-world products, it achieved a 44 percent acceptance hit rate, in part because all of these new product types had a unique and proprietary technology as their major competitive advantage.

With the new product lines to the company, the company merely surveyed the key growth categories and attempted to develop a slightly better product than already existed. Moreover, half the new product lines traveled through distribution channels that the company had no previous experience with. Their risk was significantly higher with new product lines to the company since they were not building on internal strengths but, rather, trying to capitalize on others' strengths as demonstrated in a high-growth category.

Based merely on the number of new products launched, it appears that line extensions and cost reductions have been their key survivors in the marketplace. However, until we know the revenue size and profitability of the remaining new-to-the-world and

TABLE 3-4 ONE COMPANY'S NEW PRODUCT SURVIVAL RECORD

	Number Introduced	Still on Market	Likely to Be Discontinued	Already Discontinued
New to the world	16	7	4	5
New product/line to the company	4	1	1	2
Line extensions/ flankers	18	15	3	—
Cost reductions	4	4	—	—
Repositionings	1	—	—	1
Total	43	27	8	8
Percent of total introduced	100%	62%	19%	19%

new-to-the-company products, it is difficult to fill in the grade on the report card.

Step 3. Identify the success rate—assessing new product performance against original objectives

Now the internal test begins. How successful have new products been? How realistic were the goals originally set for each new product? Is the company consistently overestimating financial-return targets only to get the capital approved to go forward? Are the goals determined according to one single across-the-board hurdle rate? Have the criteria for success been set according to the relative risk/return potential of the new product? How accurate were the forecasts?

The first challenge is to determine the original objectives that were set for the new product along both financial and strategic dimensions. The question, What's our success rate in new products? can be answered along a number of parameters. First, let's examine how closely actual financials generated resemble original forecasts. Take, for example, a $1 billion corporation that has launched three new products during the past three years. It's fairly easy to judge that the new product program has been unsuccessful since those three new products generated $6.5 million versus the forecast of $22 million in revenues and dropped only $513,000 in profits versus $2,500,000 projected.

Let's examine in more depth the three new products launched, A, B, and C, to gain further insight on performance. For product A, see Table 3-5.

TABLE 3-5 FINANCIAL PERFORMANCE OF PRODUCT A

Total Products	Forecast	Actual	Variance
Cumulative revenues	$22,000,000	$6,546,000	− 70%
Cumulative profits	2,500,000	513,000	− 80
PRODUCT A			
Year 1 revenues	400,000	550,000	+ 38
Year 1 profits	32,000	(64,000)	− 300
Year 2 revenues	460,000	635,000	+ 38
Year 2 profits	41,400	50,800	+ 23
Year 3 revenues	525,000	700,000	+ 33
Year 3 profits	52,500	56,000	+ 7
Cumulative revenues	$ 1,385,000	$1,885,000	+ 36%
Cumulative profits	$ 125,000	$ 42,800	− 66%

Clearly, from a revenue standpoint, product A far exceeded forecast revenues, however, first-year marketing costs were higher than anticipated resulting in negative first-year earnings. Thus, profits were off by 66 percent for the first three years versus forecast. But revenues and profits appear to be growing at about 10 percent per year. Was this new product, in particular, a success or a failure? The correct answer is that it may take another year or two before that can be determined. The major concern should be whether profit margins can be increased to the forecast 9 percent. Even though revenues may continue to increase, management may want to kill this product if margin improvement does not materialize. Now let's look at the performance of the second new product. (See Table 3-6.)

With product B, cumulative profits were only 5 percent off the three-year forecast, although revenues were down by 36 percent from the original revenue forecasts. In contrast to product A, profit margins on this product exceeded forecast—13 percent versus the forecast 9 percent. In this case, even though revenues are falling short of projections, product B appears to be successful and growing. Revenues should be closely monitored to determine if the original forecasts were just aggressive or something is needed to boost sales.

Finally, we turn to product C, which was a clear loser. (See Table 3-7.)

Product C is clearly unsuccessful. It has still not generated a positive cash flow, revenues are falling off, and margins are slipping owing to price competition. While the answer should be obvious, several companies in this situation will not kill the product. They will continue to feed it cash since that incremental $400,000 in revenues is now built into the annual operating bud-

TABLE 3-6 FINANCIAL PERFORMANCE OF PRODUCT B

	Forecast	Actual	Variance
PRODUCT B			
Year 1 revenues	$1,500,000	$ 950,000	− 37%
Year 1 profits	120,000	95,000	− 21
Year 2 revenues	1,800,000	1,140,000	− 37
Year 2 profits	160,000	165,000	+ 3
Year 3 revenues	2,160,000	1,425,000	− 34
Year 3 profits	216,000	211,000	− 2
Cumulative revenues	$5,460,000	$3,515,000	− 36%
Cumulative profits	$ 496,000	$ 471,000	− 5%

TABLE 3-7 FINANCIAL PERFORMANCE OF PRODUCT C

	Forecast	Actual	Variance
PRODUCT C			
Year 1 revenues	$ 500,000	$ 250,000	− 50%
Year 1 profits	40,000	(55,000)	−238
Year 2 revenues	600,000	480,000	− 20
Year 2 profits	60,000	33,500	− 44
Year 3 revenues	700,000	416,000	− 41
Year 3 profits	70,000	20,800	− 70
Cumulative revenues	$1,800,000	$1,146,000	− 36%
Cumulative profits	$170,000	$ (700)	N/A

get. If that product is killed, the revenues will have to be made up elsewhere. This is a wrong decision but one commonly made.

Total Performance

But now let's look at the portfolio of products. Granted, the forecasts were consistently higher than actuals. In addition, the overall new product program did not even come close to achieving the goals originally set. The major question is, Why weren't more new products launched during that time period? The forecast $22 million in revenues to come from new products surely was not expected to come from only three new products. Thus, overall performance relative to the company's new product growth goals is dismal at best.

On the other hand, in looking only at the three new products launched, performance appeared to be relatively good. A 66 percent hit rate was achieved, an incremental $6.6 million has been added to the company's revenues, and an additional $513,000 has dropped down to the bottom line. I'd be hard pressed to say that those three new products represented failure, even though, overall, the company clearly has a major new product problem.

Now let's examine the strategic objectives that were developed for the new product program as well as for each new product launched.

☐ *Overall Strategic Role For New Products:* Defend market-share position from competitive inroads by foreign competition.

☐ *Product A:* Preempt foreign competition by entering an emerging category segment.

      □ *Product B:* Launch a price-competitive line extension that will increase total line market share and deter competition from gaining access to distribution channels.

      □ *Product C:* Increase plant utilization to increase gross margins and decrease excess plant capacity.

      The first two strategic roles were most important to the overall mission of the new product program. Products A and B did meet the two roles. There may be some question as to whether the first two products were financially successful relative to the original forecast, but there is no question that they were highly successful in defending market position and preempting foreign competition from gaining headway in the category. Thus, for two out of the three new products developed, performance appears strong from both a financial and strategic standpoint. The real problem was that too few new products got out the door. Maybe management only wanted "winners" so only the top three new products were launched. Or maybe resources were so scarce that three new products were all that could be handled internally. Whatever the reason, the message is that what was done in new products was good—just not enough—at least relative to the objectives set for the new product program. Of course, the final variable missing from this stage of analysis is the payback. If the company invested $25 million to accomplish this program, our whole view of the relative success of those three new products would dramatically change.

      Thus, defining success and failure of new products is highly interpretive. The good news is that keeping track of how well each new product is doing as well as of the portfolio of products is the best way to establish a data base, which will then provide a tool to use in forecasting for the future. The bad news is that too often top management will use those original forecasts as a club, not a tool.

Step 4. Determine the underlying causes behind each new product's success or failure

      Accurate information is often the most difficult to collect in this step since underlying reasons behind performance change radically depending upon whether the product was a success or a failure. Information becomes highly interpretative and interdependent. The reasons why new products succeed or fail can usually be attributed to internal problems in execution, planning, testing, positioning, or forecasting. Competitive response to a new product launch can indeed negatively affect projections, but usually a product failure could have turned into a success with better internal planning and execution. The areas that should be examined to understand why a new product performed as it did include:

- □ Assumptions made in business analysis and interpretation of test results. How did information differ from observations that can now be made in the market?
- □ Data and analysis behind original financial forecasts; reasons behind changes made to forecast after test market. What is the variance between original forecasts, projections after test market, and actual performance?
- □ External factors that influenced performance—consumer-demand shifts, competitive responses, distribution-channel requirements, and so on.
- □ Internal factors that influenced performance—lack of proper funding, insufficient research, inadequate testing, no screening criteria; or positive, strong sponsorship, technology and marketing cooperation, top-management commitment, and so on.
- □ Quality of execution and coordination of the product launch in the marketplace.

Frequently, the rationale behind a new product's performance can be seen by looking at the business analysis and test-market results. If the new product is an underachiever, the cause may be competitive moves, such as raising the stakes by cutting price, adding promotions, or increasing advertising spending. Or perhaps the new product concept did not have a well-defined vision or a clearly defined positioning that the consumer can easily relate to and understand.

Assumptions behind original objectives set for a new product often do not relate to test-market results—another reason behind new product failures. Then why run a test market? When a new product does well in a test, management often assumes that with some incremental spending, volume can double. The major purpose of a test market is to simulate performance in the marketplace prior to costly roll-out expenditures. However, bullishness frequently creeps into financial objective setting. Other times the numbers increase to justify the manufacturing capital investment that has already been made—and the many different reasons continue.

Every good analysis of new products must include competitive contingency plans that spell out how competition may respond to the launch of a company's new product. Managers often fail to anticipate what corrective measures will need to be taken to counteract competitors' moves against a new product. Will competition increase advertising dollars, encourage dealer discounts, drop the price, launch a competitive "better-than" new product? This shortsightedness on the impact of competition is one reason why a new product underperforms to original forecasts. Other times a new product is launched "before its time," when too small a segment of consumers is interested in the product. For example, microwave popcorn started off slowly but recently has had a strong growth record as microwave penetration and usage have steadily grown.

Internal factors are often the cause of a new product's success or failure. The sales force didn't sell the new product aggressively enough, and therefore, when the advertising ran, the product still was not on the shelf. Or there were manufacturing problems with the product as volume increased because as through-put went up, the existing equipment could not supply adequate demand for the product. In contrast, the success of a product may be due to the technological breakthrough that came from the R&D lab, or to astute marketing that positioned the product dramatically differently from competition.

The actual launch of a product can be the factor that spells success or failure. Was the product promoted correctly? Was there enough consumer advertising behind it to stimulate trial? Were distributors and dealers given adequate incentives to get new distribution? Had enough consumer testing been done prior to launch to work out the "bugs" in the product, before it got into the hands of the consumer?

An industrial-equipment manufacturer launched a new product that was priced at $15,000 and had tested it with only two users. Both users were satisfied with the product, so the company decided to launch it nationally. However, the type of oil used by other customers caused the product to shut down automatically—the product ended up as a major failure.

Another company selling a diskette product had estimated the market growth at five times the actual, had not thoroughly tested the product, and had not anticipated competition's dropping the price. Nor was its sales force committed to selling the product. Why should they? The new diskette product offered less than half the commission rate that the regular product line provided to them. Again, the product ended up failing.

One may question how a new product can be launched in spite of these obvious barriers. That's the downside of having strong product champions who have an emotional attachment to new products. The irony is that a company cannot live without product champions, but there must also be enough checks and balances in the process so that sound business judgment—not emotion—ends up driving new product decisions.

In short, determining the reasons behind each new product's performance offers insight as to what internal strengths were exploited and which shortfalls need to be shored up. Moreover, the real benefit in examining the causes behind performance comes in identifying consistent patterns that may emerge across new products.

A chemical company's management identified six persistent problems with new product performance. These are listed in Exhibit 3-1. Some common patterns that often surface in examining the reasons behind a failing new product include: lack of clear financial and strategic objectives up front that define what the new product is expected to accomplish, and overoptimistic financial forecasts for the new product. Other reasons often cited are: inadequate market research, product-performance testing, and market testing; insufficient business analysis and inadequate understanding of competition; lack of marketing programs that appropriately support the product's launch; lack of real differentiation from existing products; and inadequate involvement of multiple functional areas during the development and launch of the product.

Thus, by identifying similar patterns behind new product performance, management is better equipped to know what changes need to be made to improve the effectiveness of the company's new product program.

EXHIBIT 3-1 New Product Performance Problems Cited by Management of a Major Chemical Company

---

Unclear career paths for commercial development/new product personnel

Unclear assignment of ultimate new product responsibility

Lack of formalized screening and measurement criteria

Concerns regarding management's real commitment to new products

Insufficient incentives to encourage risk taking

Lack of a well-defined divisional new product strategy

Step 5. Pinpoint the development time and costs for each new product—evaluate the payback period

Evaluating the payback period simply means identifying the breakeven point—when did the new product's operating profits exceed the costs required for developing it?

This step is difficult to calculate since the growth path of a new product is always tough to determine. The reason managers are often reluctant to measure payback is that it is difficult to determine how long a period of time a new product's life cycle will last.

Let's take, for example, a new ethnic food product launched in 1984. Payback on that product is easy to determine. The financials for the first three years after introduction are shown in Table 3-8.

While the company invested $1.3 million to develop and manufacture this new product, cumulative operating profits that fell to the bottom line equaled $1.3 million by the end of year 2. Since breakeven had been forecast for years 3 and 4, performance exceeded expectations. Year 3 profits of $1.7 million were purely incremental.

However, a more complex example of payback is best illustrated by another food company's line extension that was launched regionally, initially, and nationally in year 2. (See Table 3-9.)

The first question that needs to be addressed is, What was the original breakeven period established for this new product? Management had forecast payback to occur by the end of year 2. Clearly, there were performance or expectation problems: either an underestimation of development and investment costs or a misperception of what the growth trajectory would look like for this new product.

TABLE 3-8 PAYBACK ANALYSIS FOR A NEW FOOD PRODUCT ($ MILLION)

	Revenues	Operating Profits	Capital Investment	Development Expenses	Total Investment
Prelaunch			$ .4	$ .8	$1.2
Year 1	$ 3.5	$ .5	.1		.1
Year 2	5.6	.8			
Year 3	11.5	1.7			
Cumulative	$20.6	$3.0	$ .5	$ .8	$1.3

Note: Breakeven occurs by the end of year 2.

TABLE 3-9 PAYBACK ANALYSIS FOR A NEW FOOD LINE EXTENSION
($ MILLION)

	Revenues	Operating Profits	Capital Investment	Development Expenses	Total Investment
Prelaunch			$ .3	$ .5	$ .8
Year 1	$1.5	$ .1		.5	.5
Year 2	2.8	.3			
Year 3	4.4	.5			
Cumulative	$8.7	$ .9	$ .3	$1.0	$1.3

Note: Breakeven may occur by the end of year 4.

Maybe a four-year payback on this product is appropriate if its reason for being was to protect an existing product line's shelf position against encroaching competition. It has had a slow build, which may continue to grow at 15 to 20 percent per year. Assuming that the scenario is accurate, payback would occur during year 4, and by year 5 the product would be contributing roughly $700,000 in incremental profits. So depending upon the role of this line extension, management could judge its performance as satisfactory.

Too often management is either too impatient to see a return on a new product or too lackadaisical to measure payback. The impatient ones need to develop a greater understanding of a new product's growth-and-profit cycle. One way to accomplish this "learning" is to demonstrate the growth cycle taken by new products during a five- or ten-year period. In turn, management may become a bit more sensitized to the longer-term nature of new products.

In contrast, if management falls into the category of "let's not bother with payback measurement," a red flag should emerge. Is management afraid to show the "truth"? If the funds that are plowed into a new product program are yielding a negative return, management and the company's shareholders should be aware of that fact. The caution again, though, is to give a new product a realistic time frame in which to measure a payback period. A new product normally does not turn into an instant success—it takes time.

This exercise should be conducted for each new product that has been identified. Beyond determining the payback period for each new product, the ultimate test is to determine the payback for the total portfolio of new products. For example, take a specialty chemicals manufacturer that expected at least $1 million in operating profits to be generated from new products in five years. (See Table 3-10.)

In this example, top management's goal of adding $1 million to the bottom line from internally developed new products in five years was met. That goal was achieved. But how many managers would be willing to continue to support a new product program if by the end of year 3, the net return on the program was a negative $975,000? Management sees that instead of making $1 million, they have lost nearly $1 million within a brief three-year period.

Not all new product programs turn out with a happy ending, as this example did. A very plausible scenario would be that the company ended up with a $2 million loss at the end of year 5. In that case, management would have been better off to take the $975,000 loss at the end of year 3 and discontinue production. Managers who lay out a new product strategy, provide the resources and commitment needed, and track performance of new products will make the right decision the vast majority of the time.

Keep in mind that payback periods are often set by new product type in order to differentiate the relative risk, growth path, and level of investment required for each. A line extension or new addition may require, for one company, a two-year payback period, in contrast to a new-to-the-world product that has a five-year payback period and a new-to-the-company product with four-year payback period by the same company. Therefore, it is important when calculating payback periods to group the results by new product type.

The final exercise within this step is to determine the amount of time required to get each new product from concept generation to commercialization. Take, for example, a transportation company that has broken out the time required to launch three new products. (See Table 3-11.)

On average, it appears to take this company approximately two years to move new products from concept development to market commercialization. However, this development period is relevant only when compared to competition and the industry. Some industries may typically require seven to eight years to develop a new product, on account of technology and capital investments. If your company can develop a new product that is new-to-the-company in three years and your key competitor successfully accomplishes the same thing in eighteen months, your development process may be taking too long.

Development time is an important factor to consider when forecasting future new product revenues. With a five-year

TABLE 3-10 NEW PRODUCT FINANCIALS FOR A SPECIALTY CHEMICALS MANUFACTURER

	Year 1	Year 2	Year 3	Year 4	Year 5
Cumulative revenues	$2,500,000	$4,700,000	$9,500,000	$17,600,000	$28,400,000
Cumulative profits	150,000	375,000	875,000	1,950,000	3,650,000
Capital investments	(250,000)	(600,000)	(1,000,000)	(1,150,000)	(1,200,000)
Development costs	(250,000)	(600,000)	(850,000)	(1,000,000)	(1,250,000)
Total costs	($ 500,000)	($1,200,000)	($1,850,000)	($2,150,000)	($2,450,000)
Variance (profit minus total cost)	($ 350,000)	($ 825,000)	($ 975,000)	($ 200,000)	$1,200,000

TABLE 3-11 EXAMPLE OF DEVELOPMENT TIME FOR THREE NEW PRODUCTS

	Product A (Months)	Product B (Months)	Product C (Months)
Concept development	3	5	2
Business analysis	3	4	4
Prototype development	8	4	16
Test market	6	2	8
Launch	3	5	4
Total development time	23	20	34

forecast, the new product revenue stream will not even begin until year 3 if it takes two years before any new product gets launched. Granted, there may be several new products that are worked on simultaneously during the first couple of years and will be launched in years 3 and 4, but the point is still an important one. It takes time to develop new products, and during that time, cash is only flowing out—not in. Moreover, other investment opportunities may be foregone in lieu of the products under development.

There is one other time issue that should be examined during this step. How much time was spent on new products by all participants in the process? That requires an estimate of what portion of each employee's time by functional area is spent on new products during an average month. For example, this assessment might look like Table 3-12.

If later in the diagnostic audit it appears that manufacturing the new product is a frequent problem area, it may be due to the fact that manufacturing and engineering are not involved enough in the process. Moreover, if the new product objectives keep changing every quarter, it may be an indication that some senior managers need to spend more than a half day a month just getting up to speed on the new product projects. The time commitment of a few may be too short, while the involvement of others may actually be too long. The point is to identify the specific resource requirements needed to get the job done and then ensure that sufficient time is allocated to the effort by functional area.

Moreover, gaining some insight into who spends time on new products often reveals the functional strengths that are exploited in successful new products. Very often there is a direct relationship between the causes of success or failure of a new product and the amount of functional time committed to that product. If R&D spends the most time on them, new products are more often technology driven. If marketing is the major participant in the pro-

TABLE 3-12 ALLOCATION OF MANAGEMENT TIME SPENT ON DEVELOPMENT OF NEW PRODUCTS

	Number of People	Average Number of Days per Month per Person	Percentage of Time Spent on New Products per Person
Senior management	6	.5	3%
New product management	2	20	100
Marketing management	3	4	20
Research & development	5	8	40
Manufacturing	2	4	20
Engineering	2	3	15
Finance	1	2	10
Total	21	41.5	

cess, new products may be more advertising driven. There needs to be an appropriate balance between functions so that internal strengths are utilized to cover as many bases as possible.

Step 6. Identify the internal strengths exploited by the top three new product competitors

The first requirement in this step is to identify the top two or three competitors for each new product. Often, one competitor may turn up more than once as a common competitor for several new products. After developing a list of competitors for each new product launched, list the type and number of new products each competitor developed during the same time period.

Yes, that is more work because additional external research is needed. However, this information can be relatively easily obtained through annual reports and 10-Ks, trade associations, periodicals, and phone calls to security analysts, suppliers, vendors, and the like.

It's easy to brag about the three great new line extensions that have been launched by your company until you begin to assess what your competition had done in comparison. If we take two competitors in the same industry, for example, three great line extensions suddenly look rather pale.

COMPETITOR A (EIGHT NEW PRODUCTS)

New to the world	2
New to the company	6
Still on the market	7

COMPETITOR B (FIFTEEN NEW PRODUCTS)

New to the world	3
New to the company	2
Line extensions	10
Still on the market	12

Now compare the external survival rates of a competitor's products to your own company's new product survival rate. While you won't get a true evaluation of that competitor's internal new product success rate, you will get a reasonable proxy. Also, be sure to evaluate the reasons behind varying success rates.

The major advantage of identifying competitors' new product activity is to gain insight on how they might respond to new products that are launched in their category arenas. We will examine competitive new product activity again in the business-analysis chapter. But for purposes of the diagnostic audit, it is important to compare the number, type, and survival rate of competitors' new products.

NEW PRODUCT PERFORMANCE RECAP

So far, we have collected information aimed at providing a quantitative assessment of how well a company's new products have performed. Let's summarize some of the performance measures that have been discussed. The value of interpreting the performance data in total is that additional observations can be made and a better understanding established regarding why and how new products have performed in the past. By now, the following new product statistics can be assembled. Take, for example, an industrial tractor company that has $50 million in sales and has launched ten new products within the past five years. After analyzing past performance according to the six steps discussed, the diagnosis was that overall new product performance was excellent. To recap the performance benchmarks for this industrial company, a summary follows.

NEW PRODUCTS PERFORMANCE RECAP

Number of new products launched during a five-year period
Number of new products planned for launch

Revenues and profits by type of new products
commercialized (percent of revenues shown)

New to the world	30%
New to the company	40%
Line extensions	20%
Repositionings	10%
Cumulative revenues generated from new products	$5,000,000
Cumulative profits generated from new products	$600,000
External survival rate	80%
Internal success rate relative to original goals	50%
Actual new product revenues as a percent of forecast revenues	92%
Actual new product profits as a percent of forecast profits	57%
New product revenues as a percent of corporate revenues	10%
New product revenues as a percent of corporate revenue growth	65%
Corporate growth rate during the past five years	12%
Corporate growth rate without new products	1%
New product profits as a percent of corporate profits	12%
Total development costs and capital investments	$350,000
Payback period	year 4
Average development time for each new product	24 months
Number of new products launched by competitor 1	5
Survival rate of competitor 1	80%
Number of new products launched by competitor 2	3
Survival rate of competitor 2	67%

This company has a successful new product program under way. Historically, new product performance has been excellent. But how can these statistics best be used in determining how to change or alter a less successful company's program? Let's examine seven of the more important performance indicators for this same company. (See Table 3-13.)

TABLE 3-13 MOST IMPORTANT NEW PRODUCT PERFORMANCE
INDICATORS

New Product Performance Indicators	Actual
Number of new products launched versus plan	83%
External survival rate	80%
Internal success rate	50%
Actual revenues versus forecast	92%
Actual profits versus forecast	57%
Payback period	4 years
Net return on development costs	$250,000

Each indicator offers critical information on how well the new product program is working. If the internal success rate is 50 percent, the causes behind performance need further examination. The causes may range from unrealistic forecasts to underspending in marketing support. The historical new product performance statistics should be used as a tool to help pinpoint past strengths on which to capitalize and weaknesses to overcome.

Conducting an annual historical new product performance analysis provides a mechanism to monitor progress from one year to the next. This is often a valuable tool for securing additional resources and dollars for future new products. In the next example, we examine a $325 million consumer products division within a $3 billion corporation. The example shows why an audit is important. Management can be easily fooled by big revenues stemming from new products. During a five-year period, the consumer products division launched thirty-five new products, which generated $66 million in cumulative revenues, representing 20 percent of total division revenues. Thus, division management was touting the significant revenue role that new products played in its growth.

But total cumulative profits from those thirty-five new products amounted to $89,000. That's right—$66 million in sales generated $89,000 in pretax profits.

Since approximately $6.5 million had been invested in the new product program, it is clear that this division did not have a successful new product program from a profit standpoint. After further examination, one of the causes behind its poor profit performance is the predominant number of very small revenue generators. Nearly 60 percent of the new products had less than $1 million in cumulative sales, and 72 percent generated less than $500,000 in cumulative profits during the five-year period. When the profit losers were added to the new products that enjoyed some profits, albeit small, the total was $89,000. Moreover, over 40 percent of all new products launched were either profit losers or broke even at best. Only five out of thirty-five new products generated more than $500,000 in cumulative five-year profits. (See Table 3-14.)

An analysis of performance by product type helps to identify the reasons underlying overall performance. (See Table 3-15.)

By analyzing performance by product type, one of the major causes of poor performance becomes apparent: with new-to-the-world and line extensions, the company had a technological edge that provided functional benefits to consumers. Thus, sales volume was strong in these two categories. However, the company never really paid any attention to unit costs, and as a result, these new product types were running at a margin far below existing products. Moreover, with the new-to-the-company products, they put together some rather poorly executed marketing and advertising programs that did not differentiate their products from competition.

An interesting epilogue to this example was that the president of the division still claimed he had a very successful new product program. His bonus was based upon the percentage of

TABLE 3-14 CUMULATIVE REVENUES AND PROFITS ANALYSIS

	Number of New Products	Percent of Total Launched
Cumulative Five-Year Revenues		
$0 to $500,000	14	40%
$500,000 to $1,000,000	6	17
$1,000,000 to $2,000,000	5	14
Over $2,000,000	10	28
Total	35	100%
Cumulative Five-Year Profits		
Losers	5	14%
Breakevens	10	29
$0 to $500,000	15	43
$500,000 to $1,000,000	2	6
Over $1,000,000	3	8
Total	35	100%

TABLE 3-15 CUMULATIVE SALES AND PROFITS BY NEW PRODUCT TYPE

	Sales	Profits	Losses
New to the world	$25,982,000	$ 243,000	
New to the company	11,493,000	0	($919,000)
Line extensions	25,551,000	765,000	
Repositioning	3,220,000	0	
Total	$66,246,000	$1,008,000	($919,000)
Net Profit		$89,000	

revenues generated from new products. He hit the 15 percent target each year. As already stated, success in new products can be interpreted differently depending upon who is doing the evaluating and who is providing the rewards.

Once historical performance has been assessed, an analysis of future expectations can be conducted so that the two can be compared. This leads us to the final step in Stage I: identifying the new product growth gap.

Step 7. Identify the new product growth gap

The purpose of identifying the new product growth gap is to determine the portion of financial growth that is expected to come from new products. Once the growth gap has been determined, there will be a better understanding of new product program requirements. In turn, resource allocation can be accomplished more effectively. The starting point for determining the growth gap is to examine the past revenue and profit growth of the existing core business. Identifying the growth gap calls for determining the total revenues and profits that new products are expected to contribute to a company's growth during a specific time period—usually three to five years.

Take, for example, a microwave-container business that today has $250 million in sales and generates $18.7 million in profits. Looking back five years, the company had $125 million in sales and $7.5 million in profits. Thus, during the past five years, on average, the company has enjoyed a compound annual growth rate (CAGR) of +15 percent per year in revenue growth, and +20 percent per year in profit growth.

With this historical perspective in mind, the next issue to address is, Which internal and external factors will alter this growth rate during the next five years? Is competition intensifying? Are prices going up or down? Are there new competitors entering the category? Will consumer demand continue to grow at historical levels? The question to be answered is, "What is the projected growth rate of the total market category during the next five years?"

The reason this question is so essential is that it provides a benchmark to measure a specific company's growth projections. If a category is forecast to grow at 8 percent per year, and a company is projecting a 25 percent annual growth rate for a specific product line in that category, management may be filled with delusions of grandeur. However, if the company is planning to take a price reduction, substantially increase its advertising budget, expand its distribution base, or the like, then a 25 percent growth rate for the company may be feasible.

The specific factors that will propel the growth of the company beyond the category growth rate must be identified and segmented into external and internal factors. Once these have been articulated, it is then possible to estimate what impact each will have on the growth of the business. Let's return to our example of the $250 million company that has grown 15 percent per annum in sales. The microwave-container category in which the majority of their product lines compete is expected to grow at 8 percent per year for the next five years. The external factors that are expected to drive the growth of the microwave-container category are: (1) an increase in working women influencing the continued need for convenience and time-saving products, (2) continued household penetration of microwave ovens, reaching an estimated 60 percent of all U.S. households within five years, and (3) increased consumer usage of microwave ovens for cooking purposes as opposed to merely reheating or defrosting.

The company expects its microwave-container business to grow at 12 percent per annum during the next five years. The internal factors the company is relying upon to shoot its sales above industry averages include packaging, advertising, and geographical expansion of its distribution base. The company has done extensive market research, which indicates that its packaging is far superior to competition. Since microwave-container sales are heavily impulse driven, and point-of-sale consumer-purchase decisions have to be heavily influenced by packaging, the company clearly has a sales advantage in this regard. Moreover, this company is planning to spend more than any competitor in broadcast media, in addition to expanding its distribution base to West Coast markets. In this case, it appears quite feasible that this company could exceed the expected 8 percent annual growth of the category and achieve the forecast 12 percent revenue growth.

So the existing core business of $250 million in sales is expected to achieve a compound annual growth rate of 12 percent during the next five years. This means that the company expects to grow to $440 million just from current business growth.

But management has committed itself to an objective of $500 million in sales by the end of that five-year period. Expected sales from existing products will run $60 million short of that goal. Thus, new products are expected to bridge a $60 million growth gap over the next five years. Let's see it that appears feasible.

During the past five years, the company has launched fifteen new products, which accounted for a total of $12 million in cumulative revenues. Now the company is planning to generate five times that amount during the next five years. How? If the same resource structure were to remain and relatively little change occurs internally, it would seem overoptimistic to expect the company to increase its new product revenues fivefold. However, major internal changes have recently taken place that will significantly affect the management of new product development. Top management has changed, a separate new product venture team has been established, a new product director has been put in charge of new product development, and a budget of $5 million has been set aside for at least the first two or three years for new product development. There is a chance of meeting the $60 million growth gap, but it will most likely be a stretch. However, at least a clear objective has been established to focus the new product effort.

However, the $60 million new product objective, by itself, is too broad. It needs to be broken down into smaller, workable, and manageable parts. We now need to segment the $60 million in new products into objectives by new product type to determine the resources and degree of effort and emphasis required to reach these goals.

The breakdown of new products by type in this example is shown in Table 3-16.

With these objectives outlined, resources can be allocated by the degree of effort required to satisfy these aggressive revenue targets. The rather general statement that new products will make up the $60 million gap has now been tied down further by delineating how this number will be achieved.

The next step involves breaking down each new product type and analyzing revenue expectations over the five-year period within each grouping. At this point, it is important to keep in mind that these are cumulative revenue goals. The $15 million in new-to-the-world products, for example, obviously will not be gen-

TABLE 3-16 BREAKDOWN OF NEW PRODUCT TYPE AND REVENUE EXPECTATIONS

	Percentages of New Products Expected to Be Launched	Estimated Cumulative Revenue Expectations
New to the world	25%	$15 million
New to the company	30	18 million
Line extensions	35	21 million
Acquisitions	10	6 million
	100%	$60 million

erated in year 1. Instead, the breakdown in Table 3-17 is more practical.

The $15 million new-to-the-world products objective now looks more plausible. The goal is to launch two products that turn into $2 million to $3 million products. New product managers now have an objective that is workable and logical. The same type of breakdown should be done on the remaining new product categories to provide a perspective on the number and size of new products to develop.

In the line extension category, for example, where more new product launches will be required, the $21 million goal may translate into launching fifteen line extensions, each of which will generate, on average, $520,000 in sales by year 5 ($7.8 million divided by fifteen line extensions). This is indicated in Table 3–18.

Breaking down this category by line extension and revenue stream gives us a better understanding of how to manage the $21 million expectation.

The last step in setting the growth gap is to examine what the new product growth gap was historically. If management has consistently set unattainable goals for new products, it may make sense to scale down the targets now, rather than wait for the

TABLE 3-17 REVENUE EXPECTATIONS FOR NEW-TO-THE-WORLD PRODUCTS

	Revenues ($ Millions)					
	Year 1	Year 2	Year 3	Year 4	Year 5	Cumulative
Product A	0	$ .5	$2.2	$2.6	$3.2	$ 8.5
Product B	0	.9	1.6	1.9	2.1	6.5
	0	$1.4	$3.8	$4.5	$5.3	$15.0

TABLE 3-18 REVENUE EXPECTATIONS FOR LINE EXTENSIONS

Products Launched	Year 1 ($000)	Year 2 ($000)	Year 3 ($000)	Year 4 ($000)	Year 5 ($000)	Cumulative ($000)
3	$300	$ 350	$ 400	$ 450	$ 500	$ 2,000
5	0	2,100	2,500	3,000	3,400	11,000
5	0	0	1,100	2,400	3,000	6,500
2	0	0	0	600	900	1,500
15	$300	$2,450	$4,000	$6,450	$7,800	$21,000

wrath of management to descend in three years when the new product targets are not being met. Again, it may be difficult to uncover what the new product objectives were five years ago. But try to reconstruct some numbers that can be used as the reference point for determining the growth rate during the past five years. Once the growth gap has been calculated and analyzed by product type, comparisons can be made between future expectations and previous performance in terms of the first six steps of the diagnostic audit. An assessment of your company's historical new product performance in terms of revenue, profit, survival rates, original objectives, underlying causes that affect performance, payback, and competitive moves gives you a good idea as to how you've fared in this area of product management. Evaluation of future financial expectations through calculation and analysis of growth gaps should make your understanding even stronger. This stage enables you to define goals and make adjustments in financial objectives before the process is under way. This now completes the first stage of the audit. Stage II moves us into internal strengths and weaknesses.

STAGE II. ASSESSMENT OF STRENGTHS AND WEAKNESSES

Identifying those internal strengths and weaknesses relevant to building new products is a highly subjective, qualitative, and difficult evaluation to conduct. It is open to a high degree of interpretation and judgment. But that's what good managers get paid for.

Searching for new products by examining only external consumer needs and category growth opportunities will typically result in products that end up as revenue and profit mice rather than lions. The further away a company moves from its existing strengths, the greater the degree of risk becomes. Do not misinterpret this to mean that companies should not take risks by going outside their pool of strengths. On the contrary, as already mentioned, companies' most successful new products are new to the world and new to the company—the two riskiest types of new products.

However, even new-to-the-world products can draw on internal strengths. A strength may be in the form of a technology application or brand-name equity that will bring perceived value to the product or a proprietary manufacturing process that can be utilized in making the new product. Even management expertise or familiarity with a given category can represent a valuable strength that can be applied in developing new products.

Internal strengths are magnified by a product champion or entrepreneur. Often the champion's tenacity, drive, and persistence in developing a new product results in success, even if no existing strengths are utilized. The benefit of having an entrepreneurial champion in the organization cannot be overemphasized.

The assessment of any internal strength must be made relative to the importance of that strength in building a competitive advantage. Thus, identifying a company's internal strengths and weaknesses accurately calls for a sound understanding of competitors' advantages and vulnerabilities.

The best way to conduct this assessment is on a category-by-category basis. Once a company has identified specific categories that may represent opportunities for new product development, each category should be examined for the relative competitive strengths that the company could bring to future new products. After a food company had selected four categories in which to pursue new product development, it found that one category, in particular, offered immense opportunities to utilize existing strengths. Two categories afforded some internal leverage, and the fourth category seemed really far afield from any internal advantages. So there was now a priority set for the four categories, at least from a standpoint of competitive advantage.

Again, the reason for pursuing new product opportunities that build on a company's attributes is to increase the chances of success and decrease the probability of failure. Identifying strengths is a company-specific endeavor, but strengths do tend to fall into four common groups: Cost and manufacturing; Technology related; Demand related; and Marketing, sales, and distribution.

For each of the groups, there is an expanded list of attributes. (See Exhibit 3-2.) The next step in the audit is to decide how well your company stacks up in any given market category compared to your key competitor relative to each attribute. For each attribute, a score of 1 signifies that your competitor has a significant advantage over you in a given market category. A score of 5 signifies that you and your top competitor are relatively equal, while a score of 10 indicates that you have a very strong advantage over your top competitor.

The issue that must be addressed is how important each factor is in gaining a competitive edge and to what extent that strength offers a barrier that will prevent market-share gains by competition.

The scoring approach is suggested only as a means to compare degrees of strength by category. While this analysis can clearly be done qualitatively, applying quantitative rankings to the factors requires more thought and allows for simpler comparison.

First, choose a market category, e.g., major appliances, ready-to-eat cereals, children's toys; then rank your relative degree of strength. The highest attainable score is 300 points. Any category in which a company has 200 points or more suggests a solid strength base for developing new products. A score of 100 to 200 points suggests that some strengths exist but may represent a competitive threat. The key will be to examine whether the most important factors in any given market category are the ones that fall into the strengths category. Finally, any category that ends up with a score of less than 100 indicates an uphill battle relative to other categories based on internal strengths.

However, hundreds of exceptions exist. If a company has a new technology that will enable manufacturing costs to be 60 percent lower than any competitive products, chances are that few other strengths are needed. Each factor is listed in Exhibit 3-2.

EXHIBIT 3-2 Strengths-and-Weaknesses Assessment for a Market Category Relative to Top Competitor

	Company Strengths Relative to Top Competitor (Score 1–10)
Cost-Related and Manufacturing Factors	
1. *Low-cost producer:* Role that unit cost plays in the profitability of the product line. Low-cost producer scores 10; high-cost producer scores 1.	_____

2. *Patented processes:* Degree to which patented processes provide a genuine competitive advantage that cannot be easily duplicated or is costly to replicate. _____

3. *Automated equipment:* Importance of robotics and automated machinery in achieving cost economies. Compare burden or overhead costs of competitor's cost structure. _____

4. *Low material cost:* Portion of raw materials in cost stream; determine competitor with low-cost-materials advantage. _____

5. *Low-cost labor:* Portion of labor costs in cost stream; identify competitor with low labor costs _____

6. *Unique source of supply:* Determine relative substitution capabilities of raw materials and competitive strongholds with suppliers. _____

7. *Productivity programs:* Compare competitor's formalized activities and programs in cost reduction and productivity enhancements. _____

Technology-Driven Factors

8. *Product patents:* Patented products score 10. Unpatented products score 1 if patented product exists; if not, then score 5. _____

9. *Design patents:* Score 10 if design patents exist and are a key advantage in the manufacturing process; score 5 if they exist but are not important; score 1 if they do not exist. _____

10. *CAD/CAM systems:* Assess competitor's use of CAD/CAM and degree of importance of design adaptability and efficiency. _____

11. *R&D spending:* Competitor spending most in R&D scores 10, the least scores 1; weighting determined by impact R&D has had on new products developed in past within category. _____

Demand-Related and Marketing Factors

12. *Product differentiation:* The degree of perceived uniqueness of proposed product line that can be developed relative to existing offerings. _____

13. *Price advantage:* Lowest price in market scores 10; highest price scores 1. _____

14. *Packaging advantage:* The contribution of packaging in stimulating purchase; unique design or protective qualities. _____

15. *Advertising expenditures and exposures:* Importance of advertising in motivating purchase intent and total advertising dollars spent and reach and frequency achieved by competitor. _____

16. *Advertising creative:* Level of aided and unaided recall by consumer and degree to which any one competitor's creative has built awareness of the category. _____

17. *Distribution network:* Role that channel management and multichannel distribution play in product-offering success. _____

18. *Promotion impact:* The importance of consumer promotions and trade discounts in moving product off the shelf; compare competitor's spending levels for each. _____

19. *Public relations:* To what extent does publicity influence consumer trial-and-repeat purchase of the product? _____

20. *Focused market niche:* How does each competitor position its product within the category? Who has the most memorable and useful positioning? _____

21. *Brand-name recognition:* Degree to which brand name is major factor influencing purchase; competitor with highest brand-name awareness and perceived price/value benefit scores 10. _____

22. *Loyal consumer base:* A competitor who has strong consumer franchise scores 10. _____

23. *Management expertise:* Tangible and recognizable experience by managers in category that will provide a competitive advantage. _____

24. *Market research:* Already completed market research that will offer insights into a category; especially good if research is too costly for competition to conduct. _____

Sales and Distribution Factors

25. *Sales-coverage breadth:* Geographic penetration; sales-force coverage; importance of broad sales coverage in selling product. _____

26. *Channel and distribution-cost advantage:* Low-cost distributor scores 10; high-cost distributor scores 1. _____

27. *Selling costs:* Cost per sales call and selling costs per revenue dollar generated relative to competitor. _____

28. *Market/buyer clout:* Degree to which other product-line offerings or trade relationships give a competitor an edge in the category with buyers. _____

29. *Delivery turnaround time:* Extent to which quick delivery is important to buyers in the category. _____

30. *Strategic distribution centers:* Geographic coverage of distribution centers that are strategically positioned to offer lower shipping costs and better delivery times. _____

TOTAL ══════════════

After you have completed this assessment, and have a picture of how your company stacks up relative to competition in terms of new product building blocks, you are ready to move on to examining how well your company looks in terms of the key success factors for effective new product development. These factors are those most commonly found in companies that have a proven track record of hitting their new product targets—time and time again.

STAGE III. BEST-PRACTICE SCOREBOARD

Among companies that are successful at developing new products internally, there emerges a set of common attributes that influence success. This is not to suggest that successful companies always embody these attributes, nor does it suggest that the only way to become successful is to adopt all of these characteristics. However, for the most part, companies that do have certain attributes in place are most apt to succeed in their new product efforts. You can judge how well your own company stacks up by answering the questions in Exhibit 3-3. Score each factor as follows:

□ Score 2 points if attribute is currently in place and working effectively.

□ Score 1 point if attribute has just recently been established.

□ Score 0 if attribute does not exist within the organization.

EXHIBIT 3-3 Best-Practice—Scoreboard

	Success Attributes
1. *Strategic-planning process:* Is there a formalized process used by the company for strategic planning?	_____
2. *Growth role for new products:* Does the corporate-growth plan include a definition of the role of internally developed new products during the next five years?	_____
3. *Defined new product strategy:* Is there a well-defined new product strategy in writing that identifies the financial gap, strategic roles, and screening criteria that new products must satisfy?	_____
4. *Screening criteria:* Are financial and strategic performance screens established to evaluate new product concepts? Are screens based on associated risk by new product type?	_____
5. *Step-by-step new product process and consistent execution:* Has the company had a systematic and formalized, yet flexible and adaptive, new product process in place for at least five years?	_____
6. *Idea generation after homework has been completed:* Does idea generation begin after external market niches have been identified, attractive categories to compete in determined, and internal competitive strengths assessed?	_____
7. *Monitoring and tracking systems:* Does the company formally monitor and track new products relative to original objectives set and measure cost per introduction?	_____
8. *Incentive programs:* Are there compensation programs that encourage entrepreneurship, reward risk takers, and reinforce innovative thinking?	_____
9. *Clear lines of responsibility:* Is there a clear understanding of who is responsible for new products and who is held accountable for performance? Is the decision-making process understood and are go/no go approval points clearly identified and adhered to?	_____
10. *Top-management commitment:* Does top management provide consistent commitment to new products in funding and allocate the best managers, with high-powered skills and know-how, to the new product effort?	_____

11. *Separate new product organization:* Does the primary new product activity take place in an independent group that is set apart from existing business management? _____

12. *Entrepreneurial spirit:* Is there a willingness to take risks and an eagerness to break new ground and engender an independent spirit? _____

13. *Product fit with internal strengths:* Do the majority of new products play off or draw upon existing strengths? _____

14. *Product advocates or champions:* Are there individuals in the company, either self-selected or assigned, who are the sparks for shepherding the development of new products? _____

15. *Adaptive new product organization:* Does the company change the new product organization to accommodate the role and objectives set for new products by matching new product type by structure required? _____

TOTAL ════════════

Based on the fifteen best-practice characteristics, the highest score attainable in this stage is 30 points. Companies that fall above 20 to 25 tend to have the internal tools in place to succeed at new products. Companies that score in the 15-to-20 range have some strong points working for them but need to examine ways to improve their internal new product operations. Companies that score less than 15 need to carefully examine ways to improve their process and overall approach to new products.

Again, do not take these success factors as the pills for immediate cure of a previously failing new product program. Even after companies have changed their programs to include them, it may take one to two years to see some definite progress made in the new product effort.

There is no easy way out; to perform well in new products, there are few substitutes for having these factors in place. It requires planning, thinking through where you want the new product program to head, committed resources, thorough homework, consistency in approach, and rewards for the doers based upon how well new products perform in the marketplace.

The final part of the diagnostic audit is assessing the

relative degree of top-management commitment behind the new product development program. This one is the most difficult to evaluate. Often what is said by top managers is not quite reality. If top management is just not dedicated to new products, try to change that. But if after your attempt, no change results, stop banging your head against a wall and transfer to a new division, department, or company. The chances of succeeding when management is not standing firmly behind new products are limited.

STAGE IV. TOP-MANAGEMENT COMMITMENT

Once again, I invite you to judge your company, this time on top-management commitment. (See Exhibit 3-4.) The question being asked is whether top management is "behind" new products—behind it in terms of a willingness to invest, accept risk, and allocate the needed funds and talent required to make it work. And as important as the "tone" that top management sets, the attitude toward new products that is communicated throughout the organization is the key. As emphasized in Chapter 1, top-management commitment is one of the ten vital success factors.

For each of the fifteen factors score either 2 points or 0. Thirty points is the highest possible score, and committed managers usually fall into the 20-points-or-more range. If the score is lower than 20, then the specific indicators need to be further examined to determine the "real" degree of commitment. A score below 10 suggests that it may be time to hang it up.

EXHIBIT 3-4 Top-Management Commitment

	Management Commitment
1. *Long-term profitability:* Emphasized more than short-term quarterly performance.	_____
2. *Risk-taking environment fostered:* A willingness to play a longshot from time to time and an acceptance of at least a 30 to 40 percent failure rate from commercialized new products.	_____
3. *Effective communication:* This ability is essential if the company is to establish objectives, measure accomplishment, raise morale, and encourage commitment.	_____

4. *Willingness to accept failure:* An attitude that acknowledges the inherent riskiness of developing and launching new products.   _____

5. *Consistent and visible commitment of funds and resources for new products:* The important word here is *consistent.* It is not sufficient to commit human resources or financial support on a sporadic basis.   _____

6. *Adherence to formal planning process:* This requires more than establishing a process on paper; it must not be given just lip service but must be the major instrument of guidance and control in the company.   _____

7. *Reliance on strategic and financial-screening criteria:* These provide a common set of determinants to choose between one new product idea and another. They provide an objective measure of acceptability or success, which otherwise may become quixotic and unreliable.   _____

8. *Flexibility in the new product process:* Despite the need for a formally defined process, management must be willing to change direction and move quickly to take advantage of competitive moves, discoveries, or market changes. The willingness to even skip steps sometimes in the formalized process may be needed.   _____

9. *Dependence upon technology to drive new products:* In general, technology tends to produce more and better competitively advantaged products than superficial or cosmetic changes.   _____

10. *Linking of marketing, manufacturing, and distribution:* All aspects of the development effort are important to successful new products. One cannot neglect any part of the chain without endangering success.   _____

11. *Encouragement of entrepreneurship:* Individuals are given freedom and authority to make decisions on their own and are truly held accountable for new product performance.   _____

12. *Longevity of new product managers and participants:* Keep key new product people in place for at least three to five years. Make the new product function a career path.   _____

13. *Rewards for risk takers and performers:* The
individuals who take the risks get the recognition—psychological and financial, in title
and salary—that their performance deserves. _____

14. *Reinforcement for innovative managers:* The
middle managers responsible for new product development are encouraged to break
new ground in their management styles and
approaches. _____

15. *Autonomy for new product managers:* Managers have authority as well as responsibility,
without constant overseeing and second
guessing by top management. _____

TOTAL ===========

INTERPRETING THE DATA

At this point, you are in a position to judge the overall
health of your company's new product track record and, most
important, are able to determine the strong points as well as shortcomings that may need to be fixed. The new products performance
recap should help to define how and why past new products performed in the market. The growth gap will help guide the formulation of a new product strategy, which is outlined in the next
chapter. You should also have a fix on which best-practice characteristics are in place and the degree of top-management commitment to internally developed new products.

While interpretation of these data needs to be done on
a company-specific basis, a company that has conducted a diagnostic audit is usually light years ahead of a company that is still
trying to figure out why new product revenue targets were never
met.

Now let's take a look at two diagnostic audits conducted on two different kinds and sizes of companies; one company is a consumer packaged goods company in the $100 million
range; another is an industrial goods company with about $50 mil-
lion in sales. Each diagnostic audit was done differently for the
companies, but the results were similar—the information was instrumental in changing and revising the new products strategy,
process, and organization.

Example 1: $100 Million Consumer Packaged Goods Company

NEW PRODUCT DIAGNOSTIC AUDIT SUMMARY

During the past five years, the company has doubled in size, growing 14.4 percent annually in revenues and 12 percent per annum in net operating income. Company performance resulted from repositioning a major product line, making inroads into private label, and increasing sales on the company's largest product line—the backbone of the business.

The category in which the company's product lines competed had grown, on average, 7.5 percent per annum in units and 10 percent in dollars. Clearly, some healthy price increases had recently occurred in this high-margin category. In terms of market share, the company enjoys relative market shares that are more than three times the share of the second largest competitors. The company has garnered a 35 percent share of category units.

The high profitability achieved through the premium-priced brand has offset, in part, margin erosion experienced by other products outside the key category. The company shows a cash/growth balance, which points to sound performance in managing its assets profitably. While the existing business has been a cash generator during the past five years, other new ventures pursued resulted in the company's being a heavy cash user during that time.

The growth goals set for the next five years call for:

☐ Directing 50 percent of financial resources toward diversification

☐ Entering into new but synergistic businesses and product lines

☐ Reducing the company's dependence on a single product category

☐ Generating $200 million in gross sales within five years, and growing, on average, 15 percent per year, outstripping category growth

☐ Becoming a $1 billion company within fifteen years

☐ Increasing market share to 50 percent of category, which would require a stepped-up marketing plan

Moreover, the company's key category shows signs of increasing competitive intensity. The category has been superior relative to most other dry-grocery product categories, thereby attracting new entrants. Penetration outside the U.S. seems minimal since the product is heavy and costly to ship overseas, and there is not enough volume to warrant an offshore manufacturing facility.

Finally, for the existing product lines, expansion into other channels seems limited. Mass merchandisers have demonstrated a reluctance to accept the product, and department or convenience stores would never carry the product. Thus, the existing product line seems destined for the U.S. grocery-store channel.

So, how is this incremental $100 million going to be generated?

Expectations for growth in the existing product lines, which compete in one category, seem good but not good enough to satisfy the aggressive objectives set by company management. Existing business growth will be hurt by increasing competition, limited expansion opportunities through new distribution, and historical category growth of 7.5 percent in units and 10 percent in dollars. In addition, the cost of gaining market share is increasing—more advertising dollars need to be spent today to gain merely one share point.

A careful assessment of how much growth can be realistically generated from the core business shows that approximately $60 million in incremental revenues can probably be forecast. That leaves a $40 million revenue gap to be filled by new products in the next five years.

The company has achieved a solid expertise in process technologies in its current category. Process technologies in this category are capital intensive and represent an investment barrier to most competitors. The company's quality-control system should continue to enhance product consistency. Regularly scheduled preventive maintenance maximizes plant operation time and curbs costly repairs. Effective inventory management by the company reduces their fixed costs and product waste, and its low-cost source of raw materials improves yields.

Two proprietary-product technologies represent resources for potential new-to-the world products in the category. Two existing patents are pending and could represent a significant competitive advantage. However, the R&D team is currently committed to short-term cost reductions and improvements to the existing product lines.

The company has an outstanding relationship with the trade, sparked by the owner's image and sophisticated and motivating sales programs for brokers and buyers. These attributes, along with superior execution of previous line extensions, represent a strong trade lever for new product introductions in the future.

Most important, the company has a proven track record in turning a commodity—a low value-added product—into a differentiated, premium-priced packaged good. The company has shown a marked expertise in managing its marketing and sales efforts. It has a creative team of managers and several entrepreneurial people, not to mention the chairman and founder of the company. He is truly dedicated to new products and has funded new ventures aggressively during the past ten years.

The trade and consumers perceive the product lines as high quality and therefore pay a higher price than for most other competitive offerings, allowing a margin premium for the company.

However, beyond the current category, consumer recognition diminishes. The company and brand names do not appear to be leverageable or transferable to other products in other categories. Beyond the existing category, the recognition of the company name would be solely from the grocery retail trade, not from the consumer. As a result, the potential for marketing "push" in other grocery retail categories is solid, although virtually no "pull" momentum will transfer from the existing brands.

Therefore, new products established outside the existing category will most likely require a new and separate brand identity, which in turn will require incremental and heavy advertising and consumer-promotion spending.

Private ownership, a highly entrepreneurial culture, and high-caliber managers are valuable assets for several diversification options. Private ownership provides several advantages relative to larger, publicly held competitors, such as (1) minimal bureaucratic red tape—flexibility and responsiveness to competitive and industry developments; (2) secretiveness—control of information; and (3) an ability to take more risks since there are fewer owners to make decisions.

However, in considering new product development efforts, the company has potential financial constraints that must be examined. Current capital available for acquisitions and new product development and launch costs is $3.5 million. During the five-year period, a maximum of roughly $15 million will be available.

Thus, the key question now becomes, Will $15 million in funds be enough to generate $40 million in revenues during the next five years?

Moreover, beyond the existing category, the company's new product track record has been dismal at best. While very successful in the existing category with line extensions—hitting an 80 percent success rate and a 90 percent survival rate, all ventures outside the core product category have failed—a 0 percent success and survival rate.

Most important, past failures in ventures outside the key category have created a cultural impediment to internal new product development. Even though management has been extremely supportive in the past, it has recently become somewhat gun-shy, given the historical track record.

In addition, two areas of functional weakness are market research and R&D. Both areas are grossly understaffed and have no resources available to allocate to new product development efforts. This shortfall will need to be corrected early on in order to have a new product process work effectively. Moreover, success with new geographic markets outside the U.S. has been limited; thus, new product launches should, for at least a while, be confined to the U.S.

In short, several strengths exist upon which to build a successful new product program. The company's high volume provides manufacturing cost advantages and access to raw materials, process technologies, and product patents that represent key competitive advantages. Trade relationships and experience in turning a commodity product into a differentiated, premium-priced consumer packaged good suggest strong sales and marketing skills. Further, a flexible and entrepreneurial environment, directed by capable management, creates an atmosphere that is conducive to new product development, as long as management is willing to recommit itself to the endeavor and overcome its shyness caused by past failures.

NEW PRODUCT BLUEPRINT AND STRATEGY SUMMARY

Based on internal business objectives and major internal strengths, the company's new product program should be guided by both requisite and opportunistic roles. Requisite roles are those in which new products in the existing category meet competitive challenges and business requirements. Opportunistic roles are those that new products fill when they expand into new categories—beyond the core category in which the company now competes.

Strategic Roles

Requisite roles for this company should focus on protection of shelf space and expansion of market share in the core business, while capitalizing on internal strengths. (See Exhibit 3-5A.)

Opportunistic roles focus on reducing the company's dependency on a single-product business and exploit its existing strengths and resource potential. (See Exhibit 3-5B.) Requisite and opportunistic roles are weighted according to the internal strengths, which are leveraged in satisfying the strategic role. (See Exhibit 3-5C.) In turn, differentiated screening criteria are established by requisite and opportunistic roles. (See Exhibit 3-5D.)

EXHIBIT 3-5A Potential Requisite Strategic Roles

	Secure Dominant Product Share	Penetrate Canada	Enter Mass Merchandiser Channel	Increase Shelf Space Exposure	Utilize Waste By-Products	Convert Non-Users of Product
BUSINESS OBJECTIVES						
● Achieve 50% Dollar Market Share	√			√		√
● Expand Distribution and Increase ACV	√	√	√			√
● Generate $150 MM Sales	√	√	√	√	√	√
INTERNAL STRENGTHS						
● Scale/Cost	√		√	√	√	√
● Processing	√	√		√	√	
● Technology Capabilities	√			√	√	√
● Trade/Broker Leverage	√		√	√		
● Marketing Differentiation Expertise		√		√		√
● Perceived Product Quality	√			√	√	√
● Management Skills/Culture	√	√		√		

DEGREE OF DIVERSIFICATION POTENTIAL

LOW ◄─────────────► HIGH

EXHIBIT 3-5B Opportunistic Strategic Roles

	Manufacture and Market Differentiated Consumer Product	Utilize Off-Season Capacity; Offset Business Cyclicality	Exploit Existing Technology in New Way	Produce Price-Competitive Industrial Product	Establish Foothold in New Geographic Market	Utilize Existing Production Capabilities in a New Way
DIVERSIFICATION OBJECTIVES						
• Reduce Dependency on Single Product	√	√	√	√	√	√
• Enter Synergistic Product Lines/Businesses	√	√				
• Generate $150 MM Sales	√	√	√	√	√	√
INTERNAL STRENGTHS						
• Scale/Cost		√		√		√
• Processing		√		√		√
• Technology Capabilities			√			
• Trade/Broker Leverage	√					
• Marketing Differentiation Expertise	√	√				
• Perceived Product Quality						
• Management Skills/Culture	√		√		√	√

Screening Criteria

Criteria for measuring performance should be based on an intended strategic role and qualitatively assigned risk factors. To further calibrate the relative risk of each strategic role, specific opportunities and their probability of success need to be considered. (See Exhibit 3-5E.)

Homework

Here is an example that illustrates how new product ideas would pass through the framework for strategic growth. (See Exhibit 3-5F.)

The management team put the new product framework in place and established a formalized scanning system to identify category opportunities. The scanning system consists of five interrelated analyses:

EXHIBIT 3-5C Strategic Roles

STRENGTHS	LEVERAGE WEIGHT	REQUISITE						OPPORTUNISTIC					
		Secure Dominant Product Share	Penetrate Canada	Enter Mass Merchandiser Channel	Increase Shelf-Space Exposure	Utilize Waste Byproduct	Convert Nonusers of Product	Manufacture and Market Consumer Product	Utilize Off-Season Capacity	Exploit Existing Technology in a New Way	Product Price Competitive Industrial Product	Establish Foothold in a New Geographic Market	Utilize Existing Production Capabilities in a New Way
Cost Related													
• Scale	2	2		2	2	2	2		2		2		2
• Processing	2	2	2		2	2			2		2		2
Demand Related													
• Technology Capabilities	1	1			1	1	1			1			
• Trade/Broker Leverage	1	1		1	1			1					
• Marketing Differentiation Expertise	1			1	1		1	1	1				
• Perceived Product Quality	1	1		1	1	1	1						
• Management Skills/ Culture	1	1	1		1			1			1	1	1
STRATEGIC HOLD LEVERAGE FACTOR		8	4	4	9	6	5	3	5	2	4	1	5

□ Market analysis: size and growth trends, business segmentation, and growth drivers

□ Competitive analysis: profiles of the competitors and their products, industry structure, competitive costs, and pricing

□ Key success factors: cost economies of scale, quality, franchise, technology, raw materials, management and marketing ability, established channels, appropriate organization structures, and incentive programs

EXHIBIT 3-5D Potential Performance Measurement Criteria

Relative Risk Scale	Strategic Role	Leverage Factor	Potential Performance Measurement Criteria		
			Sales Potential (Dollars In Millions)	Minimal ROA (Percent)	Timing to Thresholds (Years)
Low ↕ High	Requisite				
	• Increase shelf-space exposure	9	$ 2 – $ 5	10% – 15%	1 – 3
	• Secure dominant product share	8	$10 – $20	10% – 15%	3 – 5
	• Utilize waste byproducts	6	$ 5 – $10	10% – 15%	1 – 3
	• Convert nonusers of single product	5	$ 2 – $ 5	10% – 15%	1 – 3
	• Penetrate Canada	4	$ 5 – $10	12% – 18%	2 – 3
	• Enter mass merchandiser channel	4	$ 5 – $10	12% – 18%	2 – 3
Low ↕ High	Opportunistic				
	• Utilize off-season capacity; offset business cyclicality	5	$ 5 – $10	10% – 15%	1 – 3
	• Utilize existing production capabilities	5	$ 5 – $10	10% – 15%	1 – 2
	• Produce price-competitive industrial product	4	$ 5 – $10	15% – 20%	1 – 2
	• Manufacture and market differentiated consumer product	3	$10 – $20	15% – 20%	2 – 4
	• Exploit existing technology in a new way	2	$15 – $25	20% – 25%	2 – 3
	• Establish foothold in new geographic market	1	$10 – $20	20% – 25%	2 – 4

EXHIBIT 3-5E Growth Opportunities

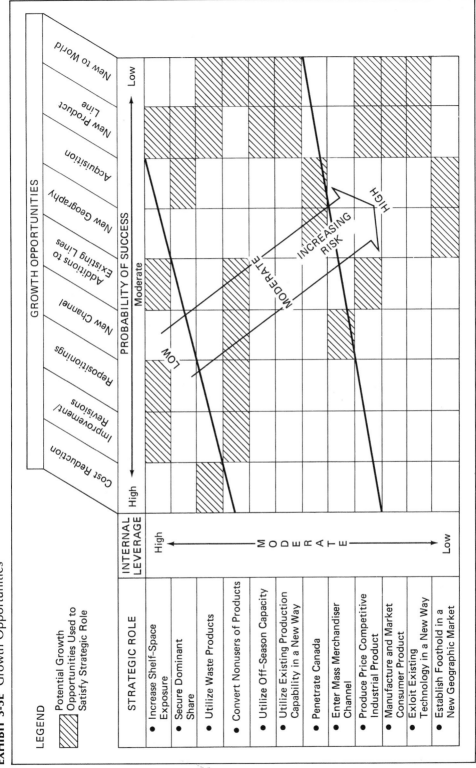

LEGEND

▨ Potential Growth Opportunities Used to Satisfy Strategic Role

EXHIBIT 3-5F

Opportunity	Roles Satisfied	Strategic Positioning
		Opportunistic
Potting Soil	• Manufacture and market differentiated consumer product • Utilize off-season capacity; offset business cyclicality	

Common Criteria ⟹

• Category growth at least comparable to inflation rate • Fragmented competitive market with few national consumer-packaged-good manufacturers • Utilizes similar distribution/transportation • No high-technology component	• 65% of US households grow houseplants; demographic shifts support 8% CAGR of gardeners; gardening sales growing at 17%	X
	• Primarily regional manufacturers and distributors—no well-known national brand	X
	• Grocery stores/mass merchants, lawn and garden centers are key channels	X
	• Uncomplicated mixing and packaging process	X

Role-Specific Criteria Opportunistic ⟹

• Regionally oriented business	• Producers constrained by shipping costs	X
	• Ingredients vary—composition and use provide differentiation potential	X
• Product with differentiated value-added or cost competitive potential	• Potential ingredients: peat, clay, vermiculite, other materials	X
• Gross margins must exceed 40% to 45%	• Differentiation provides margin potential	X

Performance Criteria ⟹

Determinant Role: Manufacture and market differentiated consumer product
Risk Factor: Moderate
Sales: $10 to $20 million
ROA: 15% to 20%
Timing to Threshold: 2 to 4 Years

Potential Sales: Potential exists to capture 5% to 15% market share of a $250 million category

Potential ROA: Dependent upon availability and proximity of raw-material source

□ Entry barriers: investment in plant and technology, proprietary products or technology, regulation, and economies scale/volume

□ Costs to serve and compete: identifies unit costs to distribute and market to trade and consumer product opportunities relative to competitive activity

Process and Organization

The new product process needs to receive top-management support, attention, and commitment. A new product task force comprised of senior management should be formed to provide counsel and guidance in the implementation of new product planning. The body should serve as a communication vehicle and review forum for guiding new product opportunities and making go/no go decisions at key points in the process.

Primary responsibility for establishing the new product process and making it work should be given to the current vice-president of corporate planning. Development of the specific process and external category-scanning system should be part of the overall corporate planning process. In this way, long-term objectives and growth avenues can be considered in concert with near-term operating objectives and strategies.

To help implement the external scanning system, the company should hire two full-time people: a market researcher and a business analyst—both dedicated to the new product effort and reporting to the vice-president of corporate planning. In addition, at least two more research-and-development people are needed, to focus attention on the application of technology for new product concepts.

Once the process is under way and additional people have been hired, management responsibility for new products should be given to a full-time executive devoted solely to new product development. The time required to implement new products effectively will be substantial, and distraction from day-to-day business responsibilities should be minimal.

Example 2: $50 Million Industrial Products Manufacturer

NEW PRODUCT DIAGNOSTIC AUDIT SUMMARY

Although this company had new product development processes, no single commonly agreed-upon approach was being used. Moreover, over twenty new product *forms* had to be completed for each new product concept. In effect, this meant that any new product idea would be smothered to death by the barrage of papers and forms. (See Exhibit 3-6.) However, the flurry of paper did not reveal the level of success in developing new products—which was virtually none.

The company had made several attempts to streamline the development process. However, success had been limited ow-

EXHIBIT 3-6 One Company's New Product Development Process

Process Steps

1. Concept testing
2. Preliminary prototype testing
3. Final prototype testing
4. Preliminary production run
5. Secondary production run
6. Final release and turnover to production

Process Forms

Requests for new or revised products
Engineering project requests
Product development work order
Project development schedule
Project plan summary report
Laboratory facility utilization schedule
Product development summary chart
Project status reporting
New product development testing and reporting
Performance, life cycle, and field testing
Design-review committee
New product release
Major-expenditure request
Preliminary engineering change record
Final engineering change record
New product sales-release planning sheet
Test report on field test or life-cycle testing
Approval for release of product to sales
First production run

ing to the lack of a well-defined new product strategy and a unified process. In short, no one knew where the company was heading in new products; on top of which, everyone was trying to get there from different directions—without a map, compass, or even sundial. The company also needed to develop a business strategy that would link its new product strategy to a well-defined marketing-and-acquisition strategy.

In this industry, new product development has tended to be evolutionary rather than revolutionary. Heat exchangers don't seem to represent the state of the art in high technology. Nevertheless, new product opportunities do exist in the industry, primarily through technology application and product adaptations. Downsizing, use of microprocessors, and laser technology are approaches used to develop new products.

The company apparently had the potential to establish a solid competitive position in the market through end-user expansion and technology applications. However, competitors were continuing to apply heavy margin pressures on the company while simultaneously launching additional new products right under the company's nose.

The bulk of the company's sales growth during the past five years came from the addition of accessories and line extensions to the existing business. Ongoing product-line growth represented only 10 percent of total company growth. Me-too new products accounted for 90 percent of the growth.

The company had several strengths, which represented a foundation upon which to build a growth platform for its future new products. Key internal strengths that could be leveraged were as follows:

□ Foreign affiliates and subsidiaries provided a strong network for technology flow and new product technology applications for domestic products.

□ Potential expansion into new category segments through low asset and burden-intensive products provided a way to broaden the scope of the product line.

□ The company had a strong after-sales service reputation, a generally high product-quality image, and customer-perceived responsiveness in the field.

□ Special orders and specific customer-product adaptations received very high marks in quality and turnaround time.

□ The Distributor Advisory Board offered potentially useful market intelligence and concept sourcing for new products.

□ Several good opportunities existed to penetrate the new-to-the-company market segments with low-cost manufacturing processes.

□ Financial resources were available and top-management commitment to launch more new-to-the-company products pervaded the management team.

During the past five years, the company introduced twenty-two new products with eighteen, or roughly 80 percent, remaining in the marketplace. During that time period, the company generated approximately 4.5 million in sales from new products. This represented 9 percent of total sales, which was comparable to the current new product goal. During the same period, 50 percent of the new products introduced yielded 5 percent of the total new product revenue. Fifteen out of the twenty-two products launched generated less than $200,000 each in revenues. Thus, there were only seven "winners" that hit the $250,000-to-$1 million mark.

In terms of new product type, the majority of the company's new products were products that responded to competition. Nine were products developed in direct response to competitive inroads; seven were adaptations to existing products, and five were licensed products (accounting for 60 percent of total new product revenues).

While the company was moderately well positioned to launch a more aggressive new product program, a strong "not-invented-here" attitude pervaded the company. Moreover, there was very little innovation; for the most part, all new products were just "better than" products. The cadre of small revenue-and-profit-generating new products probably diluted attention and resources from focusing on potential "big hits."

Without clear priorities set by new product type and strategic role, the "not-invented-here" syndrome will continue to stifle new product success. Cross-functional cooperation, a commonly understood new product plan, and clear-cut management accountability will be critical for improving new product development.

While the company had a new product steering committee in place, which seemed to demonstrate top management's commitment to the new product effort, the committee was totally ineffective. There was not a common understanding of the priorities, screening criteria, or overall role for new products. The committee seldom rejected or screened any new product, and throughout the company, the committee's influence on the new product process was seen as minimal. The lack of clear priority setting and adequate accountability tended to negate management's commitment to new products.

Responses to the company's new product shortcomings by company management included insufficient marketing input, both financial and technical, and poor coordination among marketing, engineering, and manufacturing. Moreover, the number of projects underway at one time far exceeded resource capabilities. There was no sense of urgency in middle managers, the mission was inconsistent with projects in process, and test facilities and personnel were inadequate. Accountability on projects was not clearly assigned, deadlines were never kept, insufficient market data was secured, and product design was going on after the product had been put into test market.

ACTION STEPS

Thus, it was clear that several shortcomings existed that needed immediate attention if the new product objectives were to be met: (1) improve communication and coordination among key functional areas and establish management accountability for new product development and performance; (2) establish an agreed-upon charter with new product goals, roles, and screens that will be adhered to; (3) agree upon a step-by-step development process that includes clear-cut approval points; (4) monitor forecasting and aim to improve financial forecast accuracy through better business analysis; (5) construct a new product data base and monitor performance of new products after launch; (6) develop a portfolio of new products that includes higher revenue candidates; (7) screen concepts more rigorously and conduct more competitive analysis earlier in the process; (8) separate the priority-setting and progress-review function of the steering committee from current new product resource allocation and coordination.

Beyond the development of a new product strategy, the company needs to add a market-research manager in order to identify new innovations, tap into corporate or agency research, and evaluate customer needs and potential new markets. The company needs to monitor competitive new product activity more closely and establish relationships with government and trade agencies.

Engineering must be held accountable for new product timetables and design integrity, but they need additional resources. Improved and more effective management of all personnel is a critical near-term requirement; as soon as a cadre of competent lab technicians is secured, a new lab facility should be given the go-ahead. A new lab will provide greater quality control over new products and clear the way for realistic market-simulation testing as well as allow for some experimentation and variance testing.

The new product steering committee should be dismantled. Instead, two smaller groups should be formed: a new product operating committee and a new product review committee. In concert with the new product manager, the new product operating committee would have primary responsibility for execution of new products. This committee would help to foster better coordination among sales, marketing, engineering, and manufacturing. It would track progress on projects currently under development at weekly meetings.

Moreover, this committee would be responsible for reallocating resources within functional areas to support new product priority shifts. The committee would prepare a formal monthly status update and get go/no go decisions and approvals from the new products review committee.

The new product review committee, consisting only of top management, would set priorities for new product projects, review business analyses and approve projects at specific stages of the process, hold the new product operating committee accountable for project timetables and deadlines, reward accomplishments and reinforce deadline disciplines, and meet every other month with the new product operating committee.

IN SUMMARY

Once your diagnostic audit is complete, it will provide a useful tool for correcting discovered weaknesses, better utilizing strengths, and making your new product program really work. It will also provide some indication as to whether the expectations that future new products will fill are realistic or merely a pipe dream. Moreover, the audit should provide information that will guide decision making in developing a new product blueprint and strategy—the cornerstone of a well-constructed new product program.

The diagnostic audit can usually be completed in about three months. Depending upon availability of data, access to management, and number and quality of resources assigned to the audit, it may take a bit longer. The point is that the time required to conduct the audit is relatively short and yet can provide insights and recommended changes that will affect a company's new product program for years to come.

How a company uses the results of a new product diagnostic audit is highly dependent upon the reasons why the audit was conducted in the first place. An attitude of trust, openness, and interest in understanding past performance must underscore top management's desire for an audit. It cannot be used as a club or as a device to ratchet down the new product budget. It should, on the other hand, be used as a vehicle to explore how best to improve the effectiveness of dollars spent and people assigned to the new product development process. It provides a valuable information base for getting a new product program turned around; managers may begin to get involved in the audit and generate some excitement for creating a new process or organization. Consequently, a certain degree of momentum is created, ownership encouraged, and commitment somewhat established. The mere conduct of a diagnostic audit is a signal to managers that top management may at least be willing to look at ways to improve the approaches taken to new products. Sometimes the key benefit is not the information derived from an audit but, rather, the enthusiasm and interest that is rekindled into the new product culture.

Interpretation of the results is difficult. It requires association making similar to that needed in effective concept generation. Thus, the launching pad for a successful new product program starts to be erected as soon as the audit begins.

With the information gained in the new product diagnostic audit, the company can now begin to formulate a new product strategy. When developing the new product strategy, management can use the audit to reduce the relative risk inherent in new products. The strategy must capitalize on the company's strengths and circumvent weak areas, while the shortfalls are addressed and remedied.

The next chapter will describe how to develop a new product strategy, which includes the growth gap and financial goals, strategic roles, and screening criteria that will guide market-category selection and idea and concept generation. In addition, it will discuss the importance of calibrating new product risk in a company, how to assess it, and ways to manipulate it to increase the success rate of commercialized new products.

There is nothing more difficult to plan, more doubtful of success, nor more dangerous to manage than the creation of a new system.

Niccolo Machiavelli
The Prince

4

DEVELOPING A NEW PRODUCT STRATEGY

Armed with the results of the new product diagnostic audit, management is well equipped with information to guide the development of a new products strategy. Internal strengths to exploit in generating new concepts have been identified, the reasons behind past new product performance are more accurately understood, and potential internal impediments can now be addressed. At this point, the key benefit from the audit is informed decision making and judgment that can be applied to setting up the new product strategy. A more realistic picture has been painted of what a company can expect to achieve from new products.

As discussed in Chapter 2, a new product blueprint describes the role that new products will play in satisfying the overall growth goals of a company. It should include an estimate of development expenditures and investment capital needs for at least the next two to three years, estimated human-resource and skill requirements, desired three- to five-year revenue targets from new products, and top management's expectations for and commitment to new products. In short, the new product blueprint defines the direction to take; the new product strategy describes the game plan in terms of how to get there; and the development process is the road map, which outlines the path to take to reach the ultimate destination.

CONSTRUCTING A FRAMEWORK

The new product blueprint can be compared to an architect's drawings for a new house. The architect, in concert with the future owners, discusses different ideas and gradually develops a vision of the new house. The architect takes these ideas and transforms them into sketches, which begin to give form and substance to the vision. He or she then integrates these sketches into a detailed blueprint that depicts how the owners want the house to look. However, the architect cannot build the house alone. A general contractor needs to be hired to interpret the blueprint and determine how best to segregate the tasks and coordinate the right mix of resources needed to build the house. After identifying the need for electricians, plumbers, and carpenters and hiring them, the general contractor must still work closely with the architect. The contractor now has the responsibility for getting the house built and will need to set up a schedule, timetable, and step-by-step procedure that delineates the building stages and specific duties of the subcontractors. The general contractor consistently monitors performance, tracks progress, and makes course corrections in the plan as appropriate. The contractor, in effect, develops a strategy for turning the architect's vision and resultant blueprint into a reality.

This example provides a good analogy to the new product development process. Shareholders and the board of directors in a company may be compared to the owners of the house. Top management has a vision of what is expected from new products and serves as the architect. Expectations are generated that relate to the role of new products in meeting the growth objectives of the corporation. Top management defines these expectations, which are drawn up in the form of a new product blueprint. Then top management hires a "general contractor," a new product manager, who takes responsibility for execution of the blueprint. The new product manager, like the contractor, then assumes responsibility for translating the blueprint into a strategy, execution process, and action plan.

In order to determine how best to generate and screen new product ideas that will fulfill the expectations cited in the blueprint, the new product manager must break down the objectives into manageable parts, determine which functions new products will need to perform, and decide what screens should be used to identify the best ideas. Thus, the general contractor's game plan is analogous to the new product manager's new product strategy. Subsequently, the new product manager decides on the steps to follow to get new products to the marketplace and also decides specific resources that will be needed to help execute the process. One individual cannot launch new products single-handedly any more than one good architect can build a house unassisted.

The new product strategy is intended to take the blueprint, interpret its meaning, and define in detail the new product growth gap, financial objectives, strategic roles, new product types, and screening criteria, in light of the diagnostic audit findings.

The new product strategy consists of a definition of the *revenue gap* and *financial goals* that new products are expected to meet, *strategic roles* that describe the functions that new products are to perform, and *screening criteria* that serve as a filter for determining which categories and new product concepts are most attractive to pursue.

Without a new product strategy, it is difficult to know which direction to head in; one idea may appear attractive to one person and not another. With a new product strategy, management can more quickly and effectively focus on the market categories, ideas, and concepts that match specific strategic roles. It enables managers to focus category identification and idea generation against agreed-upon targets, and it cuts down the screening time and prototype-development costs incurred by false starts. In short, the new product strategy defines how the growth objectives of the company will be satisfied by internally developed new products. It sets up the game plan to follow to get the expectations in the blueprint transformed into market realities.

DEVELOPING THE STRATEGY

Financial Growth Gap

As discussed in the previous chapter, the financial gap new products are intended to fulfill must be clearly identified. Without one, neither success nor progress can be measured; resource requirements cannot be determined. The long-range business plan usually contains some optimistic "hockey-stick" graphs and charts. At least these often lofty goals are a starting point to get the process under way. Developing realistic new product financial targets is critical. Targets that are too low tend to drag down managers' potential; targets too high create frustration and anxiety and cause the managers to lose their sense of commitment. While revenue and profit goals may be a stretch, and deliberately challenging, they should be attainable within reason. If they are not, this alone will be debilitating for new product participants, drive down morale, and weaken the new product foundation.

A five-year financial growth gap can be developed by building up the revenue projections estimated from each growth mode.

PERCENTAGE OF REVENUE GROWTH OR FORECAST REVENUES FROM:

- □ Existing businesses and product lines
- □ New product line additions, revisions, and extensions to existing products
- □ New-to-the-company and new-to-the-world products
- □ Acquisitions and joint ventures
- □ Other growth modes, e.g., licensing, alliances with other companies, minority investments

Now, percentages or absolute-revenue dollar projections can be applied to each growth mode. This framework will begin to calibrate the relative degree of importance of new products to alternative growth routes.

For example, take a power-instruments consumer durables company that currently does $500 million in sales and has been growing at an 8 percent compound annual growth rate during the past five years. The "hockey-stick" projection for the future looks at a 16 percent growth rate, resulting in a revenue projection of $1.05 billion in five years. The only breakdown in the long-range plan is between existing and new products, which are jointly estimated to generate $900 million and acquisitions that are forecast to contribute the remaining $150 million. The objective, of course, is to segment the $900 million into components that will be meaningful in framing the new product effort.

In examining the existing business, the product lines can be grouped into three product categories: power instruments, lighting products, and small appliances. Each of the groups has grown at 6 percent, 12 percent, and 3 percent, respectively, during the past five years. Power instruments and small appliances, in particular, have been under intense foreign competition from a manufacturing-cost standpoint. Higher-value new products were defined in the plan as a key way to counteract foreign competitors. Power instruments' existing business is forecast to grow at 8 percent annually and small appliances by 5 percent. Lighting products, on the other hand, are expected to grow 18 percent annually. Sales increases had to come through geographic penetration, product differentiation, and some price advantage. Apparently, this business was well positioned for future growth.

What were the financial growth expectations for new products? First, let's determine the revenue contribution to come from the existing business. Based on the forecast growth-rate projections, the current $500 million is expected to grow to $766 million, representing a 9 percent annual increase. (See Table 4-1.)

At this point, we know that the remaining $134 million is expected to come from products that are not currently in the marketplace. Within five years, this will represent roughly 13 percent of the total $1,050 million revenue base. This suggests that from a financial standpoint, the role of new products falls into the modest-new-growth-role category since the revenue-contribution expectation falls within the 10-to-20 percent range. Most important, it begins to shape the magnitude of effort that will be required to develop more than $25 million worth of new products, on average, annually.

The next step is to break out the $134 million by new product types into a realistic cut between line extensions and new-

TABLE 4-1

	Current Product Size ($Million)	Growth Rate	Five-Year Projection ($Million)
Power instruments	$225	8%	$ 330
Lighting	85	18	194
Small appliances	190	5	242
Revenues from existing products	$500		$ 766
Forecast revenues from new products			134
Acquisitions			150
Total	$500	9%	$1,050

to-the-company products in either related or unrelated businesses. (See Table 4-2.)

Thus, the growth gap for new products is about equally balanced between new products that will support and expand the existing businesses and new products that will catapult the company into new businesses.

Table 4-3 shows the company's $134 million growth gap for new products and total sources of growth.

One of the useful things that can come from growth-gap analysis is the identification of a range of financial and nonfinancial issues that relate back to the blueprint and help set the direction for the magnitude of the effort. For example, the implications for this company include the following:

☐ The new product and acquisition expectations are roughly evenly balanced. The company wants to add $150 million from acquisitions and $134 million from new products.

TABLE 4-2

New product line extensions (Including revisions and additions)		
Power instruments	$ 20	million
Lighting	15	million
Small appliances	30	million
Subtotal	$ 65	million
New-to-the-company products	69	million
Total new products	$134	million

TABLE 4-3

Sources of Growth	Revenues ($Millions)
Existing products	$ 266
Internally developed new products	134
Acquisitions	150
Total new-revenue growth	550
Current business	500
Total	$1,050

☐ Mix of line extensions and additions versus new-to-the-company products is also relatively balanced.

For this mix of new products to be developed, it is likely that a full-time new product manager will need to be hired. A separate new product department, team, or division may be needed for the new-to-the-company products, while line extensions might be managed by current product managers. If the balance was totally skewed to line extensions and additions, the new product effort might best be carried out by operating managers. Moreover, a heavier R&D budget may also be needed to support the new-to-the-company product efforts.

Total development costs and profit expectations will be higher, and consequently, the overall new product effort will have a higher risk, since new-to-the-company products represent one-half of the new product effort.

Management must recognize that new product revenues will not begin flowing in for at least one to two years. (Development time is often overlooked in setting new product targets.) Thus, the $134 million in sales from new products, in effect, are expected to be generated within a three- to four-year period. This may be an overly optimistic goal. The company wants to more than double its size within five years. With 27 percent of total revenues coming from new products and acquisitions, a high degree of focused attention and dedicated resources will be required to achieve these goals. The assumption should be that a new product team is already in the works or one will soon be under way.

The existing businesses will represent 48 percent of the incremental revenues forecast during the next five years. Thus, the eye cannot be taken off the core business. New products and acquisitions rank in about the same order of importance as the existing businesses.

The financial growth gap helps to break down and better define the new product targets. It is a way to provide a handle on the magnitude of the new products objectives and begins to provide a framework for considering financial and human-resource requirements.

Strategic Roles

New product strategic roles are largely based on a company's growth requirements and goals. That is, beyond contributing to future revenues and profits, what roles will new products play? In defining strategic roles, management must ask, "What are the functions that new products should serve in supporting the growth goals of this company?" Strategic roles help pinpoint the areas in which new products are expected to perform to either build the existing business or take the company into new businesses and categories. Each strategic role should fulfill a business requirement, whether it is to bolster existing product lines or provide a way to enter new businesses or markets. Both types of strategic roles are geared toward identifying how new products will best serve the growth objectives of the corporation. We classify new product strategic roles into two categories.

□ *Requisite Roles*—describe the functions that new products are expected to satisfy in defending, expanding, or bolstering the existing product lines.

□ *Opportunistic Roles*—define ways in which new products could propel a company into new categories, markets, or businesses.

There is often a high degree of overlap between requisite and opportunistic roles. What's important is that new product roles be developed to define what a company expects new products to do beyond increasing revenues and profits. No single role stands as a touchstone; successful companies have used a variety of new product types to satisfy a wide range of roles. Often a new-to-the-world or new-to-the-company product will satisfy opportunistic roles, whereas line extensions, repositionings, improvements, and cost reductions will be used to fulfill requisite roles. However, each new product type can potentially meet any role.

Requisite roles are usually geared toward defending or protecting a business from competition, supporting or expanding the existing business, or applying an internal strength, such as a new technology or raw-material cost advantage. In addition, requisite roles may be aimed at solving existing business problems; for example, utilizing excess capacity or waste byproducts, offsetting seasonal fluctuations in sales, or improving manufacturing costs.

Opportunistic roles describe ways in which new products can move a company into a new category, market, or business. It may represent a more significant investment than new products that serve requisite roles, but the returns are also usually greater. Opportunistic roles may include entering a new foreign country, establishing a foothold in a product category targeted to the elderly segment, or getting into the automotive aftermarket—a new category for the company with a series of new products.

To understand what new product roles are supposed to do for a company, they need to be examined from an internal perspective—in terms of the business requirements they will fulfill, not just the external consumer needs that they will satisfy. Granted, the overriding, compelling driver behind any successful new product is the ability of that product to perform better than any alternative product available in meeting a consumer's need. However, taken a given need, new products are not created equal for all companies. Consequently, companies launching similar products will most likely end up with varying degrees of success in terms of product quality, consumer acceptance, and market performance. There are four reasons why this frequently occurs: (1) the new product did not draw upon the company's internal strengths, (2) the new product did not have clearly defined objectives or roles tied to the overall business objectives of the company, (3) insufficient resources were committed to the product during the development process, and (4) execution of the product's launch was poorly performed, coordinated, or timed.

By determining *corporate* growth objectives and strategic requirements, a company can develop new product strategic roles aimed at serving specific functions that will address the company's overall growth requirements. A company is then positioned to manage its new product portfolio with the same degree of certainty and calibrated risk as it manages the existing business portfolio. A single new product may satisfy several strategic roles. For example, Quaker Oats' launch of rice cakes may have satisfied both requisite and opportunistic roles: allowed the company to enter the low-calorie segment of the snack-food business and expanded the existing snack business into more healthful foods; exploited the equity of the Quaker Oats brand name in grain-based foods; capitalized on the channel clout from the direct-sales force; and increased the total share of shelf space in retail outlets.

On the other hand, several different new product types may be required to satisfy just one strategic role. To preempt one foreign competitor from gaining market share, a company may need to introduce line extensions, cost reductions, repositionings, and new-to-the-company products. Take, for example, Black & Decker, which has been under intense competition from foreign manufacturers. In response to consumer lifestyle shifts and competition, its small-kitchen-appliance line was redesigned to fit under overhead cabinets. As a result, several products were repositioned, others were reengineered at a lower cost, some new line extensions were added, such as a single-cup coffee maker, and even a new-to-the-company product was introduced—a small kitchen fire extinguisher.

An example of satisfying opportunistic roles is illustrated by Kodak's recent launch of lithium-powered batteries called Ultralife. The new Ultralife, which lasts twice as long as batteries with alkaline cells, is expected to be highly competitive with them. This product satisfied an opportunistic role by enabling Kodak to penetrate the battery market. But it also serves as an opportunistic role for Black & Decker since that company is designing household items ranging from flashlights to smoke detectors around Kodak's new batteries.

For a soap and detergent manufacturer, new products that would protect its share of shelf space would represent a requisite role. A laundry detergent that softened fabric and controlled static could increase the company's shelf space and might deter a competitor from creeping up. In contrast, the same company might set up an opportunistic new product role enabling it to get into a totally new segment of the home laundry market, e.g., dry cleaning. In this case, a new product line that would allow consumers to dry clean their clothes at home would satisfy a more opportunistic role.

Minnetonka's introduction of Softsoap, a perceived new-to-the-world product for in-home consumer use, even though liquid soap had existed for years in public restrooms, can be viewed as a product that satisfied an opportunistic role. Preempting competition and securing a strong market share initially in a new soap category led this company into the bathroom and the kitchen. Here was a tiny midwest company up against giants and soaring ahead of them for a while. Imagine the chagrin at Procter & Gamble and Lever Brothers.

Reportedly, Kellogg established three specific strategic objectives to guide its new product development efforts during the early 1980s:

1. Build U.S. ready-to-eat cereal share in a highly competitive category.
2. Grow worldwide market share of cereal volume.
3. Diversify into food products beyond cereals.

New products developed by Kellogg helped to satisfy several of these roles, as summarized in the following example.

- □ *Requisite roles*
  Build U.S. market share
  Marshmallow Krispies, Crispix, and Nutri-Grain
- □ *Opportunistic roles*
  Grow worldwide cereal volume
  Toasted Mini-Wheats in Japan and Sustain in Australia
  Diversify into other food products
  Rice Krispies Snack Bars and Whitney's Yogurt

Marshmallow Krispies, a cereal entry positioned for children, was developed to both reinforce the strength of Rice Krispies' franchise and grow market share in the highly competitive kids' presweetened, ready-to-eat cereal segment. Similarly, Crispix not only helped Kellogg grow its market share, it also allowed the company to utilize an innovative manufacturing process. Building on their two-sided grain concept, Kellogg created a truly unique cereal.

Nutri-Grain, positioned as an adult, health-oriented cereal, represents a product designed to increase market share, take advantage of state-of-the-art technology, and serve as a vehicle to penetrate an emerging growth category—the health-and-nutrition conscious, time-constrained, dual-working household. All three of these products met the first requisite role—to protect and build the company's cereal business market share.

Aiming to diversify the business base outside of cereal, Rice Krispies Bars were launched to compete in the growing granola-bar category. Both requisite as well as opportunistic roles were satisfied by this new product: requisite, since it provided a way to further strengthen the Rice Krispies brand name to consumers from a new angle, increasing top-of-mind awareness of the cereal; and yet opportunistic, since the product provided a means for Kellogg to enter a category in which it had never before competed.

Toasted Mini-Wheats' introduction into Japan satisfied an opportunistic growth role to gain a foothold in a new foreign country. Likewise, Sustain was launched in Australia in order to grow market share and further establish a strong base in the health-oriented segment of that market.

Whitney's Yogurt clearly fulfilled an opportunistic role. It strategically moved the company into a new product category and a new grocery-store location—the dairy case. Representing a strong entrant into the high-growth and competitive yogurt cage-gory, Whitney's proved to be a favorite choice among consumers. The product was positioned as a premium-priced, high-quality product, and was consumer promoted heavily initially to establish a strong position in East Coast markets. Subsequently, as the brand gained momentum on the East Coast, the company introduced the product line in a series of regional roll outs.

These examples demonstrate how new products can fulfill various requisite and opportunistic strategic roles. They also demonstrate how the use of strategic roles in new product planning can help focus category identification, idea generation, and concept development. As will be discussed later, strategic roles can serve as a type of directional screen.

Occasionally, a type of new product that satisfies a requisite role for one company fulfills an opportunistic role for another. This is simply because companies have different resource bases, market needs, strengths and weaknesses, and so forth. They look at the same product category with different eyes, different needs, different expectations—all of which will influence their approaches to new product development. The focus comes from the internal perspective of the company. To illustrate, let's examine four new products launched by Keebler, Pillsbury, and Procter & Gamble in two product categories. (See Table 4-4.)

Keebler's introduction of Soft Batch Cookies satisfied a requisite role, largely a defensive move directed at protecting its retail market share. Nabisco and Frito-Lay had introduced chocolate chip cookies offering more chips, different texture, and a "more fresh-baked taste," intensifying the pressure on Keebler's shelf space. In contrast to this requisite role, Procter & Gamble's entry into the chocolate chip cookie market, under the Duncan Hines brand name, satisfied an opportunistic, market-driven role. It wanted to gain a new position in a growing snack-food niche, outside of its existing cake-mix base, driven heavily by advertising and brand-name identification.

TABLE 4-4

	Different Strategic Roles for Similar Products	
Requisite	Keebler	Pillsbury
	Soft Batch Cookies	All Ready Pie Crusts
Opportunistic	Keebler	Procter & Gamble
	Ready-Crust Pie Crusts	Duncan Hines Chocolate Chip Cookies

Keebler's Ready-Crust pie crusts, on the other hand, served an opportunistic role by enabling the company to expand into new dessert-related, convenience-oriented product categories where the company had no presence. Yet Pillsbury's pie crust entrant satisfied a requisite role; it was primarily developed to expand shelf exposure at retail and utilize excess flour. Thus, depending upon the internal perspective of a company, new products can satisfy either requisite or opportunistic roles, or both. These are often driven by internal, market, or expansion requirements.

An important observation is that these products were not developed merely to fill a predetermined revenue gap. Rather, they all satisfied a strategic business requirement first and served as an incremental source of revenue and profit, second. Many companies tend to drive their entire new product activity toward meeting financial targets rather than satisfying strategic roles. Hence, they miss many opportunities for bolstering their core businesses through new products. In the process of building on strategic-role considerations, a company should enhance the potential for above-average financial returns and lower the risk.

Let's look at one more company to see how roles can be used. A candy company in the Midwest had three key corporate growth roles: (1) to increase its nominal sales revenues by 15 percent, (2) to maintain existing profit margins, and (3) to realize 70 percent of projected growth from existing products and 30 percent from new products. Top management decided that to realize these goals, its corporate strategic objectives had to focus on building its U.S. market share and entering new foreign markets. The question then became, How can new products best help to achieve these objectives?

For this candy manufacturer to build market share in the U.S., new products could have played several roles: defend the company's competitive position in the marketplace, protect current share of shelf space, or capitalize on the company's existing distribution system. Management developed new-to-the-world products and new product lines to encourage brand switching and stimulate consumer demand as a means of defending its competitive posture. Moreover, they also developed line extensions and flavor flankers to protect current shelf space. All four types of new products were used to satisfy strategic roles that met the goals of the company.

It is evident, then, that both requisite and opportunistic roles are closely tied to internal strengths. Opportunistic roles, however, are driven largely by external needs, while requisite roles spring directly from a company's existing competitive advantages and disadvantages.

LINKING THE DIAGNOSTIC AUDIT TO THE NEW PRODUCT STRATEGY: TYING THE PIECES TOGETHER

To illustrate the process of linking a diagnostic audit with the development of strategic roles, let's look at a consumer nondurables company with a strong share position in the household-tool category.

In 1982 the company enjoyed a 25 percent dollar market share. The company had a steady revenue growth of 18 percent annually during the last five years, but encroaching foreign competition, coupled with the growing risk of dependency on virtually one supplier, made management realize that a rigorous and disciplined new products planning process was necessary to protect future margins and growth.

As a result, the company conducted a thorough new products diagnostic audit. Among its findings, it learned that over the last five years, the company had generated $10 million from new products. A good record but one that fell far short of competition. Numerous ideas not related to tools but aimed at the do-it-yourself market had been floating around without direction. Many good opportunities had been lost because this market had not been targeted by the company. Yet people had been working on these ideas anyway. In addition, an "unwritten" requisite goal, reducing dependency on one supplier through new products, had not been met, and furthermore, dependence had increased. Also included in this self-assessment were those internal strengths the company could bring to bat in its new product program. An examination of technologies and patents owned, manufacturing and marketing advantages relative to competition, and competitive market analysis revealed five areas where the company had a competitive edge upon which to build its new products program.

□ *Cost/Scale Advantage*—Even though a major raw material was purchased solely from one overseas supplier, the company enjoyed significant unit-cost advantages through scale economies. The business was volume-sensitive and the company's leading market-share position provided economic cost leverage. Moreover, increasing volume through-put, in tandem with processing improvements, would result in even further cost benefits to the company.

□ *Technology*—The company's existing CAD/CAM design capabilities were truly state of the art. They offered precision in tooling and cost-effective development of new products from the drawing board to finished prototype. Moreover, the company had several product and process patents pending that could provide some big-hit opportunities.

□ *Distribution and Sales Coverage*—With current distribution in hardware stores, mass merchandisers, do-it-yourself stores, and a wide mix of specialty-tool stores, the company was well positioned to launch additional new products in existing channels. The sales force had established strong trade relationships with sales reps and buyers. It was always running well-received contests for these customers. These factors, combined with brand-name equity, meant that gaining shelf space on new products in these channels would be relatively easy.

□ *Consumer Position and Brand-Name Equity*—Consumer perception of product quality was extremely high. Competitors did not enjoy the same high standing in perceived quality or brand-name recognition. The company had spent heavy advertising dollars to bolster high-quality brand-name awareness. It was feasible that this brand-name equity would be transferable to new products. In fact, its brand name alone would communicate quality to consumers even before they understood the new products' specific benefits.

□ *Entrepreneurial Environment and Committed Management*— Management was willing to take the risks associated with moving out of the existing core-products base. Over $20 million had been allocated to developing new products during the next two years. Venture teams were established that consisted of some of the top talent across functions within the company.

These findings had tremendous value when it came time to develop a new product blueprint and strategy. Using this information, the company developed its blueprint, corporate plan, market research, and so forth. Through a series of educated extrapolations and informed projections, it then developed its new product strategy. (In this particular case, there was some overlap between goals for the existing business and expectations from new products.) Contained in their strategy were business objectives, financial gap (percentage mix of revenues and profits to come from new and existing products), identification of internal strengths, initial list of categories, and strategic roles and screening criteria.

High margins generated through premium-priced products and a strong cash/growth balance in managing assets led the company to set aggressive growth targets for the future. The company had developed a new product blueprint from its corporate plan. It then identified five major strategic goals to be satisfied through its new product program:

1. Achieve a 20 percent increase in dollar market share from existing and new products.
2. Generate $50 million from new-to-the-world products not yet in the marketplace.
3. Diversify into do-it-yourself-related product categories besides tools.
4. Expand tools distribution to the West Coast market in do-it-yourself retail outlets through existing and new products.
5. Reduce dependency on one source of supply.

The company had basically developed several requisite and opportunistic strategic roles to guide its growth program. It determined that first it must protect its existing business to maintain its current clout in the market. Several requisite roles were formulated to protect and expand this business by capitalizing on internal strengths. They ranged from increasing market share to developing lower-cost tools, utilizing new supply sources to compete with foreign competitors through the development of new products.

Opportunistic roles, such as exploiting existing technology and entering new do-it-yourself retail niches in the U.S. market, were developed to launch the company into new product lines and new business categories.

The next step was to calibrate the relative degree of risk for each new product associated with specific strategic roles. To assess the risk for each strategic role, management developed a weighting system based on the company's internal strengths. The leverage of each internal strength was valued, and the weights given indicated the degree of importance a particular strength had in contributing to strategic roles. The requisite and opportunistic roles were then ranked in order of relative importance to the business objectives, and performance criteria were developed based on the assigned risk factors. The lowest risk is associated with a cost reduction that is intended to play the role of securing a dominant market share and compete more effectively with foreign competitors. The highest risk is attached to a new-to-the-world product designed to establish a foothold in a new geographic market.

Yet the findings from the diagnostic audit proved instrumental in getting the whole new product project off to the right start. In a sense, it provided a foundation for the architect and contractor. They clearly saw that to meet these challenges (especially with respect to generating an additional $50 million), they needed a separate new product team, *written* plans, and clear accountability.

Separating the "can do" from the "would like to do" involves measuring the relative degree of risk of each potential new product matched to strategic roles. Strategic roles provide direction for how to grow a company with internally developed new products. The roles also provide a way for top management to offer input on the direction of the new product efforts without getting involved in the nitty-gritty stages of development. As you can also see, new product strategic roles link the entire development process to corporate growth and financial objectives. The diagnostic audit provides the other necessary ingredient. In simple terms, it gives you a clear understanding of what has gone on in the past and what to expect in the future. With increased planning and commitment early on in the new product direction-setting process, companies can remove a good deal of uncertainty and really manage new product development.

Screening Criteria

Screening criteria should be developed in order to set priorities on market categories and new product concepts. By setting screening criteria to measure the attractiveness of new product concepts, a company increases its chances for new product success. While most companies tend to use sales revenues, profit contribution, and return on invested capital for screening a new concept, other financial criteria may be even more appropriate, such as margins, payback, and return on sales or assets. Regardless of the specific performance measures chosen, successful companies identify a common basis for agreeing on screening criteria and then stick to them—for each new concept under consideration. Strategic roles and new product types must also be linked to financial screening criteria. As one new product director for a consumer durables company noted, "First, strategic objectives are set, and then we establish screens that differ by role and new product type."

For example, the Toro Company uses several different techniques to generate new product ideas and calibrate risk. Some are formal and systematic, while others fall more into the ad hoc brainstorming category. Most of the time, however, they establish strategic roles. For them, this boils down to asking, What business objective should new products satisfy? Their snow products and lighting businesses may have resulted from this strategic role: utilize off-season capacity and offset sales cyclicality.

Identifying a simple direction can often provide successful new product results. That is because managers are united. They share a common, focused direction—one that can be interpreted differently but one that keeps new product players working toward a commonly agreed-upon set of objectives.

Beyond establishing strategic roles, Toro well understands and utilizes screening criteria to filter out the less attractive opportunities and concentrate on higher potential-return ventures. The first type of screen Toro uses is a comparison of each new product concept under examination with the corporate mission statement for new products—their blueprint. To paraphrase the mission statement for their Consumer Products Division, Toro wants new products to be outdoor, gas-powered maintenance-related equipment. Quality and pricing must communicate upscale and premium price/value. No "cheap" products are allowed.

This mission statement, in and of itself, represents a fine-meshed sieve for screening new product ideas. If a concept is not an outdoor machine that helps the consumer with some type of chore, then it probably won't pass to the next stage of development. This is an extremely cost-effective screen. Whether it is too fine meshed is always open for discussion. But the point is, a lot of time will not be wasted nor dollars spent on concepts that wander into areas that will never receive top-management support and financial commitment.

After a concept passes the Toro corporate mission screen, it then has to pass a quantitative screen on potential sales revenues and profits. A minimum sales- and gross-margin threshold has been established that every new product must satisfy. Subsequent to satisfying the minimum financial criteria, in-depth business analysis is conducted on the concept to determine the following:

☐ Who will buy it—market potential and target customers?

☐ Why will the customer buy it; how is it different from competitive offerings?

☐ Is the product unique; does it truly have superior benefits?

☐ Does the innovation yield a product that will allow the task to be done by the customer better than ever before?

If the concept passes through the business-analysis screen, then it is placed into the formal new product development process. At this point, additional competitive analysis is undertaken to pinpoint the desired product characteristics. While Toro admits that sometimes the structure and formality of the process get a bit cumbersome, it is clearly an outstanding strength of the company's new product planning process. It gives focus to the new product program and ensures that new products satisfy corporate objectives and that money is not wasted on products that have little potential for fulfilling real market needs. Management does recognize the need for the process to be flexible at times, given competitive new product entrants, and will occasionally alter the step-by-step stages in the process.

Typically, at Toro ideas come very early on in the process. Often they precede category idea generation. In other words, product ideas lead to category identification and subsequent product lines to compete in an entire category. Of course, many other companies will begin with category identification first, as a way to focus idea generation. This approach allows a way to identify new product ideas by focusing on attractive categories, thus tying idea generation more closely to those categories a company has already targeted.

Similar strategic roles and screens are often adopted by companies once a market trend has been identified. In 1982 and 1983 new product efforts by many food companies focused on nutrition- and health-oriented consumer trends. Many food companies set strategic roles to get into nutritional foods—whether the nutritional component was real or perceived. Low-salt, low-sugar, and low-cholesterol products began to fill the shelves in 1984 and 1985. Aspartame-sweetened products, fruit juices, and health snacks continue to be rolled out onto the grocery shelves even today.

Many companies have crowded the shelves with items for the fitness-oriented and diet-driven consumers—such things as Banquet's Hot Bites, Fleischmann's No-Cholesterol Cream Cheese, Planter's Lite Peanuts, and Armour's Classic Delites.

However, beyond nutrition, consumers were also trending toward foods that offered single serving sizes and gourmet "grazing" products. Both of these trends indicated that the single-person and dual-working households were increasing, and meal times were dramatically changing from the three-meals-a-day pattern to the eating-less-but-more-frequently approach.

The proliferation of single-serving-sized frozen entrees, smaller frozen pizzas, individually wrapped danish, and ice cream bars separately packaged supported this consumer trend. This signaled increased competition for share of shelf space, share of voice, share of market, and share of stomach.

Why do some of these new products work and others fail miserably even though they all satisfy the same strategic roles? The answer is that products that build upon existing internal strengths and comply with screening criteria usually end up as the success stories in the marketplace. However, the point is that the development of strategic roles and screening criteria are sometimes triggered by market trends. Companies identify a trend, jump on the band wagon, and then develop roles and screens to guide or provide checks on new product idea generation. While this is more of a seat-of-the-pants approach to managing the new product process, as opposed to a preferred step-by-step and more systematic approach, at least roles and screens are used in these situations. Latching onto a new consumer trend or need is only part of the success equation. The winners are those companies that still make sure they match these market trends to the company's internal capabilities and desired new product objectives.

The purpose of screening criteria, therefore, is to provide a consistent way, with limited management emotion and bias, to compare new product opportunities against one another. If companies had unlimited funds and resources, there would be no need at all for criteria and performance benchmarks. A company would just launch every new idea that it came up with. That not being the case, companies must make trade-offs and choose those opportunities that offer the highest utilization of scarce resources. Screening criteria, then, become the common language that can be spoken by new products and top management.

While any new concept can be forced to fit established screening criteria by changing the market, cost, consumer demand, or competitive assumptions, at least the ground rules are understood and can be used to test the underlying assumptions that are being made. Companies use screening criteria to prioritize categories and new ideas and concepts. The purpose of screens is to enable managers to compare one opportunity to another to determine which ones potentially offer the best fit to the company's objectives, internal strengths, and return requirements. Screening criteria are usually applied at three stages of the execution process: (1) setting priorities for category selection, (2) concept development, and (3) after-business analysis. Exhibit 4-1 shows the relationship of screening criteria to these steps in the new product process.

The potential danger of screening criteria, and the reason many new product managers shy away from them, is that they have been burned by top management too often when the performance of the product in the marketplace does not perform

EXHIBIT 4-1 New Product Development Process

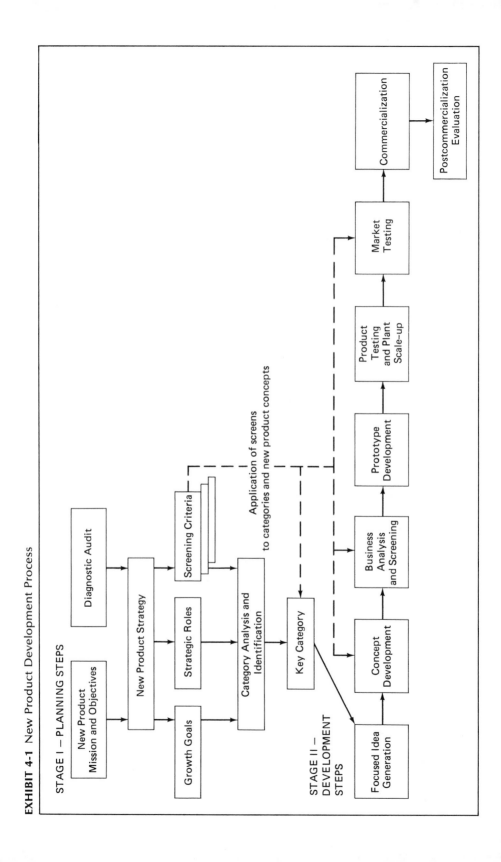

as expected. It is much "safer" for one's career to base personal-performance evaluations on objectives—for instance, to launch five new products each year or develop products that will provide a new business opportunity to the company. These types of meaningless objectives can most often be achieved. However, it takes a totally different risk posture to be held accountable for generating an incremental $50 million in revenues and $4 million in profits from products currently not on the market. Consequently, top management must set an appropriate tone and foster a supportive environment that allows mistakes to be made in the new product area. Likewise, new product managers need to be willing to take some stances, put their butts on the line once in a while, and launch high-risk products with potential high returns. Screening criteria serve as the common ground to bring the two closer together.

TYPES OF SCREENS

Different types of screens can be used to evaluate and prioritize new product opportunities. Screens can be applied to entire categories or individual concepts. As shown in Exhibit 4-2, examples of six types of screens include the following:

- □ Growth-role screens
- □ Category screens
- □ Strategic-role screens
- □ New product type screens
- □ Internal-strengths screens
- □ Financial-risk screens

Once a company has determined its expectations from new products and decided what management is planning to get from the effort, selection of one kind of screen or a combination of screens needs to be made. Some companies use several screens in one way or another, while other successful companies use only two or three sets of screens.

It is also important to determine how new product managers will be rewarded; if the wrong incentive benchmarks are set, screens can become major obstacles to overcome rather than guideposts. One problem that often arises in setting performance benchmarks for new products is establishing criteria that are too rigid and cumbersome. Again, if screens are used as clubs to elimi-

EXHIBIT 4-2 Types of Screening Criteria

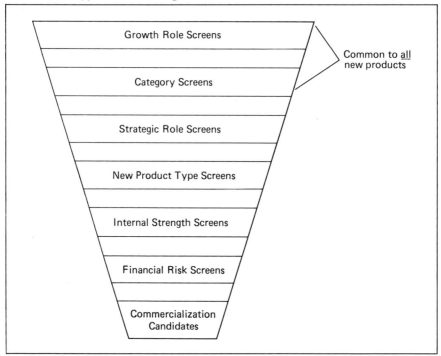

nate all new concepts, risk is reduced to zero, but so is growth from future new products. The use of screening criteria must be kept in perspective. Screens would not be needed if risk weren't a factor, and yet it is important to try to balance this risk factor so that screens are an asset—so that they assist managers, not hinder them unduly. However, even the new entrepreneur, who may not have well-defined written screening criteria, uses intuition and past experience as the screen against which to judge his idea or concept.

A company could be successful at new products without a formalized screening process, as in the above entrepreneurial case, *if* management did not change, *if* competition remained constant, *if* all team players involved in new products had the same thorough understanding of the business and experience in it, and *if* judgmental criteria were applied consistently and interpreted uniformly across all concepts. Rarely is that ever the case. Thus, in an attempt to standardize risk and provide a common language for managers within a company, screens are a valuable tool.

The screening criteria in Exhibit 4-3 show how a con-

EXHIBIT 4-3 Strategic Roles/Screening Criteria

REQUISITE	OPPORTUNISTIC
• Secure dominant product share • Penetrate Canada • Enter mass–merchandiser channel • Increase shelf-space exposure • Utilize waste byproduct • Convert nonusers of existing product	• Manufacture and market differentiated consumer product • Utilize off-season capacity; offset business cyclicality • Exploit existing technology in a new way • Produce price-competitive industrial product • Establish foothold in new geographic market • Utilize existing production capabilities

COMMON CRITERIA FOR ALL ROLES

- Category growth at least comparable to inflation rate
- Fragmented competitive market with few national consumer packaged goods manufacturers
- Utilizes similar distribution/transportation network
- No high-technology component

• Premium-priced, high-margin, value-added differentiated consumer product • Distributed primarily through grocery trade • Raw material related to product • Production process similar to product • New product—shelf life four to six months • Minimal coverage of competitive product by existing broker force • Gross margins must exceed 35 to 40 percent	• Regionally oriented business • Product with differentiated value-added or cost-competitive potential • Gross margins must exceed 40 to 45 percent

sumer packaged goods company first established a set of common screens that all new concepts had to satisfy, and then applied various role-specific screens, depending upon the type of business requirement that the new product concept would be potentially addressing.

Growth-Role Screens

The first screen cited in Exhibit 4-2 is the growth-role screen. The purpose of growth-role screens is largely to provide the first "rough-cut"—to define the "universe" of new product opportunities that are acceptable to the company. The screens should be broad, very simple, and straightforward. Yet they are crucially important because they identify the specific direction all new products must follow and establish firm benchmarks in terms of how the company plans to use new products to grow its business.

For example, some new product growth-role screens

for categories and concepts for the Pillsbury Company have included: (1) to introduce innovative new food products, (2) to enter a totally new food category that would represent a new leg to the current portfolio, and (3) to expand the company's global market share of refrigerated and frozen new products.

The common link among those growth-role screens was that new products had to be food items. At first glance, this appears to be a rather naive screen; since Pillsbury is in the food business, it makes sense they would want new products to come from food categories. However, it reinforces Pillsbury's commitment not to stray from this objective. Thus, if the Pillsbury new product development team was examining new power tools or new kitchen appliances, these screens would quickly serve as a sharp ax to delete those ideas from consideration. These growth-role screens are broad; their primary purpose is to define areas which the company should not enter. They are not tight enough to direct a company to a specific category or concept, but they usually depict the general direction that all new products should take.

When developing growth-role screens, it is important to identify top management's personal aspirations, biases, and desires for the corporation. The strategic long-range plan may list the "boiled-down," pat version of the company's mission, but these objectives should be further clarified and crystallized after they are discussed individually with top managers.

Determining top management's risk posture is also essential. If the new product manager gets a feel for how much they are willing to put at risk in terms of corporate funds and management talent and time, a risk profile will emerge. The real answer being sought is whether they *accept* failures as part of the. new product process. Their attitudes toward the expected success rate for internally developed new products will also shadow the risk posture. Some considerations in shaping the growth-role screens are management's expectations for new product margins, returns, asset intensity, geographic coverage, and investment level.

To summarize, the first set of screens should be aimed at providing a rough-cut definition of what types of new products can potentially be developed and what general growth objectives the new product program will have to achieve. These screens are basic and focus on broad objectives. Some can be applied equally to an assessment of entire categories and individual concepts, while others apply solely to one or the other. Finally, while they are broad and simplistic, they are important because they narrow the range of opportunities to be considered and provide the first step in narrowing down a wide array of possibilities.

Category Screens

We will discuss market-category identification and screening in depth in the next chapter. However, there are several types of screens that can be developed for category selection and priority setting. Category screens may cover internal strengths that a company wants to exploit, or market or competitive characteristics that represent the amount of risk the company is willing to take. For example, if low advertising budgets are common with your company's new product launches, then categories should be screened out if they require high degrees of advertising to compete effectively. For the most part, qualitative rather than quantitative screens should be used for category identification. Without a specific new product in mind, it becomes difficult to measure sales and profit performance; financial screens should be saved until a specific new product idea has been delineated. The category screens should be simple and relatively broad. Remember, the entire screening process should be thought of as a funnel—wide at the top and gradually narrowing. As new concepts are poured into the funnel, the tapered screens catch the "bad" ideas, leaving the ones with the highest potential flowing out of the base of the funnel.

For a look at category screens, criteria established by a consumer packaged goods company include:

□ There is intense consumer need in the category for the solution to a particular problem.

□ Twenty percent of all U.S. households must relate to the problem and represent potential purchasers.

□ Competitive market structure is reasonably fragmented—no competitor having more than a 40 percent share of existing market.

□ After entry, category will average at least 10 percent revenue growth annually.

□ Opportunity offers a distinctive cost, functional, or time-saving benefit to consumer.

□ Category opportunity is expected to remain in a growth posture for at least five to seven years.

□ Product opportunity does not require an advertising and sales ratio that exceeds 20 percent during the first two years as gauged by current category advertising expenditures.

The company decided that any category opportunity should be able to pass all of these screens, which provide direction and yet are relatively loose.

Until a concept has been generated, it is difficult to determine definitely that a category is bad or good. While this caveat should be kept in mind, category screens at least provide a first step in the "funneling process." The greater the extent to which new product development can be focused on those categories where management is willing to place some bets, the better the chances for internal success and effective resource allocation. The real purpose of category screens is to provide managers with informed judgment in choosing new areas to explore.

Exhibit 4-4 illustrates how a food company has set priorities on key categories in which to pursue concept development. The screens assisted management in deciding which categories to focus on first.

Let's look at another set of category screens—this time for a cheese manufacturer who has segmented category screens by product and market.

PRODUCT

□ Consumer food—dairy or frozen.

□ Category offers true product differentiation, uniqueness, and/or superior perceived quality and taste.

□ Category lends itself to high-end, top-tier price positioning.

□ Category fit with established equity in brand name.

MARKET

□ Singular, fragmented, or nonexistent competition in category.

□ Affordable consumer- and trade-support requirements relative to degree of risk involved.

□ Distributed via existing channels.

□ No unresolvable key broker conflicts.

Strategic-Role Screens

Strategic-role screens can be applied to categories *and* to specific new product concepts. They are predominantly nonfinancial statements that pinpoint competitive, market, or other key business requirements new products will have to fulfill. Growth-role and category screens are, for the most part, used to identify the target categories in which to pursue new product development. Exhibit 4-5 illustrates a consumer packaged goods company with four strategic roles driving its new products program. In turn,

EXHIBIT 4-4 Screening Criteria for Category Priority Setting

Market Categories	Strategic Roles		Risk			Internal Strengths			Market			
	A	B	C	D	E	F	G	H	I	J	K	L
1. Health Snacks	+	+	+	+	+	+	+	+	+	+	+	+
2. Dietetic main meals	+	+	+	+	?	NA	NA	+	+	+	+	+
3. Frozen novelties	+	+	+	+	+	?	+	+	+	+	+	?
4. Yogurt	+	+	+	+	+	?	?	+	+	?	+	?
5. Pizza delivery	+	+	+	+	+	?	+	+	NA	+	+	+
6. Ethnic appetizers	+	+	O	+	+	+	?	+	?	+	+	?
7. Single-serve desserts	+	+	+	+	+	+	?	+	?	+	+	?
8. Tofu	+	+	+	+	O	O	?	+	?	+	+	?
9. Sauces	+	+	+	+	O	?	+	+	?	+	+	?
10. Peanut butter	+	+	+	+	O	+	+	+	+	+	+	+
11. Cheese snacks	+	+	O	+	+	?	?	+	+	+	?	?
12. Baby food	O	+	O	O	+	?	?	+	+	?	?	?
13. Branded produce	O	+	O	+	+	+	+	?	?	?	+	+
14. Condiments	+	+	+	+	+	+	+	?	?	+	+	+
15. Meat substitutes	O	+	+	O	+	?	?	?	?	+	+	+
16. Coffee	+	+	+	+	O	?	?	?	+	?	+	?

Legend: + Screen is satisfied.
? Screen may not be satisfied.
O Screen is not satisfied.
A Category is different from those in which division currently competes.
B Category offers branded niche segment.
C Category trends allow a minimum of $25 to $40 million in annual sales within five years of launch.
D ROCE of at least 45% by year 5 could be generated.
E Breakeven could occur prior to year 5.
F Technology advantage and opportunity application offered.
G Competitive manufacturing cost position achieved within three years after launch.
H Twenty percent of U.S. households relate to problem and represent potential purchasers.
I Solution presented to an unsatisfied consumer need.
J Reasonably fragmented competitive market structure.
K Average of at least 10% revenue growth annually during the first five years.
L Idea generation to start of market test realized in three years or less.

EXHIBIT 4-5 Consumer Packaged Goods Company

New Product Strategic Roles	Product Screening Criteria	
	Sales Threshold	ROI
Enter the Emerging under-21 Market Segment	$20 Million	20%
Establish Foothold in a New Geographic Market	$10 Million	25%
Increase Share of Shelf Space at Retail	$ 5 Million	15%
Utilize Off-season and Excess Capacity	$ 2 Million	12%

Reprinted with the permission of Booz Allen & Hamilton, Inc.

each strategic role has differentiated screening criteria based upon varying levels of perceived risk by each role.

Once categories have been selected, strategic roles are often the first set of criteria to use against any new idea that emerges within selected categories. They are the bridge to a company's corporate objectives, as they describe what a company expects from any new product. Apart from the desire to increase revenue and profit growth, strategic roles help to explain, Why are we focusing attention on new product development and what do we expect to gain from our efforts?

Strategic roles must be agreed upon by all levels of management. Otherwise, new product development is chaotic. Disagreements over directional interpretations and priorities will lead to mass chaos and poor communication with each manager pursuing his or her own strategic goals. The company ends up spending dollars and committing people to projects that are "out of sync" with its best new product interests.

The following examples of strategic-role screens are from three companies: an equipment manufacturer, a consumer packaged goods company, and a consumer durables company. These strategic roles define which business requirements new products are expected to satisfy. Any new product concept must satisfy one or more of these strategic roles.

EQUIPMENT MANUFACTURER

☐ Defend core business against competitive inroads and ensure company survival.

☐ Expand target customer base to secure new users.

□ Strengthen company's position in supplier attractiveness to current target customers.

□ Decrease cyclicality of earnings.

□ Fill obsolescence gap in product line.

□ Utilize excess plant capacity.

□ Offer way to move company into other high-growth, high-margin product categories.

This company selected strategic roles which were largely aimed at strengthening the company's existing operations. Only the last role is opportunistic, reflecting the company's concern with using new products to first bolster its business before branching out into new areas.

CONSUMER PACKAGED GOODS COMPANY

Requisite roles—improving existing business

□ A way to increase presence and penetration in the dairy case.

□ A way to increase penetration and strength in the cereal category.

□ A way to improve branded-product margins.

□ A means of reacting to competitive new product offerings to protect existing share of shelf space.

Opportunistic roles—diversifying the business

□ A way to enter new, higher-margin cereal, cereal-related, and dairy categories.

□ A way to move the company into refrigerated and frozen areas that offer higher margins than the dry shelf.

□ A means to further utilize the breading- and beverage-packaging-equipment investment.

□ A means to position the company as an innovative entity that offers more new-to-the-world and new-to-the-company products and fewer line extensions.

This company has chosen to separate its strategic roles into requisite and opportunistic roles, as we discussed previously in the chapter. For this company, new products were needed to defend the existing business as well as to launch into new diversification. Clearly, this company saw new products as tools to build market share. That's not to say that advertising, consumer promotions, and trade deals were not critical in this category to defend market share from competition; it's just that they saw more of a longer-term competitive edge coming from new products.

CONSUMER DURABLES COMPANY

□ All new-to-the-world or new product lines must be technologically superior to any existing product on the market.

□ New products should be limited to consumer nondurable branded, packaged goods.

□ All new product lines to the company must be in categories where competition is fragmented unless product has unique benefit.

□ Stay away from high-spend, advertising-intensive competitors unless product is unique.

□ Must be able to reach distribution channels economically.

This company chose not to establish any category screens; thus, their strategic-roles screens were applied to categories as well as to new products. However, these roles do not describe exactly what the company expects to accomplish from new products as well as the first two examples. However, in examining their corporate mission statement, they have a very clear articulation of new product expectations. As a result, between their "mission screens," which are similar to growth-role screens, and their strategic role screens, the company has covered its bases on setting the direction for the new product effort.

Financial screens can also be established for strategic roles. As the investment required and the probability of failure increase for any product satisfying a specific strategic role, the performance expectations should go up. A useful approach in assessing risk relates the required investment level to the probability of failure for each new product; the calibration of risk varies by strategic role. For example, a new product that utilizes excess capacity, fits the current distribution, and requires minimal investment can be assessed as low risk. (See Exhibit 4-6.) Establishing a foothold in a new country may also require little investment; however, the probability of failure is higher, and therefore the new product would be assessed as a moderately high risk.

Each role may have a return estimate tied to it—based on different perceived levels of risk:

□ Low risk (15 percent ROI required). New products that will utilize excess capacity.

□ Moderate risk (20 percent ROI required). New products that will serve to combat a new, competitive entrant.

☐ Highest risk (25 percent ROI required). New products that will enable the company to establish a foothold in a new country.

This company has clearly decided that as its financial strategic roles become more risky, it will in turn require higher ROI performance from those new products selected to fulfill each role. The screens become stiffer and more difficult to pass as risk increases. To summarize, strategic-role screens are broad state-

EXHIBIT 4-6 Relationship Among Strategic Role, Investment, and Risk

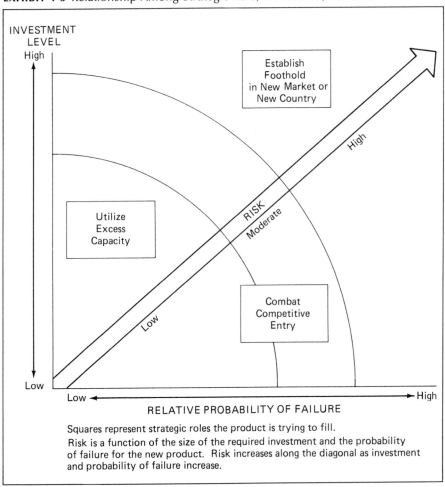

INVESTMENT LEVEL

High

Establish Foothold in New Market or New Country

High

RISK Moderate

Utilize Excess Capacity

Low

Combat Competitive Entry

Low

Low ←———————————————→ High

RELATIVE PROBABILITY OF FAILURE

Squares represent strategic roles the product is trying to fill.
Risk is a function of the size of the required investment and the probability of failure for the new product. Risk increases along the diagonal as investment and probability of failure increase.

ments that put forth various business conditions new products will have to fulfill in order to pass through the screening process. They are largely nonfinancial but do include finance, market and competitive concerns, internal requirements, and the like. They are strategic in nature because each one contains some basic element or issue of vital concern to the company.

Screens For New Product Types

While each new product type has a different level of risk, the smart company will adjust the financial return expected by the product type to reflect the varying risk level. For example, the revenue and profit minimum should be substantially less for a lower-risk line extension compared to a high-risk, new-to-the-world product. Here, in particular, the issue of differentiated screening criteria becomes relevant. The point is to establish financial screens that reflect the relative risk to the company by each new product type.

Sometimes, the screens may be rather simplistic, as illustrated in the following example. However, the screens for new product types illustrated in this case are well understood by all management in this company. They have been discussed several times and agreed to by all managers involved in new product planning. Managers in this company understand why these three new product types are the only ones included in their screens, and they have agreed to work within the framework of options.

SCREENS FOR NEW PRODUCT TYPES

☐ *New to the world*—rests on the premise that consumer needs are best met in a whole new way. Consumer must be able to see or understand the benefit of the product and its use.

☐ *New product line*—must be perceived by consumer as outperforming competitive product. Exceptional price/value relative to need.

☐ *Flanker*—Expands consumer interest in existing product line.

For a company that has been extremely successful at commercializing new-to-the-company products, the relative risk of this new product type may be less than even a line extension.

The determination of risk level by new product type should be a function of three factors: company past experience with a new product type, internal strengths that will consistently be brought to each new product type, and a balance of new product types in the planned portfolio. (If a company wants to introduce only new-to-the-world products, the risk level for those new product types is substantially higher than it might be if other lower-risk new product types were also part of the new products strategy.)

The following example illustrates how some companies establish qualitative *and* quantitative screens by new product type *and* strategic roles, as shown in Exhibit 4-7.

In this case, while the consensus of top management in a consumer durables and nondurables company was that the use of new product screening criteria would help focus the new product effort and increase the chances for new product success, no distinction was made between strategic role or new product type. Five screens were established for all new concepts and categories.

☐ New products should be limited to consumer nondurable packaged goods.

☐ All new-to-the-world or new product lines must be technologically superior to any existing product on the market.

☐ All new product lines for the division must be in categories where competition is fragmented.

☐ Stay away from high-spend, advertising-intensive categories and competitors unless product is unique.

☐ Must be able to reach distribution channels economically.

☐ After commercialization, new product projects must be formally reviewed if they fall below $500,000 in revenues or under 20 percent profit margins.

These five screens provided just enough guidance for this company to keep a handle on its new product efforts. However, further breakdown by strategic role and new product type would have given the company more focus and direction, and made their screening process more beneficial.

Internal-Strength Screens

As discussed in Chapter 3, a new concept should take advantage of as many internal company strengths as possible. If homework has been done and a diagnostic audit conducted, the transformation of the internal strengths or weaknesses identified into internal-strength screens may begin. Internal-strength screens should not be viewed as veto screens as much as support arms. In other words, the screens should not be set up with the intent of

EXHIBIT 4-7 Example of New Product Screening Criteria for a $300 Million Durables Company

		Qualitative Screens	Quantitative Screens (by year 3 after launch)
STRATEGIC ROLES	Preempt competition and defend share	Must generate at least a 2% market-share increase	20% ROIC
	Expand into foreign market	Affords the formation of a new consumer business	25% ROIC
	Utilize waste byproduct	Must be distributed via existing channels	12% ROIC
NEW-PRODUCT TYPES	New-to-the-world	Must utilize in-house technology patent	$5 million sales, 40% gross profit margin
	New-to-the-company	Competition must be fragmented; no two competitors with over 70% share	$3 million sales, 35% gross profit margin
	Line extensions	Must be perceived by consumers as better than competitors' offerings	$.5 million sales, 25% gross profit margin

automatically scratching ideas that do not pass through all of them. Some might be more essential than others. But on the whole, the more internal-strength screens an idea passes through, the better. If it barely makes it through, it should trigger an alert so that the idea is then judged more closely. The more internal strengths a new concept draws upon, the greater the chances of success. Internal-strength screen for a company might include: utilization of patented technology, increased use of a low-cost manufacturing process, and sales via existing, strong direct sales force.

Financial-Risk Screens

Several different types of screens are used effectively by companies to assess the relative attractiveness of categories and new product concepts. Exhibit 4-8 depicts the most frequently used financial screens by a sample of 100 companies surveyed who were active in new products. A combination of at least two financial screens are commonly used.

The financial screens should be the final set of screens a new product concept is passed through. After the business analysis has been completed, and there is a moderate degree of

EXHIBIT 4-8 Financial-Performance Criteria Used Most Frequently by 100 Companies

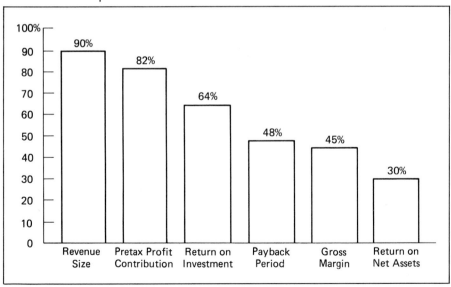

Survey conducted by Kuczmarski & Associates, 1986.

comfort established regarding the demand and cost dimensions of the concept, a pro forma statement can be assembled. With a projected income statement in place, a new product concept can be evaluated against the new product financial screens. Exhibits 4-9 and 4-10 show the different kinds of financial benchmarks that can be used and the great range in numerical sizes and expectations. Obviously, risk profiles vary dramatically among companies, a fact reflected by the degree of risk companies are willing to take with financial screens.

The lack of specific screening criteria may have contributed in the past to a diffusion of new product efforts—the management has made major strides in developing more precise criteria by new product type. (See Exhibit 4-9.)

After business analysis and product costing, new product concepts must pass the quantitative screens before prototype development and plant testing. (See Exhibit 4-10.)

As Exhibits 4-9 and 4-10 demonstrate, financial screens are most often tied to new product type or strategic role. In this way, financial screens can be differentiated according to varying levels of risk. A higher financial hurdle will be set for the roles or new product types that will require longer development and investment time and costs and less clearly defined consumer demand. Launching line extensions that increase plant capacity should involve relatively low hurdle rates. Thus, implicit in the screens is a calibration for the varying degrees of risk.

The reason it is important to set differentiated screens rather than a single hurdle rate is that missed opportunities usually occur as a result of companies setting up one standard performance benchmark. A consumer packaged goods company has consistently stated that it will only launch new products that represent a $25 million new product opportunity within three years. They have just as consistently not launched any new products during the past four years. Are there no profitable $18 million new products that would make sense for this company to launch? The point is that when one single standard is set for all new products, many potentially successful new products are neglected and ignored. Yet developing some sort of financial screens is essential to ensure that the financial expectations surrounding new products are viable.

CHALLENGING THE SCREENING CRITERIA

Exhibit 4-11 provides a check list that should be used once screens have been developed. Challenging the integrity and comfort level of the screens will reinforce a company's adherence to them in the future.

EXHIBIT 4-9 Financial Screens by New Product Type

Product Type	Revenue Size ($Million)	By Year	Minimum Operating Profit Margins	By Year	Payback Year
New-to-the-world	$5 to $25	3	20%*	5	3
New-to-the-company	$5	3	20%*	3	2
Flanker (protect business)	$1	2	5%	1	2
Line extension (adds to)	$.5	2	At least equal to existing margin	1	2
Repositioning	At least equal to existing product	1	At least equal to existing product	1	1
Cost reduction	At least equal to existing product	1	At least equal to existing product	1	1

*And/or a minimum ROCE of 30%.

EXHIBIT 4-10 Quantitative Screens

Minimums	New-to-the-company	Line Extensions	Flankers	Resale
Revenue volume by year 2	$500,000	$250,000	$100,000 (By end of year 1)	$500,000
Cumulative revenue volume by year 3	$1,500,000	$750,000	$350,000	$1,500,000
Gross profit	24%	21%	20%	20%
Pretax Margin	6.0%	5.5%	5.0%	5.0%
Breakeven—payback on development and launch costs	3 years	2 years	1 year	3 years
ROIC	5-year payback	3-year payback	3-year payback	5-year payback

EXHIBIT 4-11 Challenges to Screening Criteria

> Are the new-to-the-world criteria too aggressive? Using the criteria es-
> tablished, are there past successful new products that would have been
> screened out?
> Will the use of screening criteria be perceived within the division as a
> mechanism that cuts off the "creative juices" or helps direct them?
> What would be the impact of the criteria upon new product projects
> currently on the books?
> Are corporate financial objectives consistent with the new product
> screening criteria?
> How will the screening criteria be adhered to effectively?
> Have we left any noticeable gaps in the criteria, and if so, why?

DEVELOPING SCREENS—FIND OUT FIRST

A final note on screening criteria: It is important to find
out from management what they perceive as the key criteria upon
which to judge new product opportunities. You may be surprised
at the results. Usually, managers have several screens in mind that
they will elaborate on when asked. Whether the criteria have ever
been communicated to other managers is another issue. But talk
with at least three or four managers to see if any patterns emerge.
This information can also provide a starting point for listing and
formalizing a set of screens management can ultimately agree on.
You will probably want to talk with managers in all functions related to new product development, including research and development, corporate/divisional business planning, finance, sales and
marketing, and human-resource management. Begin by making a
check list of questions to guide each interview. Afterwards, compile a draft of potential screens and the pros and cons for each
screen, and circulate them to all interviewees. After comments
have been collected and you have had a chance to synthesize and
develop a final group of screens, you should find greater acceptance of them since people have had the opportunity to take part
in developing them from the outset. Don't forget senior-management involvement; you may decide to involve senior management
in this process for "political" reasons, even when senior managers
have little direct involvement. This will give you some "political
protection" down the road.

Interviews with people involved in new product development can yield other insights too, aside from just helping develop screens. When asking managers in a company what the set of screens is for new products, responses often reveal why no new products get out the door. For example, it is often the case that everyone has different criteria and the managers' collective set of screens prevents any new product from making it through—the criteria are far too limiting. The following screens were mentioned by six managers in one consumer durables company.

Two times better than competitive product's quality.

Around $2 million in revenues.

Between $5 and $10 million in revenues.

Achieve 25 percent pretax margin payback in three to five years.

Distribute via existing channels.

As Exhibits 4-12 and 4-13 also illustrate, management often has totally different perspectives on growth expectations and screens for new products. Needless to say, a company cannot run a successful new product operation when management people are all thinking differently—often with conflicting points of view. In this case, management needs to find out where it stands and then move to build consensus and common understanding. The following responses were cited by top managers when asked, "What is the single most important criterion that your new products have to meet?" The range of answers included:

Offers superior performance relative to current products used.

Benefits must be recognizable and justify value before purchase.

Satisfies biggest problem of product class far better than all competitors.

Projected to capture top one or two share points.

Provides technological protectable position.

Offers 15 percent annual revenue-growth opportunity.

Low capital intensity.

Needs a 50 percent gross profit margin.

Generates a 30 percent return on invested capital.

EXHIBIT 4-12 Over the Next Five Years, What Percent of Growth Should Come From Each of the Following?

	A	B	C	D	E	F	G	H	I	J	K
Existing businesses	20%	10%	50%	15%	5%	75%	10%	25%	70%	80%	64%
New to the world	15	5	10	20	—	—	20	15	8	2	5
New to the company	15	10	5	20	10	13	15	10	9	2	8
Flankers	10	5	20	5	25	3	5	7	4	2	7
Line extensions	10	55	10	20	50	5	50	8	5	2	10
Repositioning	5	5	5	10	5	3	—	10	2	2	3
Cost reductions	5	5	—	10	5	1	—	—	2	2	3
Acquisitions	20	5	—	—	—	—	—	25	—	8	—
Licensing	—	—	—	—	—	—	—	—	—	—	—

LEGEND:
A Chairman
B President
C Vice-President, marketing
D Vice-President, engineering
E Vice-President, manufacturing
F Vice-President, R&D
G Vice-President, sales
H Vice-President, finance
I Manager, new products
J Manager, acquisition planning
K Manager, facilities

EXHIBIT 4-13 What Should be the Minimal Annual Revenue Target by Year 2 for Each New Product Type?

	A	B	C	D	E	F	G	H	I	J	Breakeven year
New to the world	$5	$5	$5	$1	$5	$4	$2	$2	$3	$5	4
New to the company	5	5	3	5	1	8	8	5	5	2	3
Flankers	1	.5	1	1		.4	.8	.5	1	.5	1
Line extensions	1	2	.1	.2	.5	.4	.5	.5	.1	.5	1
Repositionings	1	.5	.1	.1	.5	.4	.3	.5	.1	.5	1

LEGEND:
A Chairman
B President
C Vice-President, marketing
D Vice-President, engineering
E Vice-President, manufacturing
F Vice-President, R&D
G Vice-President, sales
H Vice-President, finance
I Manager, new products
J Manager, acquisition planning

Without priorities clearly established that earmark which of these factors are most important, it would be virtually impossible for any new product to satisfy them all. In another company case, the top eight managers gave a wide range of answers when asked, "What financial screening criteria are used to evaluate new product projects?"

The diversity of answers underscores the problem facing a committee charged with setting new product priorities and guiding/managing the process.

> Financial benefits are weighed against projected development costs. Costs for tooling, patterns, and dies are evaluated against potential sales income or reduction in manufacturing costs.
>
> Costs versus projected return on investment.
>
> Projected sales are evaluated versus projected costs.
>
> Simple ROI and payback.
>
> Total cost versus total profit.
>
> Sales develop the financial criteria.
>
> ROI better than interest rate. Sales dollar projections for three years. Sales/costs versus gross margin and net profit.
>
> ROI, payback.

Now, isn't that list unbelievable! There are few new products that could ever meet all of those screens. The real problem is that top management carried those screens around in their heads. A new product that might pass two managers' sets of screens could never make it past two others.

Identifying the screens that management is currently using for new-product selection should be done before any discussion on screening criteria occurs. Following are the responses by managers in an industrial-equipment company to the question, "What benchmarks are currently used to evaluate new product concepts?" The wide range of answers reflects the confusion that constantly existed in the company as to which new products were most attractive. When management doesn't have a clear view of the screens being used, the likelihood of getting new products out the door is slim.

> ROCE, effect on existing business, impact on future earnings.
>
> Assessment of real potential to reach target profitability in four to five years.

Ability to support total program: ROI, ROCE.

Percent profit, ROI, minimum sales level.

Dollar growth impact on other products, profit dollar contributions, percent profit margin.

Payout in five years at 5 to 30 percent gross margin and/or cash generated, even if product falls below minimal margin requirement (low margin but high cash based on high volume).

20 percent ROI.

Sales, profit, percent to sales, ROCE, investment required to break even, including manufacturing, development, and advertising investments.

Consequently, companies must set down on paper the list of screens and criteria that all will use to determine the relative attractiveness of a new product opportunity.

The point is that by documenting a list of screens, you can make sure no holes exist, the screens are reasonable, and everyone agrees to live by them. In this sense, they serve as the game rules for the new product development process.

USING SCREENING CRITERIA TO CALIBRATE RISK

Thus far, we have discussed the notion of risk without delving into its meaning or isolating it and examining its role in new product development. Let's now take a closer look at the role of risk in the new product equation.

Risk is determined by comparing required investment and potential return to the probability of failure. Risk levels vary by company objectives, strategic roles, and new product types. Risk taking is necessary to succeed at new products. Yet at the same time, companies should be adopting approaches that reduce risk to increase the probability of success.

As discussed earlier, once the strategic roles have been developed to guide new product concepts, screening criteria must be developed from these strategic roles to "validate" new product concepts and ventures. Screening criteria force management to examine a new product idea against a number of specific parameters before any investments are made. This works as a safeguard against shooting from the hip—it reinforces the need for sound business analysis. Use of screening criteria can reduce the number of new product failures, which affect not only the earnings of the company but the morale of management and the sales force. So, as you can guess, using the criteria reduces the level of risk associated with new products.

The underlying question to be answered when analyzing risk is, How much are you willing to stake for a certain level of return? Yet risk itself is complicated; many factors affect it as the following example illustrates.

A veteran gambler in Monte Carlo may be willing to bet only 20,000 francs at baccarat since he knows the house has the odds in that game. On the other hand, he may bet 100,000 francs at blackjack since he can count the cards and therefore has a slight edge over the house. Finally, he may end up investing 500,000 francs in the Grand Prix because he used to race himself, knows all of the cars and drivers, and won the last two years. The last bet has the lowest risk for *him*.

However, in the following year we suddenly see that the Great Gamblino has totally changed his betting strategy. Why? Because external factors have changed, and therefore he has shaped a new game plan. He now knows the baccarat dealer and has a substantial edge over the house—cheating. His baccarat bets have increased fivefold to 100,000 francs. He also knows that the roulette wheel and the house favor red, so he's up to 50,000 francs for each of these bets. However, for the Grand Prix, he's betting only 10,000 francs, since most of the drivers have changed and he doesn't know anything about them this year. So he decides to risk only a small amount on the Grand Prix.

Our gambler has established betting criteria to determine how he will risk his money. In the new product arena, these criteria are considered screens.

Every opportunity must be evaluated and passed through screens as internal and external factors change. A concept that didn't make it a year ago may now pass quickly through the screening criteria. It's not that the criteria changed but rather that the assumptions about the opportunity changed.

So by establishing a consistent set of screens, managers have a way to calibrate the relative risk of any concept, even ones previously rejected—and change their bets. As already mentioned, screening criteria can be used as a tool or club. The only effective way to use screens is as tools to assist managers in setting priorities on opportunities, balancing the overall new product risk, and better allocating resources.

Most companies tend to define themselves as either new product innovators or followers. The *innovator* establishes competitive new product leadership by building on technological advantages, undertaking preemptive marketing strategies, and investing heavily in the development and launch of new products. The *follower*, however, maintains a low-risk profile, and reacts to competition by generating "second, but better" new products. Either or both of these approaches can provide successful new product results—one is not necessarily better than the other. But neither approach provides a practical direction for the role new products should play in meeting corporate growth roles.

The problem that these definitions often raise for companies is the discrepancy between calling yourself a product innovator and then acting like a product follower and vice versa. To set a direction for a company that suggests the overall role of new products is to establish a reputation for being an innovative and creative developer requires risk taking and funding to back it. Once an "innovator" culture has been established, the worst thing possible is to jerk the team back into a follower mode. It is essential to attempt to define clearly which camp a company wants to land in and then nurture that specific direction for as long as possible.

RISK AND SELECTING NEW PRODUCT TYPES

As discussed in this chapter, a company must also examine the types of new products they want to pursue that will satisfy strategic roles and accommodate the risk profile of the company. As shown in Exhibit 4-14, each new product type can be defined according to its relative degree of newness to the company and perceived level of newness to consumers. As would be expected, new-to-the-world products enjoy the highest degree of newness to both a company and consumers. In contrast, an improvement to an existing product may not even be perceived as a change by consumers. The result is that as the degree of product newness increases from low to high (along either measure), the relative riskiness of the new product increases. In addition, there is usually a correlation between the risk line and new product types. Usually, the highest development cost comes with a new-to-the-world product; the lowest with a line extension.

As the relative degree of *newness* increases for both the company and consumers, the degree of risk of that new product type escalates. Thus, if a company chooses to pursue nothing but new-to-the-world and new-to-the-company product types, the new product portfolio is a high-risk one. On the other hand, if a company spreads its mix of new products across different types of new

EXHIBIT 4-14 New Product Types

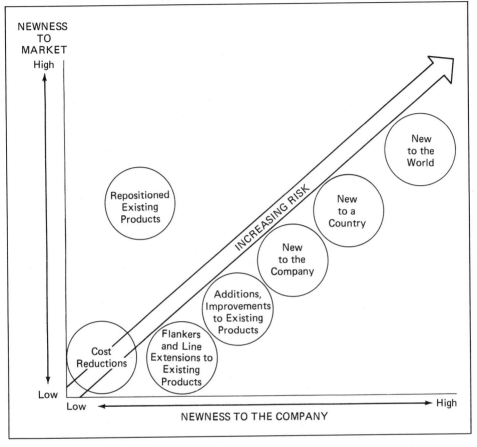

Reprinted with the permission of Booz·Allen & Hamilton Inc.

products, the risk is better balanced, and chances for a successful new product program are enhanced.

Successful companies tend to balance their new product portfolio. They go after the higher big-hit, new-to-the-world opportunities along with lower-risk line extensions, cost reductions and product improvements. It's no different from investing in the stock market by having 25 percent of the portfolio contain high-growth and high-beta stocks that represent high risk, matched with 75 percent of the portfolio containing blue chip, lower-risk and lower-return stocks.

Even though the risk associated with new product introductions is fundamentally role specific, the type of new product chosen to fit the role can increase or decrease the probability of the new product's success. The trick, therefore, is to fill a new product strategic role with the new product type that simultaneously satisfies the role, offers suitable return on resource investment, and resides within the risk tolerance framework of the company management.

Companies are more likely to develop a new-to-the-world product than any other type if the intent of the strategic role is to maintain a position as a product innovator or to exploit technology in a new way. This is especially evident in high-technology companies, such as information processing, where advances in electronics have prompted the outgrowth of many new-to-the-world products during the past five years.

Typically, a company's new product program includes a mix of new product types—from low to high risk. However, one should not just evaluate the new product types according to risk. The other part of that equation is potential return. Thus, while new-to-the-world and new-to-the-company products usually represent the highest risk, they also offer the potential for the highest margins and returns. Risk management is the cornerstone of successfully managing a company's new product portfolio. Consequently, a strong portfolio contains a mix of high and low risk-and-return new product types.

Managers often lose sight of the return side of the equation in higher-risk new product types. They succumb to the lower-risk me-too syndrome. But in examining hundreds of new products across companies, it is consistently found that companies' most successful new products are usually new-to-the-world or new-to-the-company—the ones with higher risk. Concomitantly, many companies' biggest failures also fall into these two new product category types. But the fact remains that unless risk taking is woven into the fabric of a new product organization, the upside return from new products will be limited. "No pain, no gain" is a fitting adage.

MANIPULATING NEW PRODUCT RISK

New-to-the-world products or new-to-the-company product lines typically have a higher risk than, say, cost reductions or repositionings. However, the relative risks involved with each new product type is not unalterable—a company's previous experience with the various new product types can change the relative risk of each type for that company.

Risk can be manipulated in the following ways:

□ Develop a portfolio of new products that cut across different types and varying levels of risk.

□ Draw upon internal strengths and past new product experience.

□ Increase the number of launches; the more attempts, the higher the probability becomes for a success.

□ Define and agree upon the internal new product direction.

With truly innovative new products, there is a greater variability of return and outcome. But risk often brings big profit. New-to-the-world and new-to-the-company products most often provide companies with the big hits. While they frequently represent the fewest number of launches, they have the greatest potential for return.

As an illustration, let's look at Blair Paints, a manufacturer of indoor and outdoor paints. Management has determined that one strategic role for its new products is to preempt competitive moves in a new geographic market. From the new product diagnostic audit the company conducted, the new product director determines that the company has low-cost production capability, better perceived product quality than local competition, better packaging design than competition, and capital resources necessary for manufacturing. However, the company does not have a comprehensive marketing program, a sales force in the new geographic area, nor management in place with knowledge of the markets.

As we will discuss in Chapter 6, one reason that new product development is often separated from current business operations is the associated risk of new products. Moreover, company compensation systems are geared to risk aversion—the two don't mesh if one is trying to stimulate risk taking in new products and margin maintenance in existing products. If managers are given responsibility for existing products as well as new products, they will concentrate their time and attention on the existing line since the risk is lower and the probability of their investment outcome more positive.

Manipulating the new product portfolio is a key risk-reducing action step. Combining different levels of risk into the new product plan makes the overall risk of the program lower than it would be for any single given new product. The chances of success for the overall new product effort are far greater than the probability of success of any one new product. Diversification can reduce risk, and screening criteria serve as the filters to further reduce that risk. But let's not forget the role that company experience and internal strengths have in assessing risk. These two factors probably represent the most valuable risk-reducing valve that any company has.

The variability of profit return is greatest for new-to-the-world products, followed by new-to-the-company products, line extensions, additions to existing products, repositionings, and cost reductions. A distribution of returns is associated with each of these new product types. New-to-the-world products have the highest frequency of outcome in the high- and low-return ranges.

Although specific new product categories typically display a distribution of returns like the ones above, the distribution of returns for any given new product is company and category specific. A firm's functional and new product experience, as well as its comfort level in making the required investment, influences the relative riskiness of the new product type. Consider two companies each evaluating the same two new product opportunities. The first opportunity is a new-to-the-world product; the second is a new product line. Company A has a higher level of experience in developing new product lines and good technical background for both products but little experience in the level of investment required for the new-to-the-world opportunity. For this company, the new-to-the-company product is more attractive as evidenced by a higher expected return.

Company B, however, has a higher level of experience in developing new-to-the-world products and has a poor manufacturing base relative to the new product line opportunity. This company does have the experience and comfort level in making major investments—especially in the range required for this new-to-the-world opportunity. For this company, the new-to-the-world product is more attractive.

Although a new-to-the-world product may have a high variability of return, a new-to-the-world opportunity may be a relatively low-risk venture for a company with high experience in developing new-to-the-world products and strong internal levers to pull that development.

Why are new-to-the-world products usually fraught with higher risk? Because these products often lack information concerning consumer attitudes, purchasing behavior, usage, and the like. After all, if a company already has a product in the market against which another company proposes a new-to-the-company product, the second company can find out consumer reactions, purchase frequency, and attitudes toward use, and make the appropriate changes to be more competitive. When dealing with a new-to-the-world product, those data do not exist.

For innovative products that require a change in consumer behavior, risk is high because consumers must be educated, and it is difficult to assess whether the education will have the desired effect. New-to-the-world products diffuse slowly through the population because they often require a change in values and habits. While new-to-the-world products fill consumer needs, the consumer may not have the ability to understand or the willingness to acknowledge the product benefit or advantage. Likewise, high investment spending is required to support the launch of a new-to-the-world product; reinforcement and repetition of message and consumer education are needed to change behavior patterns, and that's costly.

Whether a company chooses to be a new product innovator or an imitator is also a key element of measuring the riskiness of their respective new product programs. In choosing one approach over another, companies tend to establish common patterns, as illustrated in Exhibit 4-15. However, we take a firm stance on believing that companies must first be innovators and then imitators—it's not an either/or issue. How can most companies afford to sit back and just react to new products that have been innovated by others in the hope that once the product has been introduced, they will find some way to make it better? They can't. But that approach certainly is a lower-risk stance to take. On the other hand, companies that are launching better-than, me-too imitations will need to develop three, four, or ten times as many as

EXHIBIT 4-15 Patterns that Companies Establish in Their New Product Programs

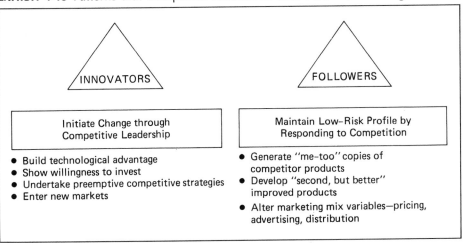

INNOVATORS

FOLLOWERS

Initiate Change through
Competitive Leadership

Maintain Low–Risk Profile by
Responding to Competition

- Build technological advantage
- Show willingness to invest
- Undertake preemptive competitive strategies
- Enter new markets

- Generate "me–too" copies of competitor products
- Develop "second, but better" improved products
- Alter marketing mix variables—pricing, advertising, distribution

Reprinted with the permission of Booz Allen & Hamilton, Inc.

one or two new-to-the-world or -company products to achieve the same financial results.

Companies must take the risk of developing innovative products. The payout is too great to let potential hits go by. Granted, the downside is a lot less for the line extensions and me-toos, but so is the upside. Of course, truly innovative products demand more time, resources, and money—the three variables most cherished by corporate management. Well, the old adage "You get what you pay for," is applicable to the new product game.

Who ends up with the bulk of the revenues and profits? Not the company that enters the market as number four with one more me-tooer. Even from a pricing standpoint, the company that provides the innovation to the consumer is the company that can command an impressive gross margin—at least until the competition follows. Innovators, not imitators, are the companies that, over time, end up with the higher returns and, ultimately, lower risk. Risk is substantially lowered, regardless of the category, competitive environment, company strengths, or investment level, if the product really solves a problem that current offerings inadequately address. It's as simple as that.

Studying consumer behavioral patterns is another way to reduce risk in managing the new product effort. Look at the trends in beverages. Hard-liquor sales have fallen dramatically during the past five years, while white wine and champagne sales are way up. Fruit juices and nonalcoholic beverages are the new trend. And, lo and behold, we find California Cooler, Slice, and Bartles and Jaymes on the retail shelf. Ocean Spray has put some of its juices in aseptic packaging, as have others in retail grocery. That hasn't happened totally by accident. Keeping track of where consumers' tastes, habits, and recreational activities are heading often leads to an innovative product. But it is hard work; you have to be able to make associations and link two observations together along with two others to find an innovative idea. Catering to the consumer requires not only an understanding up front of how the product will meet the consumers' needs better, it also calls for catering to the consumer in the product launch. That's what test markets are for—to try different approaches in communicating the product benefits to the consumer.

As a means of summarizing this discussion of screening criteria and risk, Exhibits 4-16 and 4-17 present the screening criteria for a food company and for a low-technology industrial/commercial manufacturer. While the depth and breadth of screens vary between companies, both screens have been tailored to the specific com-

EXHIBIT 4-16 Screening Criteria for a Food Company

STRATEGIC ROLES

Improving Existing Business
   A way to increase presence and penetration in convenience stores
   A way to increase penetration and strengths in snack category
   A way to improve branded gross margins beyond 35 percent
   A means of reacting to competitive new product offerings to protect existing share of shelf space

Diversifying Business
   A way to enter new, higher-margin breakfast foods and nutritional, health-oriented food categories
   A way to move into other refrigerated and frozen areas that offer higher margins and draw upon current process technology and manufacturing expertise and imagery transference
   A means to further utilize equipment, plant, investment
   A means to position the company as innovative (offering more new-to-the-company and -category products and fewer extension new products)

FINANCIAL SCREENS/LINE EXTENSIONS

	Screen
Sales dollar volume by year 3	$1,000,000
Cumulative dollar volume, first three years	$2,500,000
Gross margin guideline	32%
New product profit contributions	10%
Breakeven on development and launch costs	1 to 2 years

---

pany's needs and have been in place for more than three years. Both companies are churning out successful new products.

As we have already said, U.S. corporations need to shift their thinking and risk posture. They must be willing to stand up to shareholders and say, "Earnings will be down this year because we are investing in the future." While few CEOs would have the guts to make a statement like that, innovation cannot occur until that mentality is instilled into the minds of corporate managers.

IN SUMMARY

As summarized in Exhibit 4-18, we have reviewed, thus far, the direction-setting stages for successful new product management. Stemming from the new product blueprint and diag-

EXHIBIT 4-17 Screening Criteria for an Industrial Commercial Manufacturer

These initial screening criteria are common to all growth opportunities and match the company's overall corporate goals.

COMMON SCREENING CRITERIA
Strategic

New products and services must fall under the category of "information processing and office supplies."

Initially, new products must be sold through existing distribution channels.

High-technology-based new products will be allowed into the core business only if they remain cost competitive or offer improvements in quality over old products.

New products must have limited product liability.

New products must capitalize on internal strengths.

Patented technology
Service/distribution
Commodity-type products
High volume
Currently loyal customers
Professional and broad-coverage sales force

New products in the core business have priority.

Financial

New products must generate a positive cash flow within two to three years of launch.

New products must have a 15 to 20 percent ROI after three to five years.

The difference between gross profit and total incremental costs to carry a product line as a percent of sales should be 8 to 10 percent of the pre-tax profit.

New product expenditures over $500,000 must be reviewed by the officers.

TYPE OF PRODUCT
Role

Cash generator/diversification.

Strategic Screens

Must fit into information-processing or office-automation supplies category.

Must have similar selling characteristics as core business.

Must be able to be sold to existing customer base.

Must be adaptable to direct sales and distributors, and current customer base must be using it in large quantities.

Must have long-term, secure relationship with suppliers.

Must be a high-quality product.

Financial Screens

Minimum return on investment is 10 to 15 percent by year 2.

Revenue threshold is $500,000 by years 2 and 3.

Pretax margins of 8 and 10 percent by year 2.

Inventory turns must occur a minimum of seven to eight times annually.

INTERNALLY DEVELOPED NEW PRODUCTS

Role

Long-term growth/diversification and protection of core business.

Strategic Screens

Must be in the information-processing or office-automation products category.

Must provide adequate diversification to core business.

Must have long-term growth potential.

Must be as good as competitive products.

Must fit with current customer base.

Must be at least as profitable as core business (profit margins).

Must be compatible with current sales force.

Financial Screens

Minimum return on investment of 15 to 20 percent.

Timing to break even in two to four years.

Pretax margins should be minimum of 10 to 12 percent by year 3.

ACQUISITIONS

Role

Protection and growth of core business/long-term growth/diversification.

Screens

Acquisitions must offer increased capacity, cost savings, and/or resources that complement current operations, i.e., customer base, sales force, technology, and so on.

Acquisitions should be in distant geographic areas such as the East or West Coast.

Acquisitions may require higher returns (ROI) of 25 to 30 percent, as opposed to core business, which might require an ROI of 15 to 20 percent.

Acquisitions in new business must provide adequate diversification from core business.

nostic audit, the new product strategy, like the overall game plan that the contractor uses to build a house, enables management to guide and direct new product development.

All too often, companies want to overlook the material presented in these past three chapters. Rather, they want to skip the preliminaries and start with the new product process discussed in Chapter 5: "Just tell me how to develop new products—what are the steps I need to set up to get new products out the door?" The development process itself is virtually worthless unless adequate time and energy have been expended up front in shaping the direction for new products.

The new product strategy, therefore, is the vital link that companies need to translate corporate goals into new product realities. The strategy enables a company to work from the inside out— first to focus on internal strengths, strategic roles, and screens, and then move outside to understand potential consumer needs, identify attractive categories, and generate new product concepts. More and more, best-practice companies are improving the effectiveness of their new product dollars by spending the time initially in planning, and molding the casts for future new product investments. A product's fit with external market needs must be coupled with a company's internal strengths and strategic business needs. Marrying the two decreases the number of new product divorces in the market. Developing a role-targeted strategy requires much more analytical time and effort, but the advantages are well worth it. First, by linking an explicit new product strategy to corporate objectives, idea generation is focused, which means fewer new concepts need to be evaluated and passed through the costly stages of the development process.

The efficiencies gained on the front end mean that a smaller share of total new product expenditures is allocated to unsuccessful products. A second advantage is that differentiated screening criteria can be established for new products, providing a mechanism to assist concept priority setting. Third, an agreed-upon strategy builds greater management commitment, further ensures continuing support, better allocates resources, and presents a more consistent direction to new product managers. Finally, a new product strategy provides a trade-off framework to improve the allocation of capital and evaluate alternative use of funds. Boosting the advertising budget on an existing line may increase profitability more than searching for the "golden egg" new product. But, without a few "golden eggs," there may not be enough growth hatched for the future.

EXHIBIT 4-18 Direction-Setting Stages For New Product Management

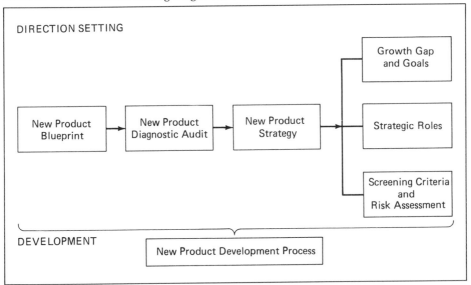

Well-defined strategic roles provide the link between the product itself and the growth objectives of the company. They are derived from the strategic business requirements of the company. The determination of business requirements depends largely upon a company's growth needs—that is, what percentage of a company's growth will be realized from new products and what portion will come from existing products or through acquisition. In conjunction with the findings from a diagnostic audit, the development of a well-defined new product strategy also sets the stage for developing screening criteria to assist the new product development process. This, in turn, helps reduce the risks associated with new product activities.

Chapter 5 describes the recommended steps in the development process, ranging from category selection and idea generation to commercialization.

Unnerved by the success of foreign competition and the fast pace of technological change, executives around the country are recognizing the need to alter their product approach. Such activity will accelerate in the post-recession 1980s as executives focus on developing products that better fit their company's technology, manufacturing, and strategic orientations and also do a better job of satisfying market needs.

Reprinted from the February 21, 1983 issue of *Business Week* by special permission; copyright © 1983, McGraw-Hill Inc.

5

MANAGING THE NEW PRODUCT PROCESS

PROCESS STAGES: DIRECTION SETTING AND DEVELOPMENT STEPS

Stage I: Direction Setting

Managing new products successfully requires a commonly applied, disciplined process that is consistently used and understood by all managers. Companies use a variety of approaches to develop new products. While no single process is suited for all companies, there are common elements among effective processes that serve as guideposts for constructing a company-specific new product process.

A new product management process can be compared to a road map. It provides the direction and the routes to take to get to the final destination—commercialized new products. With enough resources backing it, just about any process will work. However, given limited human and financial resources, the process needs to be tailored to a company's specific needs. Any new product management process should include the following two stages: direction setting and process development. Often, companies tend to start with development and never take the time to establish the direction setting needed to optimize the allocation of resources. Rather, they believe that a cauldron of hot new product ideas is the right place to begin. Unfortunately, for those types of companies, the boiling pot continues to be stirred, but few successful new products are ever cooked up. One reason most companies tend to experience a 33-to-50 percent failure rate in commercialized new products is insufficient direction setting up front. As shown in Exhibit 5-1, the new product management process must begin with the direction-setting stage so that managers know how to focus development activities.

This first stage of the management process tells managers where the company wants to head with new products and the role they should play in meeting the company's objectives. Driven by longer-term objectives and business strategy, the direction-setting stage comprises five key steps, as we have discussed in the previous chapters:

☐ *New Product Diagnostic Audit*—evaluates the past new product performance, strengths, and weaknesses, and pinpoints internal impediments.

☐ *New Product Strategy*—defines the growth gap for new products, goals, strategic roles that new products will satisfy, and screening criteria to be applied to categories and new product concepts.

EXHIBIT 5-1 New Product Management Process

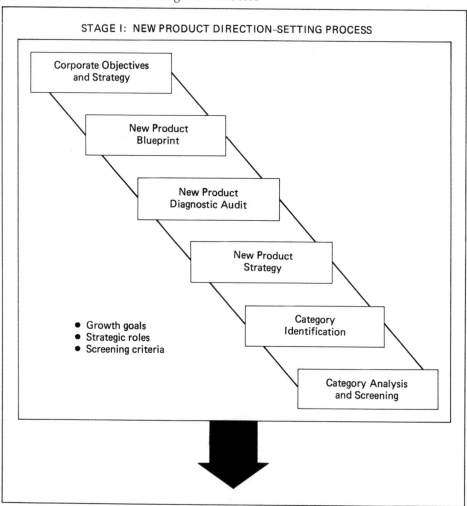

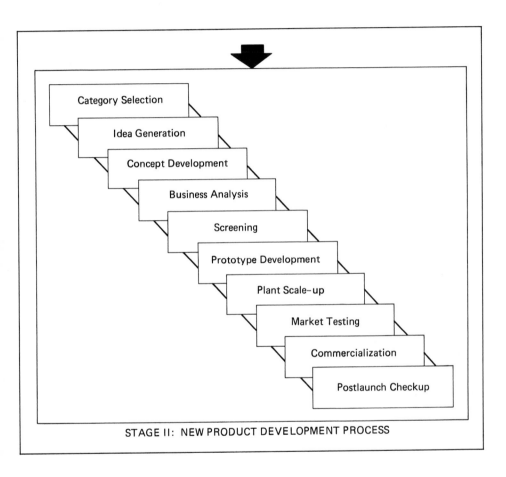

STAGE II: NEW PRODUCT DEVELOPMENT PROCESS

◻ *Category Identification*—identifies a range of categories that may warrant further examination for new products.

◻ *Category Analysis and Screening*—develops business visions, analyzes categories identified, and screens catagories down to the most attractive ones.

These gearing-up steps may require anywhere from three to six months to complete. Again, a company cannot afford to give short shrift to this stage of the process. Once these steps are finalized and top management has given its blessing to the direction, new product strategy, and category priorities, the direction-setting part of the process should now guide development activities for at least the next twelve to eighteen months. New products should not necessarily be calendarized like current business. Often it is much more productive to leave a new product strategy untouched for two years to enable the new product team time to work against the same objectives. However, there is nothing wrong in updating the steps in stage I on an annual basis. Just don't totally redirect the new product charter each year. If you do that, the only new product will be a planning document.

A balance is needed. Once a solid directional plan is prepared, adopted, and approved, then delve into the development process and stick to it. Of course, frequent referral to the new product strategy, screens, category analyses, and so on, is paramount in order to keep the development activities and concept progression on track.

The major outputs of this first stage of the process are a new product strategy and a prioritized ranking of attractive categories. The new product strategy will have incorporated many of the findings and conclusions from the diagnostic audit into all facets of the plan. The new product strategy should represent the blueprint that will guide the "construction" of new products.

The category rankings will be driven by the category business visions, the category analyses, and application of the examined categories against the category screens. These two major outputs represent the overall new product plan and should enable development of concepts into product realities.

Once the direction-setting stage is completed, management will have a road map to guide development activities. This stage enables new product participants to know the agreed-upon game plan and the routes to take to get there. The blueprint and new product strategy will be used throughout the development process. They must be referred to and checked to ensure the new product activities are kept on track.

Stage II: Development Steps

A recent client, who was the new product development manager for a $300 million food company, wanted to get going with idea generation since he had some aggressive new product objectives placed upon him. He saw no need to prepare a new product strategy. He firmly believed that a strategy was the planning department's job. Top management quickly informed him that the value of the blueprint was to solicit from other functional managers their perceptions of the role for new products. This step really helped to build ownership among managers to the development process.

The blueprint and strategy are not merely planning exercises to keep the strategic planners employed. They are the first and most important steps of the new product development process. They set the direction and growth role for new products, define the way new products will be managed, and identify the resources needed to get the job done. The blueprint and strategy provide a reference guide or checkpoint to focus the execution and the development process.

With the new product direction set, the ten-step development process offers a logical approach for taking a selected list of potentially attractive categories and generating ideas from them that will eventually become new products. These ten steps include:

1. CATEGORY SELECTION. *Analyze and rank potentially attractive categories.* Study the role of new products in the company and choose categories that will provide the most attractive arenas for idea generation.

2. IDEA GENERATION. *Generate ideas in selected categories.* Through a variety of problem-solving and creative approaches, generate new ideas that fit the identified categories.

3. CONCEPT DEVELOPMENT. *Develop concepts, conduct initial screens, and set priorities.* Take ideas that pass initial screens and develop a three-dimensional description of the product.

4. BUSINESS ANALYSIS. *Conduct business analysis of selected concepts.* For each concept formulate a market and competitive assessment that leads to a pro forma for two to three years.

5. SCREENING. *Screen concepts to determine prototype candidates.* Keeping in mind financial forecasts developed in the business analysis, pass the remaining concepts through all performance criteria.

6. PROTOTYPE DEVELOPMENT. *Develop prototype.* Finalize development of product and run product-performance tests.

7. MARKET TESTING. *Determine customer acceptance and run market test.* Determine consumer purchase intent; test the product in either a simulated market or actual market roll-out.

8. PLANT SCALE-UP AND MANUFACTURING TESTING. *Initiate plant scale-up and production.* Determine roll-out equipment needs and manufacture product in large enough quantities to identify bugs and problems, and run product-performance tests.

9. COMMERCIALIZATION. *Develop launch plans and introduce product.* Introduce the product to the trade and consumers.

10. POST LAUNCH CHECKUP. *Monitor performance.* Monitor performance of the new product six and twelve months after launch relative to original forecasts; after one year, performance is monitored annually.

Each step is described briefly in the following pages.

1. *Analyze and rank potentially attractive categories.* Regardless of the strategic roles established for new products, there is a range of market/product categories that for any company may represent high-potential areas warranting business analysis and concept development. While very often additional categories will be added to the "considered set" and others deleted, a company needs a list of market/product categories that in one way or another fit the new product blueprint and strategy.

For example, a consumer durables company has directed its overall new product charter at products that can be used in the home to provide assistance in completing a task or chore. With this type of new product charter in place, the list of categories could range from vacuum cleaners to wallpaper. However, the category list would not include such things as food, clothing and furniture. In other words, even though the category-attractiveness list may be broad, it provides yet one more fence post to guide and focus idea generation and concept development. As depicted in Exhibit 5-2, companies can identify potentially attractive categories through a variety of analytical approaches. Later in this chapter, we will discuss category identification and selection in more detail.

2. *Generate ideas in selected categories.* Now there is a road map in place to begin the creative, brainstorming, and association-making process to develop new ideas. New ideas hardly ever seem to be lacking in companies. However, there are a number of tools and approaches that can be used to solicit emerging ideas:

EXHIBIT 5-2 Ways to Identify Potential Product Categories That a Company Can Consider

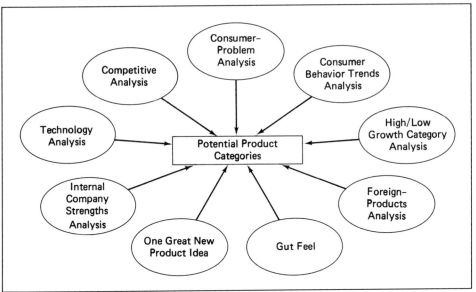

□ One-to-one interviews or group sessions with:
Employees across functional areas
Management
Suppliers
Customers
Competitors
Sales representatives
□ Patent searches
□ Warranty cards
□ Questionnaires and surveys
□ Trade shows
□ Trips to foreign countries
□ Purchased and customized consumer research
□ Focus groups

      3. *Develop concepts, conduct initial screens, and set priorities.* At this point there could well be dozens of ideas that have been generated in each potential category. Turning an idea into a concept means giving the idea form, substance, and shape. Knowing what the product will look like—a rough sketch; the type of package, the price, and so on. The concept must describe the real, functional, or perceived benefits of the new product concept. The task is to apply screening criteria *loosely* to each concept. *Loosely* is the appropriate word. All of the in-depth business analysis should be completed later in the process. That then becomes the data base to screen out or in specific new product concepts.

The process of developing new products is iterative. As a result, some initial screening takes place here to determine which concepts warrant business analysis. Granted, a dose of judgment is required at this stage in setting concept priorities, but keep in mind that a number of screens—those aligned by strategic role or new product type—have already been developed to assist in this process. Implicit in being able to screen concepts is the need to have some "homework" completed on each concept to be able to develop a rationale for attractiveness. Thus, a minimal amount of analysis, including an examination of competition, relative market shares, key success factors, growth of the category, degree of capital intensity, and the like, should have been preliminarily examined by now for any concepts under consideration.

4. *Conduct business analysis of selected concepts.* Business analysis of a new product concept requires examining the dynamics of the category and competition, cost positions, consumer buying patterns, and fit with internal strengths in order to develop financial projections of the new product concept. Specific components of business analysis should include the following.

- □ Market trends and growth potential
- □ Competition
- □ Distribution structure
- □ Environmental considerations
- □ Complementary product performance
- □ Barriers and costs to enter and serve the market
- □ Success and risk factors
- □ Product unit costs
- □ Product-performance rating by consumers
- □ Consumer segments and concept reactions
- □ Fit with company strengths
- □ Financial projections—income statement and capital requirements

5. *Screen concepts to determine prototype candidates.* Once the business analysis has been completed for a concept, it should then pass through the quantitative financial screens that were established in the new product strategy. Moreover, this is often a good go/no go point to get approval from management to proceed further to the prototype development stage.

6. *Develop prototype.* Very often a mock-up, a sample, or some type of prototype has already been developed by this stage in the process. But now is the time to design a product that is finalized to the extent that cost of materials and manufacturing can be accurately figured. Moreover, manufacturing must be actively involved with the research lab or engineering staff by now. Much wasted time occurs when manufacturing is handed a product that just won't work outside the lab.

The objective at this stage of a new product's development is to get one or more prototypes that are in final form for consumer testing, can be costed, and can be made. New product managers must remain involved—they cannot just turn it over to the technicians. A product champion must nurture the product concept through this stage, especially since coordination among several functional departments is required.

7. *Run product-performance, customer-acceptance, and market tests.* Companies often forget this stage. Excitement, anticipation, competitive threats, and management emotion begin to creep in. A product has now been developed, it passes the screens, management "knows" that it is going to be a winner, so why perform more tests?

The answer is to make sure it really is a winner and to make the product even better. The objective of a test market is to determine whether a new product will fly and to identify what changes need to be made prior to launch. However, the real advantage is to provide real-life direction on how to improve the positioning, packaging, pricing, advertising, shelf placement, and so on. In this way, a company reduces the risk of failure during commercialization. While test markets do take time and money, the question that a company has to ask if avoiding this stage is, Can we afford *not* to test this product? What are the potential upsides and downsides if we don't?

8. *Initiate plant scale-up.* At this point, the decision to launch or not must be made. Additional equipment may need to be purchased, factory lines shifted, new tooling added. The product needs to be tested in the plant in large enough quantities to ensure product quality prior to launch.

9. *Develop launch plans and commercialize new product.* Timing, coordinated and carefully planned execution, and communications are the cornerstones of a successful launch. Once the test results have proven adequate to make the decision to go forward, the sales force must be brought up to speed and properly motivated to garner their commitment behind the product. Often companies neglect this important step. The sales force must be "sold" just as the consumer must be persuaded to buy.

Moreover, the execution of the launch must be properly timed, adequately supported, and closely monitored to make adjustments to the initial program. Identification of the target customer, product positioning, and competitive advantage must be factored into the development of the roll-out plan. The underlying cause behind many product failures is poor execution during this phase of the process. A new product may still be further refined during the first six to nine months in the marketplace.

10. *Monitor performance regularly against the original plan.* This step, often overlooked by companies, can provide significant leverage in the development of successful new products. Management frequently "revises" forecasts once the new product has been in the marketplace for six months. The original financial estimates are forgotten, and by year 2 no one in the organization has any recollection of what they were, never mind measuring performance against them.

ENCOURAGING DISCIPLINED CREATIVITY

The "creative," right-brain manager may dream up ideas all day rather than follow through with those ideas and create a tangible product. After shooting down a formal approach to new product development, that manager might shout, "You're stifling creativity and innovation with all these processes, screening criteria, approval points, and business analyses." The reality is that a number of different approaches can work. The important thing is that a company choose one process, agree to the steps and approval points, and stick with it so that ideas are carried through to commercialization or are killed along the way with a sound rationale—not by emotional irrationality. That attitude of irrationality commonly develops unless a company brings managers along to reach a common understanding of the process to be used. Top management runs the risk of being brainwashed into believing that constant change in the process and a "mucking-around" approach to new products yields the creativity needed to come up with the big winners. What a lot of bunk.

What do these naive creativity prima donnas think corporations are in business for—to come up with hundreds of new ideas that remain creative gestures? Successful new products absolutely *do* result from heavy doses of creativity. But creativity more reliably occurs when there are stimuli, such as information, inputs, feedback, analysis, conjecturing, deadlines, emotions, and association making. Each of those stimuli can nurture and spark idea generation. Most companies create practical ideas more frequently when there is a formalized process in place. Disciplined creativity breeds successful idea generation.

Corporations have limited funds, resources, and time. Yet the creative dreamers believe that they should be given free reign to magically produce new ideas. Most companies are not short on new ideas—they are short on ways to assess, screen, prioritize, and execute them.

Some new product people have somehow deluded management into believing that new product management is not a multidisciplinary process but rather a creative free-for-all. This must stop if a successful, well-managed new product program is desired. First, find a sound business leader—a seasoned manager with strong leadership qualities in charge of new products, along with a systematic process that receives top-management commitment, and you can dispense with the free spirits.

STICKING TO ONE PROCESS

One distinctive characteristic of successful companies is that they keep the same process in place for a period of years. You can't have a bunch of new product managers all going in different directions, using various approaches to generate the next great invention of the decade.

Successful companies have a systematic and orderly process with sequential steps that guide the development of an idea into a commercialized new product. It is a step-by-step process, and at the same time, it is an iterative process. That is, the outputs of each step can be looped back to the previous step in the process. While each step of the process is distinct, each overlaps and is tightly linked to the other steps surrounding it. For instance, after you have finished concept development, you may have moved to business analysis; but if in conducting this step, two additional ideas are generated that look promising, these ideas need to be recycled back through the concept-development stage at a later time.

Using the *same* process uniformly yields the most productive results. While companies use a wide variety of processes and approaches to develop new products, the most successful companies are those that have kept the same process in place for more than five years. A new product development process provides a thinking and action framework for transforming new product objectives into commercialized new products.

Management is often enamored with changing the new product process. It believes that if the *way* new products are being developed changes, increased creativity will result. The opposite occurs. New product managers become confused, often lost, disillusioned, and frustrated. The art of managing new products is a creative and "flowing" activity in and of itself. Therefore, companies need some anchor to hold onto—structurally sound and sturdy girders that new product participants can erect around the program.

At this point, you may be asking yourself, "So, should a new product development process be structured, systematic, orderly, disciplined, and done by steps, or should it be adaptive, flexible, iterative, and tailored to company objectives?" The correct answer is yes. All of those attributes depict a sound process.

The major benefit of having one process in place for a period of time is that it produces economies of scale. Managers involved in the process develop a comfort level after working with the process for a few years; they see why category analysis works; they understand the purpose of strategic roles better. They increase their efficiency during every stage of the process. The best companies are those that are able to keep the same team of new product managers in place for a relatively long time—that's how a company really gets leverage from its new product people. Once a new product group is functioning as a team, the game quickly shifts from a losing score to a win. In addition, once a new product team has generated a couple of hits, team members increase their collective and individual self-confidence base. Top management is also apt to feel more confident in this group and, therefore, to be more committed to the new product effort.

Yet for some strange reason, many companies continue to perpetuate a certain attitude: New products is only an area to get your feet wet for advancement purposes in the company. You don't want to stay there long, though, because you need to be in an operating unit to get promoted. How short-sighted. Give me a manager any day who can generate and launch a successful new product. It takes more skill and more seasoned managerial capabilities to effectively manage a multidisciplinary team working on new products than to run a momentum-driven, well-defined existing business.

Companies need to emphasize that new products *is* a promotable and career-advancing position. While the risks are higher, the benefits that accrue to successful performers should be recognized. The best people should be in new products for at least three to five years—it must not be a revolving door for less effective managers who are placed in a corporate career holding pattern.

Among most companies there are basically three approaches to a step-by-step new product development process. They can be described as consumer driven, competition driven, or technology driven, as shown in Exhibit 5-3.

The consumer-driven approach represents most closely the normally thought of conceptual process of new product devel-

EXHIBIT 5-3 Approaches to the New Product Development Process

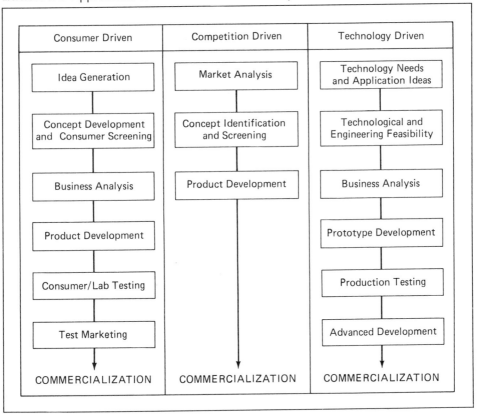

Reprinted with the permission of Booz·Allen & Hamilton, Inc.

opment. One thing that has changed over the last decade is that a host of market-research techniques have been devised for each stage.

The competition-driven approach begins not with idea generation but with an analysis of the marketplace to determine what competitive niches and product opportunities exist. Once new niches are identified, they are further screened, and concepts are developed. Very often test markets are eliminated under this approach since lead time to the marketplace is a critical success factor. This process is more often used by followers than by innovators.

Third, in the technology-driven approach, a new type of technology can either be applied across a number of different businesses or, in and of itself, serve as the impetus for a new product. Engineering feasibility follows business analysis, prototype development, production testing, and, in most cases, some type of advanced development, precluding any test marketing.

SOLVING COMMON PROBLEMS IN THE DEVELOPMENT PROCESS

Once a company conducts a diagnostic audit, the flaws and shortcomings in the new product development process can be more clearly seen; however, even then, it may be difficult to "sell" the changes that may be needed for enhancing the effectiveness of the process. To ensure that your company is not the lone wolf in the wilderness—the only organization that has problems—here are some of the problems commonly found in the development process across large and small companies:

☐ Prototype development is well under way before in-depth market analysis has been completed and business potential determined. If the decision is not to go ahead with the product, R&D managers react negatively when they consider all the time they spent that now goes down the drain. A frequent complaint expressed by R&D people is, "Why didn't they estimate the size of the market and discover that the competitive barriers were too great before telling us to spend three months developing a prototype? Why wasn't market analysis done prior to giving us a mandate to develop this concept?"

☐ New product priorities often shift, and not all new product participants are aware of the change or understand the rationale behind the new priorities.

□ Subjective, emotional, and political judgments influence critical-path decisions too heavily; screening criteria are overlooked and circumvented.

□ Process steps need to be simplified and streamlined. As with one company that we worked with, a process that consists of forty-three development steps is too cumbersome and counterproductive.

□ The process lacks flexibility and adaptability. A process that is rigid and regimented will curtail individual thinking, product championship, and motivation.

□ Clear approvals and go/no go decision points lack closure and specificity since screening criteria are loose.

□ Variations in interpretation of the process and meaning of the steps exist across different functional areas; marketing's interpretation of the business analysis is different from that of research and development or finance.

□ Not enough focus and attention placed on test marketing—often perceived as unnecessary. "This product is so great, let's just roll it out nationally, before our competitor discovers the idea."

□ Too many approval points and checkpoints in the process. Top management becomes an obstacle to getting anything done—approval is always needed before moving to next step.

□ R&D and marketing not working jointly or closely together from idea generation to test market.

□ Sales and manufacturing input not secured or used until the plant scale-up and test-market stage commence.

□ Infrequent and ineffective communication mechanisms, thereby leaving new product participants working in the dark.

This litany of common development-process problems support the need for a commonly understood and adhered-to process. Here is one area where discipline and structure are required. You cannot have new product managers running around a company developing new products according to their own approach. There is plenty of room for creativity—in idea generation and concept development—but not in the approach taken in developing new products for commercialization. Establish an effective process and then leave it alone. It is fine to maneuver around it at times, but leave the goalposts in place so that the new product players know on which end of the field they should be playing.

The following example, which summarizes the obstacles to the development process identified in one consumer durables company, may help you spot problems in your own company.

The company had been failing at new products for at least the past five years. While several factors were contributing to poor performance—not just the process—several process shortfalls surfaced that are fairly common. The major issue was that the company still did not have a systematic process or method in place for managing and controlling new product development. It just more or less "happened" in the lab, the focus group, the conference room, and the manufacturing plant. While there was one new product director and a new product team that met monthly, the focus was on status updating and the progress made since the last meeting on the assigned new product projects. Several of the shortfalls that management identified in its process included the following.

□ Lack of strategic guidelines to focus new product and acquisition efforts. There were no "guideposts" that managers could use, nor was there a road map to follow.

□ Lack of clear accountability and responsibility for new product development.

□ Lack of overall direction and coordination of the steps in the process.

□ Idea and concept generation was hit or miss rather than deliberately focused on a category, strategic role, growth area, or anything.

□ Very limited business analysis prior to prototype development. The tendency was to "let the lab people get started on this thing. It always takes them so long." Of course it took the lab people a long time. They were being inundated with superfluous new product concepts.

□ Weak communication, coordination, and sporadic involvement among functional areas in shepherding a new product from concept to commercialization.

□ Lack of communication with, and especially feedback *from*, "new product participants," including customers, sales, manufacturing, marketing, packaging, and brokers.

□ Lack of lead time for development and distribution of sell-in materials to the sales force for a new product launch.

□ Realistic timetables and deadlines not set or not adhered to during the steps along the process.

☐ Limited pilot testing and market testing prior to commercialization.

☐ Limited product performance testing, e.g., quality control, shelf-life stability, packaging, or consumer acceptance prior to roll-out.

☐ Cost analysis conducted too late in the process. Volume and profit projections were not tied into concept development.

☐ No written or formalized screening criteria for setting priorities, evaluating concepts, or measuring performance. Many low-volume products and discontinuations resulted.

☐ Insufficient project accounting or monitoring system. No idea of how much development costs were running.

☐ Inconsistent tracking of postcommercialization performance of new products launched. No understanding of why new products succeeded or failed.

☐ Capital investments made in equipment before new product had been thoroughly analyzed.

☐ Lack of decision-making forum at top-management level to steer strategic direction of new products activities.

This company addressed the new product problem with its board of directors and was soon on the search for a full-time new product manager. Once he was hired, the company underwent many changes to its process. Three years later, new product results were impressive: twenty new products launched; $38 million incremental revenues from new products; $2.5 million in incremental profits.

One of the best ways to determine why the current new product process is not working as planned is to distribute a written survey to top management that solicits their own perspectives on the way the current process works. The often telling results of such a survey allow top management to see clearly the discrepancies that exist among the ranks. There has to be agreement among the top players on some of the basic elements of the process. That is one of the major causes underscoring a failing new product process—everyone in a company is coming from a different direction with different "internal rules and regulations."

The following sample of responses from ten top managers in a consumer packaged goods company that conducted a survey reflects the differing views of key decision makers in this company.

"HOW ARE PRIORITIES SET IF MULTIPLE NEW PRODUCT PROJECTS REQUIRE FUNDING?"

The determination would likely come from Jim, but it would be discussed with the senior-management team.

Funding would be made on a selective basis, bearing in mind the current operating budget, the attractiveness of the project, and our overall long-range, financial objectives.

Product need, potential sales volume, potential profit, time frame, and management direction.

This is not my department. Who knows?

By the person heading the given project.

I assume that it would be based on the overall return on investment.

A subjective look at which new product offers the best opportunity.

Gut feel and the greatest expected ROI.

Now, how can a company ever set any priorities in a rational way when top management demonstrates this degree of diversity in knowing how to establish priorities and resultant resource allocation?

There also needs to be a uniform and common understanding of new product financial goals in order for the entire team to push forward together effectively. Managers in this company cited a range of 10 to 60 percent when asked, "What percent of total 1990 sales are expected to come from products not currently in the marketplace?"

The next question can often pinpoint the most critical problems challenging the smooth operation of the new product process.

"WHAT ARE THE MAJOR STUMBLING BLOCKS IMPEDING AN EFFECTIVE NEW PRODUCT PROCESS?"

We do not have a formalized plan that gets everyone working in the same direction.

Communication.

Getting it off the ground. Too many committee meetings. Too much inertia.

Lack of manpower. One or two individuals assuming too much of the responsibility. Lack of money.

No real leader seems to exist to supervise and guide the entire process. Commitment and communication are very poor.

Discipline of all players. Quick-draw philosophy. Unwillingness to face losers.

Thus, identification of process problems is a key step in improving the effectiveness of new product management. Once the problem areas are agreed upon, solutions can be created that will then become integrated into the new product process.

KEYS TO PROCESS EFFECTIVENESS

Any successful new product development process is structured and systematic. It needs to be accomplished in logical steps and in an orderly way. New product participants must be able to envision the progress of an idea through to market launch and to plan the route to be taken. Flexibility should underscore the process to accommodate external market changes, such as competitive moves, entry into a foreign market, or a new patent discovery.

Moreover, the process should have distinctive steps through which concepts pass. New product people need to know what stage of development a new concept is in at any given time. Management also should require separate steps to ensure that clear approval points can be established, for example, after business analysis, prototype development, and test market.

Most important, the process must be applied uniformly by top management and new product team members. A clear understanding of how the process should work must be established to enhance day-to-day new product management. Furthermore, new product participants should feel that they have some room to move within the process—unless they have some freedom, creativity and championship will not emerge. However, the freedom provided must have some boundaries—it must work in a given framework.

Used consistently and interpreted similarly by senior managers as well as by functional and new product managers, the process must include frequent communication mechanisms. Constant communication, feedback, and dialogue with new product team members and top management is needed to keep all informed and abreast of progress made and obstacles observed. A mix of formal and informal communication vehicles is usually most effective, i.e., monthly meetings and stopping by an office to see how things are going.

Clear approval points should be set up in the process to clarify the go/no go decision points for any new product concept. Moreover, the process should spell out *who* makes the go/no go decisions and how those decisions are made. Tied to the approval points is the need for the process to be definitive in describing accountabilities for new product activities during each step of the process. Who is responsible for tasks and coordination efforts must be outlined at the outset.

Successful processes are iterative. Each step loops back to the previous one as well as back to the idea-generation stage. Postcommercialization evaluation cycles back to each step to determine why a product succeeded or failed.

The consumer durables company discussed earlier, after having identified the shortfalls in its new product development process made several changes to the way it went about structuring innovation. Some of the action steps implemented that resulted in a successful track record follow.

□ Decide, agree upon, and implement a commonly understood step-by-step development process that includes clear-cut approval points.

□ Ensure adherence to process steps in a consistent and timely fashion.

□ Begin prototype development after market assessment and business analysis of concepts have been completed.

□ Increase input from potential customers at the concept, prototype, and test-marketing stages.

□ Adhere more closely to screening criteria and terminate unattractive product concepts early on in the process—don't let them linger.

□ Conduct rigorous and in-depth market research tied to competitive, business, and market-opportunity analysis.

□ Tighten the integration and communication link between sales, marketing, R&D, and manufacturing.

□ Increase testing on new products prior to scale-up production.

□ Conduct more frequent field testing prior to commercialization.

□ Define coordinating responsibilities and accountabilities.

Having checkpoints throughout a process is a good way to keep people on track and enables top management to have access to the process.

Often, a more streamlined process may be appropriate for certain types of new products. For example, line extensions, flankers, repositionings, and cost reductions may very well be better served and the product more expeditiously gotten to market if the process is revised. However, if a dual-process approach is established, it is critical to make sure the new product definitions are clearly determined up front. "Is this a line extension or a new-to-the-company product concept?" The aggressive new product manager may want to take the new-to-the-company concept through the line-extension process to circumvent more time-consuming steps found in the new-to-the-world process.

As illustrated in the following consumer packaged goods company example, management established two processes: one for new products in areas the company did not compete in, and another for new products related to existing products.

The first process, described in Exhibit 5-4, is the step-by-step approach used for new-to-the-world and new-to-the-company products. However, a more streamlined process, shown in Exhibit 5-5 is adequate for line extensions, repositionings, and cost reductions. Both processes are used simultaneously. Once a new product concept has been selected as a priority, the process used will depend upon what type of new product it is.

Typically, one of the key missing ingredients in a company's process is adequate homework—homework being defined as compiling external market and customer information that will serve as the backbone for decision making, assumptions development, and screening. If new concepts are selected on the basis of gut feel, the risk jumps exponentially. That is not to say that intuition is not an important factor, because it is. But concepts cannot be passed through screens unless the competition, market, consumer, and costs are examined. Yet this part of the process often gets relegated to the librarian, researcher, or even summer intern. It's fine to use these resources to assist in the data collection required, but new product managers and the team should be the analyzers and synthesizers. The people managing the process need to get their hands dirty in the category and business analysis. They need to think, look, and listen as they continue to shape and mold a new product.

After a new product has been approved for commercialization, there should be continuous new product performance

EXHIBIT 5-4 A Development Process for New-to-the-World and
New-to-the-Company Products

Establish growth goals, strategic roles, and category ideas.

APPROVAL POINT

Step 1: Opportunity identification—initial idea generation
  Category/competitive analysis
  Market research and consumer problem analysis
  Technology advancements
Step 2: Market/needs assessment
  Ease of entry; competitive barriers
  Feasibility of technical development
Step 3: Concept development
Step 4: Preliminary business analysis and screening
  Initial cost analysis; rough-cut P&L
  Opportunity priority setting

APPROVAL POINT

Step 5: Prototype development
Step 6: Pilot plant scale-up

APPROVAL POINT

Step 7: Market testing

APPROVAL TRANSFER POINT

Step 8: Plant scale-up
Step 9: Commercialization

---

monitoring. Monitoring performance will allow management to make course corrections, product or marketing changes, and adjustments to the product. If the product encounters severe problems early on, a monitoring system will detect them, thereby limiting potential losses. Changes in the product or even termination could result from monitoring. Monitoring performance of new products relative to original objectives will result in better forecasting because of the lessons learned and the new product track record that is established.

Bolstering forecasting skills through better business analysis is a commonly perceived need. Of course, if there were any sure-fire way to project accurately the future performance of a

EXHIBIT 5-5 A Streamlined Development Process

Define new product strategic roles for businesses.

APPROVAL POINT

Step 1: Concept generation and feasibility development

Step 2: Business analysis and screening

APPROVAL POINT

Step 3: Prototype development and plant scale-up

Step 4: Market research (not test market)

APPROVAL POINT

Step 5: Commercialization

new product, the risk element of the entire process would have been eliminated a long time ago. However, the statistical black-box models that clutter the new product testing and forecasting fields are not the solution. Statistical models cannot be guaranteed to do much better in forecasting what a new product will do than someone who objectively develops assumptions and examines various external and internal factors.

While there are no money-back guarantees in forecasting, looking back at the performance of new products in the past and comparing actual to originally projected forecasts provide a way to measure the variance that usually occurs. After some practice, a new product manager should discern some patterns. For example, most forecasts, for certain types of products, were over, under, or within a close range of target projections.

Screening new product concepts more rigorously, conducting more competitive analysis earlier in the process, and market testing products prior to commercialization represent the most neglected parts of the process.

CHOOSING CATEGORIES

An effective approach to idea generation is to focus on three or four categories that represent attractive opportunity areas for a company. In this way, new product concepts are already focused on predetermined high-potential categories. The concepts themselves still need to be passed through additional screens, but far more efficiency will result.

In the following case history, I discuss a consumer durables company that established a blueprint for its new product program. With a $5 million annual new product budget, management wanted to be sure that some "big hits" would occur. Their new product strategic roles focused on identifying attractive categories that would offer unique products to be used for household tasks or time-consuming projects.

The thrust of the company's new product strategy was to launch new products that would create a totally new business for the company. Line extensions, product improvements, and repositionings had characterized the new product program in the past. Now, the management wanted an aggressive effort placed on new-to-the-company or -world products, not just modifications to existing products.

As a result, the following guidelines were established to focus all category identification and new product idea generation.

☐ Identify, evaluate, select, and commercialize new business opportunities for branded nondurables as well as small, hand-held durable goods. They will be sold to consumers for use in tasks or projects performed at home.

☐ Primary focus—identify opportunities that form the nucleus of new consumer businesses.

☐ Secondary focus—develop new product additions that re-new, defend, or expand current product lines.

☐ Enter markets or market niches where opportunity exists to become the dominant or leading player with the line of products.

The identification of potential categories for new product opportunities should *precede* the generation of ideas and concepts for individual new products. The company's new product strategy should guide category identification. (See Exhibit 5-6.)

Identification of potential categories can be accomplished by a variety of approaches. Some companies search for categories that satisfy market criteria, such as size, concentration, or growth rate. They may seek markets that

☐ Are very large and have diverse customer needs—Playboy's entry into casual and athletic clothing.

EXHIBIT 5-6 Identifying Potential Categories For New Product Opportunities

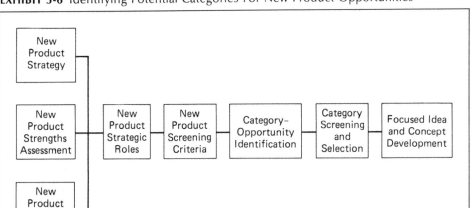

□ Have niches too small to be of interest to major players—Black & Decker's entry into kitchen fire extinguishers.

□ Have no dominant competitor (less than 40 percent market share)—Quaker Oats' entry into pet treats.

□ Have a single dominant competitor (greater than 50 percent market share)—Sargento Cheese's challenge to Kraft in the branded-cheese category.

□ Have been growing very rapidly—IBM's entry into personal computers.

□ Have experienced very slow growth—Miller Brewing's creation of Lite Beer; Campbell Soup's entry into gourmet soups.

Some companies let consumers and competition drive the identification of new-product categories. Potential categories result

□ As a response to consumer needs—Abbott Labs has developed a test for AIDS.

□ As the solution to a problem—microwavable cooking accessories.

□ From a desire to preempt a competitive threat—Gillette preempted Bic with the disposable razor.

☐ As a response to a competitive threat—U.S. automobile producers have added small-car lines in response to Japanese imports.

☐ From a desire to capitalize on a current fad or trend—several companies are producing "gourmet" ice cream bars, e.g., the DoveBar.

Others take an internal focus and generate ideas for new product categories based upon company strengths. They pursue categories that will

☐ Utilize excess capacity—Kellogg expanded its cereal business to foreign countries.

☐ Complement current product lines—Head branched out from sporting goods to athletic clothing.

☐ Achieve a current strategic objective, such as gaining access to a new channel, technology, geographic region, or target-customer segment.

Esprit clothing and New Balance running shoes have gained access to new channels by opening their own stores.

Entemann's entered a new geographic region by purchasing local bakeries.

Oshkosh B'Gosh targeted a new customer segment by creating a line of adult clothing.

☐ Leverage an internal strength, such as marketing or distribution expertise.

Texas Instruments used its experience in pocket calculators to enter the digital watch market.

Dow used its knowledge of industrial chemicals to enter the home-cleaner and bug-killer markets.

☐ Make use of a byproduct—Dole Fruit'n Juice Bars.

Many products that do well in foreign markets can be equally successful in domestic markets. Aseptic packaging had been used in Europe and Australia for several years before U.S. firms would try it. Products that could not survive in the past occasionally do well in the present—Sara Lee launched a gourmet ice cream in the 1970s that failed. Today, such products thrive. New products sometimes result from a fortuitous accident—American Cyanamid stumbled onto a powerful roach killer while working on an antimalaria drug.

Regardless of the approach used on categories that are identified, market information is critical before developing new product ideas and concepts. Questions that should be answered on each category under consideration include:

☐ What are the current entries and who are the key competitors in the category?

☐ Where in the category are there currently gaps waiting to be filled?

☐ Who is the consumer (defined psychographically, not demographically)?

☐ What differentiates currently successful products from those less than successful?

☐ What benefit is being sought in the category by consumers?

☐ What new product trends are currently seen in the category?

Successful companies focus their attention on a small number of categories; thus, some type of screening criterion is needed to prioritize category attractiveness. It is not practical to apply strict, quantitative screens to a category. Attractiveness of a category ultimately results from the degree of competitive advantage of specific new products that are launched into a category. However, categories are often ranked in order of potential according to degree of financial risk for the company, competition in a category, and internal strengths that can be applied to category opportunities.

Let's examine three levels of category screens as one way for setting category priorities:

FIRST-LEVEL SCREEN: HOW MUCH RISK TO THE COMPANY IS THERE IN THIS CATEGORY?

☐ How capital intensive is entry into the category?

☐ How advertising intensive is commercialization?

☐ How much advertising exposure and expenditure will be required to enter the market, and is there advertising expertise (e.g., if the company's strength is in print advertising but entry will require largely television)?

☐ How long will it take to enter the market?

Design time
Tooling time
Time to set up channels
Time to inform consumers about product
Time to build sufficient inventory

☐ Will the market last long enough to recoup the investment?

☐ Is the technology changing so rapidly that the products will be obsolete?

☐ Is this just a fad?

☐ How seasonal is this category?

☐ Are consumers likely to understand the products, or will they have to be educated?

☐ Is the market large enough to permit production at minimum efficient scale?

☐ What is minimum production scale, in units, for this market?

☐ What is the size of the market in units? in dollars?

☐ How many sources of raw material are there, and are they stable?

☐ How entrenched is competition?

SECOND-LEVEL SCREEN: WHAT IS THE NATURE OF THE COMPETITION IN THIS MARKET?

☐ How much room for expansion is there in the market, and how many other companies are competing aggressively for it?

Who are the current competitors?

Who are the likely new entrants?

Do we want to compete with them?

☐ Does the competition have an insurmountable competitive advantage?

Patent

Low-cost structure

Brand-name recognition

Captive-distribution network

☐ What is the likely response of competition to entry? Will it have harmful effects on our existing products?

How likely is it that the competition will retaliate by attacking our existing markets, lowering its product prices, increasing trade promotions, and so on?

How effective will they be if they do?

Technology?

Marketing?

Distribution?

☐ Are there barriers that can be erected to impede competitive inroads?

☐ Does the category satisfy all or most of the requirements set forth in the new product strategy?

☐ Does the category satisfy any or all of the current strategic goals?

☐ Does this category take into account existing limitations?

Size and specialization of labor force

Technology available

Management time available

Capital available

☐ Are the requisite marketing skills, manufacturing capacity, and product-testing abilities available? If we do not have them now, can we acquire them at a reasonable cost?

☐ Can products in this category be sold to existing customers?

What are the characteristics of consumers who would buy products in this category?

Do our current consumers have these characteristics?

☐ Can products in this category be sold through existing channels?

There is more involved in the process of category identification than just listing a few attractive categories that appear to offer opportunity. To do it right, it may take a new product group anywhere from three to six months to give adequate time to this important step. The time investment in category screening will pay off once idea generation begins.

The most essential part of category identification is thinking carefully through the development of business visions. Take, for example, the business vision of air-purifying equipment. A company is looking to expand into the retail home market and decides that its technology can be used to make air purifiers for the home. However, after looking into that category, the company sees that sales in air purifiers have declined during the past five years, consumers are unhappy with the effectiveness of given purifiers, and foreign competitors have entered the field. So management decides not to enter this category.

Unfortunately, the business vision had not been carefully expanded or thought out. If the opportunity had been defined differently, that is, the business vision had been broadened, the company might have found itself developing successful new products in a growing category. Air deodorizers and air fresheners had been growing at more than 15 percent per annum in dollars during the past five years. This is the category that would have been identified if the business vision had been expanded. A different business vision could have provided a strong opportunity for this company since it had a technology that could be applied to a small table-top model that not only absorbed odors but also released a fragrance to cover any remaining telltale odors in the air.

The business vision might better have focused on products that would provide consumers with a way to extract and control odors in the air. With this starting point, there is a good chance that some preliminary category analysis would have uncovered the attractiveness of the deodorizer and freshener category—not air-purifying equipment.

Therefore, let's examine the steps that can be helpful in category identification before idea generation for specific new products begins. They include:

☐ Begin to collect ideas, problems, issues, and potential opportunities from a variety of external and internal sources. These can be used to initiate the flow of creativity. Brainstorming is the key here.

☐ Develop a "gut-feel" list of initially attractive categories with a selected group of internal managers—a top-of-mind list of categories without any analysis conducted. Any company should be able to generate at least ten or twenty different categories that might be feasible for new products.

☐ Next, further expand the list of potentially attractive categories, perhaps to twenty or thirty, through individual interviews and group meetings with

R&D

Top management

Sales

Marketing and business unit managers

☐ Judgmentally prune back the list of categories to fifteen or twenty that fit the new product strategic charter of the company, which has already been defined.

☐ Conduct preliminary analysis on the first-cut categories to establish a data base and rationale to determine potential attractiveness.

☐ Develop qualitative category screening criteria to be applied to each of the fifteen to twenty categories.

☐ Select five or six categories that fit the charter and category screens and have an internal champion sponsor.

☐ Review the target categories with top management to solicit its insights, comments, and consensus.

☐ Begin idea generation and concept development within the identified categories.

The need to formulate business visions prior to any preliminary category analysis cannot be stressed enough. The business-vision definition is as important as the category analysis.

Once the business definitions have been developed, the categories should be examined to understand the characteristics of the category better. The following factors exemplify the type of information that should be selected for each category under consideration. Market data collected and analysis conducted can then be applied to each category to identify the most attractive ones.

The following areas should make up the category analysis.

☐ *Business vision*—define the parameters of the category and describe the potential opportunity.

☐ *Applicability of technologies*—examine current and nearly perfected technologies in the company that could be applied to the category opportunity.

☐ *Estimated size of opportunity*—determine size of category in which opportunity exists; sales volumes; unit volume; number of consumers participating; average price; frequency of purchase; how can vision expand category? recovery dollars needed to convert; if nonexisting market, then potential number of households participating and frequency of use.

☐ *Growth trends*—examine historical five-year sales and margins; next five-year sales and margins forecasts.

☐ *Geographic limits*—examine opportunity relative to regional or national distribution; degree of geographic concentration.

☐ *Distribution channels*—examine estimated percentages of volume sold through each channel; past and future trends.

☐ *Competition*—find out names of competitors; assess their strengths and weaknesses in category; market shares; competitor's technical- and manufacturing-cost strengths and why; sales and distribution clout.

□ *Barriers to entry*—identify barriers that will impede entry.
Capital and marketing costs
Competition
Communications
Technical patents
Obstacles after launch
Timing

□ *Advertising to sales ratios*—Marketing cost; past advertising levels; expected future advertising levels and rationale.

Once these preliminary category analyses have been developed, the list of categories can be applied to a company-specific set of category screens. The following example demonstrates the types of criteria that might be developed.

Category-Screening Criteria

STRATEGIC-ROLES SCREENS

□ A category that offers branded, nondurable products or small durable products.
□ A category that offers opportunities for products that will be used to simplify or enhance household tasks or projects.
□ A category that expands the scope of the division—is new to the division and different from existing product-line categories.
□ A category that affords the formation of a new consumer business.

INTERNAL-STRENGTHS SCREENS

□ Category offers technology application.
□ Category offers low-cost manufacturing.
□ Category offers ability to market superior-quality products.
□ Category offers distribution through existing or low-cost channels.
□ Category opportunities will exploit current management talent.

MARKET/PRODUCT SCREENS

□ Reasonably fragmented competitive market structure—no two competitors having more than a 60 percent share of market.

☐ Intense consumer need exists for the product, which is currently inadequately satisfied.

☐ Higher end, premium-price point positioning.

☐ Value in existing brand-name equity that can bring immediate benefit to product.

☐ Affordable consumer- and trade-support requirements relative to degree of risk involved.

RISK SCREENS

☐ Size and projected growth trends of category allow a business to reach a minimum of $25 million to $30 million in annual sales within three to four years of launch.

☐ Products launched within category would generate an operating profit of at least 20 percent by year 3.

☐ Products launched would break even on development and launch costs prior to year 4.

☐ Return on invested capital would hit, on average, 20 percent per year.

Categories that survive the screening stage are ready for idea and concept generation. Companies can take several approaches to idea generation. The key component to idea generating is making associations. One thought leads to another and sparks a new thought from someone else in the group. Most important, idea generation is a group rather than an individual endeavor. Sitting in a dark room by yourself while contemplating new product ideas will usually yield few results. However, through the power of group dynamics, creative ideas can quickly surface.

There are several ways to prepare a group for idea generation. A group needs to be warmed up before it can generate new ideas. Beyond the need for strategic roles, and the like, to provide some order and structure to idea generation, group members need grist for their minds. Opinions and information from a wide variety of sources can be instrumental in sparking ideas. This body of information should be distributed at least one week before the idea group meets to allow time for some association making. Some background sources include interviews with suppliers, brokers, distributors, customers, noncustomers, focus groups with potential customers or distributors, and a company suggestion box. Other sources include questionnaires/surveys, purchased market research, and visits to other parts of the country or world.

Often, informal one-to-one interviews or group sessions stimulate new product ideas and offer additional background for an idea-generating session. Special insights may be contributed by

□ Sales representatives

□ Employees—marketing, engineering, manufacturing, service

□ Management

□ Suppliers

□ Customers

□ Competitors

□ Department meetings

While this list is far from exhaustive, it suggests that there are many underutilized and untapped resources that companies can draw upon to sharpen creativity and the ability to generate new ideas. Once a few categories have been selected, additional analysis of the category can uncover ideas and opportunities that can be factored into the idea-generating sessions.

After categories have been selected, the development steps are used to generate ideas, develop concepts, analyze the business opportunity, screen, develop prototypes, market test, and commercialize the new product.

IN SUMMARY

Managing the new product development process can be enhanced by grounding the development steps in a direction-setting framework. Establishing a step-by-step, structured process will enable new product team members to follow an orderly approach, increasing efficiency of the effort. While creativity is an essential component of any new product process, a certain degree of discipline is healthy. Moreover, it is imperative that a company does not keep changing its development process. Consistency in using one process is more effective than trying to redo the process frequently. While a variety of approaches work, companies that follow and adhere to the steps established will be more successful in commercializing new products.

New products fuel sales and earnings. . . . If you don't change, you'll lose your position with the consumer. But they're not all Ivory Soap successes. Without failures, you're not really working. You must have failures with success.

R. Gordon McGovern
CEO, Campbell Soup Co.
Chicago Tribune
December 3, 1986

6

STRUCTURING AND LEADING THE ORGANIZATION

So far we have discussed the value and importance of setting up a blueprint and game plan for managing new products. But, the best-laid plan is worthless without a motivated and committed team of players to execute it. Creating a supportive environment for new products is tantamount to success. In this chapter, five organization factors will be discussed that heavily influence the ability to manage the process effectively.

1. Organization, structure, and teams
2. Accountability
3. Skills mix
4. Leadership sharing
5. Top-management commitment

New product management is a complex and subtle process. In many ways, successful and unsuccessful companies often share common elements in their approach to new products. They may introduce the same types of new products and spend about the same amount of dollars, as a percent of sales, on research and development for new products. They may even use a similar step-by-step process and similar criteria to measure performance. So if it isn't the development process, what is the secret? What distinguishes the winners from the losers in the new product game? To find the answer, we must move inside the winner's circle and look not at the process they use but at how they *implement* the process. That is often where the real difference lies. Success rests upon creating the right environment, one that is conducive to taking risks and supportive of the individuals who take them. Senior management, in winning new product companies, recognizes that problems inherent in introducing new products can be solved only by taking an interdisciplinary team approach. Sensitivity to the organization dynamics involved in new product development is a must—it is a delicate process requiring a blend of pulling and pushing people in a common direction. Freedom and autonomy may stimulate one type of new product manager, while deadlines and tight controls may be more effective for another. Judging what works best for each manager is the key ingredient for leading a successful new product organization.

A CHANGING CULTURE

To succeed in new products, companies must capitalize on accumulated experience and make the long-term commitment required to provide the necessary funds and managerial know-how. In addition, establishing a culture—a management leadership style, organization structure, and incentive reward system—linked to the new product strategic roles, will be crucial for improving new product performance.

During the past two decades, the new product management process has undergone a gradual cultural evolution in thinking and approach. In the 1960s companies looked *internally* to create new products. They believed that management expertise, technological know-how, and production and distribution superiority would breed successful new products. Only now, from the vantage point of years of evaluation, can we see that effective management of new products requires the integration of multiple functional areas.

In 1963, Polaroid introduced one of its biggest hits, the Color Land Camera, a popular innovation in amateur photography. It was a classic example of a company's using one of its greatest internal strengths and capabilities—technological innovation—to create a new product that met a market need. By combining its sales and marketing know-how with its technology, R&D, and manufacturing acumen, Polaroid capitalized brilliantly on what it did best—going after a market need with a technological strength.

By the 1970s the focus for new products had shifted to identifying *external* consumer needs in the marketplace. With the advent of sophisticated market-research techniques and segmentation analysis, companies looked for high-growth markets and niches that new products could satisfy. The driving forces behind new product development were becoming more complex.

In 1976 Miller Brewing Company introduced Miller Lite not just because it knew how to brew beer superbly or because there were many beer drinkers to satisfy but because there was an identified consumer "need" for a low-calorie beer that provided, "Everything you always wanted in a beer and less." What had changed from the 1960s? Rigorous tracking of demographics, scanning of lifestyle trends, market-research testing, behavior-patterns analyses, and consumer segmentation uncovered the calorie-conscious beer drinker. This focus stimulated companies to look outward—first, to identify high-growth markets and then to develop the products that would satisfy them. Polaroid's and Miller's successes attest to the fact that during the 1960s and 1970s many U.S. companies were becoming better and better at identifying what the market—or more correctly, market segments—wanted and at filling those needs.

Today and in the 1990s the underlying principle guiding new product development combines both these views. Matching *external* market needs with *internal* functional strengths allows companies to develop a new product portfolio that satisfies corporate strategic objectives.

In the early 1980s, 3M introduced Post-It note pads. This new-to-the-world, internally developed new product now approaches $200 million in sales revenues. Product conception was driven by an aggressive corporate objective of generating 25 percent of total sales revenue within five years. Conceived in the laboratory, Post-It's use of microadhesive technology featured a light-tack adhesive. 3M "fused" this internal technology with the external need for office workers to have attachable note and scratch pads that would not ruin a document when removed. The company had successfully matched the office need for efficiency with an advanced technology. Combining externally driven needs with internal economies or functional strengths offers companies the best foundation for a new product launch. The cultural evolution of new products has sharpened their approach and focused it more highly.

Another example of the transformation that new product thinking has undergone is embodied in Theodore Levitt's focus on external aspects of the marketplace. His classic article, "Marketing Myopia," first published in 1960, resulted in a near preoccupation with identifying external market needs. Levitt concluded that companies needed to look at themselves differently and more broadly in order to identify and exploit external growth opportunities. His theory centered on the belief that growth and even survival depend upon a company's ability to reach outside itself and develop new products that satisfy consumer wants and needs.

Levitt's article has left a dramatic mark on industry's view of the importance of marketing. Across the board, we have seen heightened corporate sensitivity toward identification of consumer needs. Market-research techniques have proliferated, with increased sophistication. Sales personnel are even trained as marketing problem solvers—listening carefully to their customers and developing client-specific solutions through modified products and services. In fact, a product's fit with external market needs is considered the primary factor contributing to a company's most successful product in the majority of cases.

However, Levitt's glass was half empty. Or perhaps the glass was twice the size it needed to be. He identified only part of the success formula for managing new products effectively.

Matching a new product to customer needs is only one-half of the equation.

Management must realize that to succeed in today's complex and competitive world, companies must base new product development on a solid understanding of their own strengths, economic cost advantage, and functional capabilities. That is why the majority of the more successful companies cite, as a vital factor in developing a successful new product, the ability of that product to draw upon internal strengths.

Implementing this perspective, the more successful companies are managing new products from an internal purview, emphasizing the strategic roles that a new product concept should fulfill. They are working from the inside out: first, they focus inside to determine their internal strengths, financial objectives, and strategic roles; then they move out and scan the external environment to understand potential consumer needs better and identify attractive categories and emerging product-opportunity areas.

As a result, structuring and leading a successful new product organization requires that managers have the ability to critique the internal strengths and levers. Those strengths and levers can provide the grounding for external opportunities. The right environment must be created. That is, a culture that recognizes new product management as a difficult and different business discipline, not an existing-business maintenance, and rewards people for their performance.

CREATING THE RIGHT ENVIRONMENT—OVERCOMING INTERNAL BARRIERS

Top management in the best of companies creates and supports a positive environment for new product development. In the less successful firms, a threatening climate is often induced by top management when it focuses on short-term results, demonstrates risk-averse tendencies, and fails to communicate priorities. Senior management in successful firms generates a positive climate by taking actions such as assigning the best managers, supporting entrepreneurial behavior, compensating managers consistent with long-term goals, and treating the process as an investment rather than an expense. This positive climate fosters superior dedication and enthusiasm for success. (See Exhibit 6-1.)

Most successful new product efforts are clearly enhanced by top-management commitment. That commitment is often demonstrated by senior-management involvement in devel-

EXHIBIT 6-1 Factors Affecting the Right Environment for New Product Development

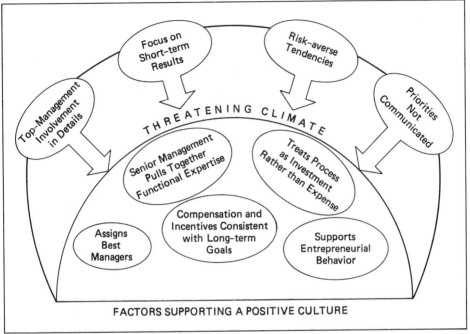

FACTORS SUPPORTING A POSITIVE CULTURE

Reprinted with the permission of Booz·Allen & Hamilton, Inc.

oping the new product strategy with well-defined new product roles, implementing comprehensive measurement criteria, instituting new product organizational incentives, and enforcing a formal yet adaptive process. The combination of a positive corporate environment and top-management commitment provides most successful companies with a distinct competitive advantage.

Staying alert to changes in the marketplace and restructuring management approaches to match those changes are important tools for fine-tuning a successful new product program. But a successful program is contingent first upon management's belief in the importance of new products. That may seem like an obvious point, but it is one that should be underscored.

The biggest obstacle to new product success today is management's emphasis on short-term profitability. Succumbing to the pressures of current business, managers constrain innovation by channeling dollars away from new products. While such an attitude may bring high profits for existing products, it can be paralyzing to a new product program.

As management looks to new products to fuel future growth, it must overcome this short-term orientation and narrow-minded focus. It must commit to a sustained flow of outstanding new products and keep the pipeline full. That commitment must come from senior management, and it must come in the form of the long-term funding and resources necessary to realize long-term new product successes.

In determining the appropriate level and extent of senior-management support and involvement, companies should examine the particular types of products under development and the management approach in use. For example, when risk-taking efforts are openly facilitated in order to achieve greater profits, as they are with an entrepreneurial approach, top management must provide the highest level of support, and a strong commitment to, and involvement in, the new product effort. Top management must be willing to push responsibility down to lower-level employees by providing a high degree of autonomy to a venture team. Such a group can focus its efforts. Similarly, strong support from top management and extensive participation in new product decision making can strengthen the stature of new products within a company.

Though the level and nature differ from product to product, top-management support and commitment are an imperative force in a successful new product program. A strategy is useless if the funding and personnel to implement it adequately are not available.

In working with a consumer durables company to improve its new product track record, middle managers expressed a concern that top management was not fostering a team-oriented environment. Comments included:

> The screening criteria and process steps are too systems oriented and not people oriented.
>
> Players and coaches make football teams—not referees and rule books.
>
> We need more emphasis on what the company can do to help people create and execute growth opportunities.
>
> The we (middle management)-versus-they (top management) syndrome needs to be addressed.

Moreover, managers expressed concern that funding for new products was sporadic, competition for internal resources by company business managers was curtailing new product progress, and the process was missing a market-driven thrust.

EXHIBIT 6-2 Obstacles to the Right Environment as Perceived by Managers

Management commitment, involvement, and accountability are absent.
"We-versus-they mindset."
"Partner-versus-judge atmosphere."
"They don't foster an esprit de corps."
"Why not, 'How can we help?' instead of 'What's wrong with it?' "

Critical need to establish clear, commonly understood objectives, strategic direction, priorities, and financial targets grounded in a centralized mission.
"Goals and targets need to be written."
"Performance needs to be monitored."

Organizationally, new product responsibility should be clearly defined, specific managers held accountable, and ownership assigned.
"Shared responsibility does not work."
"Need a single new product director."
"Everyone needs to know who the number-one accountable guy is."
"We need to define responsibility better and then adhere to it."
"Make people accountable and then be willing to delegate authority."

New product process is inadequate and "bulky."
"System itself, with multiple checkpoints, is a major obstacle."
"Process is inconsistently interpreted and used differently throughout the division."
"Interfunctional communication is weak and priority setting is missing."
"Process needs to be based on market-opportunity analysis."
"We now put the cart before the horse."

Major conflict exists between operating current businesses and managing new products—from time and mindset standpoints.

Division needs delegation in decision making.

Inadequate support exists in human and financial resources; need more marketing resources.

Emphasis on protection versus innovation—risk taking is not reinforced.

As shown in Exhibit 6-2, middle managers' perceptions of the internal obstacles to an appropriate new product environment were fairly disconcerting. Clearly, top management had a few things to fix before growth targets could ever come close to being reached.

EXHIBIT 6-3 New Product Performance Problems Cited by Mangement at a Major Chemical Company

Unclear career paths for commercial development/new product personnel

Unclear assignment of ultimate new product responsibility

Lack of formalized screening and measurement criteria

Concerns regarding management's real commitment to new product

Insufficient incentives to encourage risk taking

Lack of a well-defined divisional new product strategy

At a major chemical company, managers' barriers cited indicated that, here too, the right environment had not been created for managing new products. The top concerns expressed are summarized in Exhibit 6-3.

Regardless of the barriers in a company, the key issue is to knock them down as quickly as possible. Some of the barriers might just be givens, but even then, at least talk to new product managers about them. Don't let internal barriers fester and turn into major blockades. Shrink them so that managers can at least walk over or around them.

The president of a $100 million office products company summarized the key characteristics of his ideal new product environment, as shown in Exhibit 6-4. Environment is an attitude, and one that demands constant attention.

It also involves making changes. That requires changing the company status quo, somehow circumventing the historical modus operandi. New product managers will need to challenge the status quo, and top managers will need to give them freedom to function as entrepreneurs. In turn, the entrepreneur or product champion will serve as the internal catalyst to spark innovation.

"There are more and more people at a company who can say no, and very few who can say yes," laments the president of an advertising agency. "Everyone has developed a corporate timidity," claims another. B-school mentalities promulgate little risk taking. Consequently, graduates who enter big corporations often feel more secure just riding with the current wave rather than trying to make their own mark in the sand. Nurturing risk taking and recognizing new product participants will go a long way toward creating the right environment.

EXHIBIT 6-4 Example of a Company President's Perception of an Ideal New
Product Environment

Top-level endorsement and high visibility for new products

New products tied to long-range corporate objectives and financial
plans

An agreed-upon new product charter covering objectives, category
arenas, and screening criteria

"Small-company" flexibility and expediency

Clear identification of responsibilities

A high level of communications and interdepartmental cooperation

Collegial, *teamwork* involvement

A front-loaded process

Includes a portfolio of product improvements, line extensions, and
"new" products to balance risk

An atmosphere where failures are accepted along with the successes

The resources and consistent commitment to do the job—money and
people

CHOOSING A NEW PRODUCT ORGANIZATION STRUCTURE

Over the years, various organization structures have
been used to guide new product programs. Booz·Allen & Hamilton, for example, describes them as: (1) free-standing or autonomous units such as multidisciplinary teams, separate new product
departments, and venture groups; and (2) functionally based units
that are part of existing planning, marketing, R&D, or engineering
departments. (See Exhibit 6-5.) Companies also use a variety of
multiple management styles.

The choice of management style and organization
structure helps to create an atmosphere conducive to the successful
development and introduction of particular types of products.
Each new product's performance is significantly enhanced when
organization configurations are chosen that complement the strategic roles identified by company-specific growth objectives.

Successful companies also select management styles
appropriate to meeting the needs of new product development.
Further, they periodically revise and tailor those approaches to
changing new product opportunities. In general, companies use
some form of one of three approaches to managing new product
development. The following example is reprinted with the permission of Booz·Allen & Hamilton.

☐ *An entrepreneurial approach,* associated primarily with developing new-to-the-world products

☐ *A fraternal approach,* associated mainly with adding new-to-the-company products to existing product lines

☐ *A functional approach,* mostly closely associated with developing new products that are closely linked to existing businesses

EXHIBIT 6-5A Free-Standing Structures for New Product Management

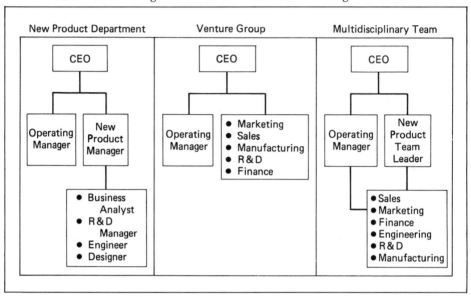

EXHIBIT 6-5B Functionally Based Structures for New Product Management

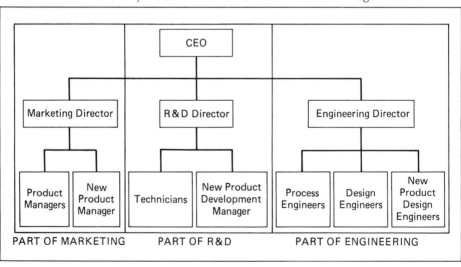

The first approach supports entrepreneurial behavior, thus creating a positive environment for risk taking. Moreover, new product managers in this environment enjoy incentive systems that reward success. As a result, they want to remain in the new product development function, which provides continuity and accumulation of new product experience.

For example, developing new-to-the-world products and developing new product lines are riskier ventures with relatively long payback periods. Such new product types require a fairly unstructured, entrepreneurial style to generate the necessary creativity and focused discipline needed. In an entrepreneurial style, an autonomous new product group may be established, reporting to a general manager. It consists of a multidisciplinary venture team with representatives from areas such as marketing, sales, production, R&D, and finance and is headed by an entrepreneurial new product manager capable of integrating diverse functional skills. Less attention is paid to formal business planning, and there is less dependence upon formal financial planning criteria to evaluate new product opportunities.

Entering new businesses and adding products to existing lines may be better suited to a fraternal style. The fraternal approach is characterized by strong senior-management participation in new product decision making; strong top-management support of risk taking; commitment to, and support for, a new product effort; and a formal new product process to guide the effort and ensure discipline. It is characterized also by a clear commitment across functional lines to provide whatever is necessary for success and to make decisions quickly.

In the typical fraternal style, a management board consisting of four or five senior managers and the new product director oversees major new product decisions. Usually, anyone in the company can bring an idea to the management board. The procedures the board uses to evaluate new product ideas are clearly established and communicated throughout the company. This team approach provides strong top-management support and a long-term commitment to new product efforts. Because senior management makes the new product decisions there is support for risk taking and a clear commitment across functional lines to provide whatever is necessary for success.

The problem of developing products that are closely tied to existing businesses, such as repositionings and cost reductions, is most appropriately met by a functional approach. This approach utilizes a hierarchical management structure that involves lower levels of management and provides strong top-down direction to the new product effort. The emphasis is on functional leadership, strong business planning, use of a formal and less flexible new product process, and a heavy reliance upon formal financial criteria to evaluate new product opportunities.

The functional approach is well suited to the management of existing businesses, and it meets near-term financial objectives because it rewards successful new product managers with quick promotions. But this approach is restricted to new product endeavors of low-risk variations on existing products. It also provides less continuity than the other two approaches because new product managers are often promoted to other functions.

Are companies really capable of letting the structure and style of management fit the types of new products pursued? Consider the case of a diversified office products company. In the mid-1970s the company found itself in a declining market for one of its product lines, in a modest-growth market for another, and in a strong-growth market for the third. But in the latter, it had a poor competitive position. To remedy the situation, senior management set two major new product objectives: consolidate the company's position in existing markets and enter new business categories that would utilize its strong distribution network and capitalize on its existing loyal customer base.

A strong new product environment simply did not exist in this company; operating divisions did not interact, senior management was highly risk-averse, and the new product process worked from the bottom up.

The solution was, for this tradition-bound company, extreme. A senior-management board was created to oversee all new product projects in excess of $1 million. All new product ideas were evaluated formally, using stringent measurement criteria, and final decisions were made by consensus.

Such strong top-management support of, and involvement in, new product decisions created a fraternal environment in which necessary risk taking could flourish. Moreover, decisions could be made quickly, and priorities were carefully set for specific new product projects.

But no matter how carefully managers match structure and style to product type and strategic role at a given time, they must be alert to changing marketplace opportunities and the need to adjust their corporate cultures accordingly. Companies, therefore, must evaluate their new product environment periodically and systematically and tailor their approaches to support emerging new product objectives. Sensitivity and an appropriate response to the need for change will produce environments that directly support new product programs.

The stories of two companies that successfully adapted their corporate cultures to exploit changing opportunities are good case histories.

First, let's examine a U.S.-based industrial-parts firm. In the late 1970s the company was a market leader in all three of its product lines and held a strong competitive position in existing segments. But the market was changing. An influx of electronics technology to automate factory systems had brought an end to the manufacturing/volume orientation of the business. There was also a growing need to design automated systems for their costumers. Recognizing these trends, senior management developed new product objectives that would position the firm in this emerging market by integrating its current capabilities, thereby allowing it to enter new segments that could be linked to the new system.

The company's historical approach to new products could not meet the entrepreneurial needs of a shift to technical innovation. A formal new product process used stringent financial criteria to evaluate new product performance. The company maintained a strong business-planning orientation, and management was decentralized. A risk-averse senior management further complicated a move toward highly innovative new products.

The remedy required a restructuring of the company's new product process, beginning with a new strategy to push the company into a more entrepreneurial direction. A new venture group was established within the existing structure to implement that strategy. Entrepreneurs rather than managers were recruited, and less stringent performance criteria were developed for projects that met strategic criteria. The stage was set for innovation.

By adopting a more informal entrepreneurial approach, the company was able to successfully change its orientation. Communication among divisions increased. Even more important, strong top-management support and an incentive system created an environment conducive to necessary risk taking.

The opposite problem, however, was faced by a consumer durables company. It, too, was a market leader and enjoyed a strong competitive position, but some of its high-technology market segments were maturing. Foreign competition had become brisk in its traditional markets. Market requirements were changing as well; consumers wanted the same performance at a lower cost. Clearly, greater complexity and higher technology were not the answer. The emphasis now had to be on effectively managing the existing business, and for that, a top-down functional style was the best approach.

Autonomous product lines where each product manager took total responsibility for new product decisions, coupled with little integration among product groups, had resulted in significant duplication of effort. Moreover, little formal business planning and incentives still encouraged risk taking.

A new formal strategic-planning process that included long-range product plans and annual product-line objectives formed the foundation of the company's changed approach. Strategic plans were reviewed by divisions and corporate leadership to ensure that they were in line with corporate objectives, integration was encouraged through a functional roundtable, and a formal new product process established set procedures for identifying and pursuing new product opportunities. In addition, the support and involvement of top management was increased, and the company achieved a much needed business orientation.

From an organizational standpoint, the new product structures of companies vary widely, ranging from having a new product department reporting to a division president, to a functional organization where new product activities are housed in research and development or marketing. And in some cases, a separate venture group is set up reporting directly to the CEO. In many cases, this type of structure also has other new product activities decentralized further down the organization.

Perhaps one of the most interesting observations made by examining successful and failing new product companies is that the organization structure itself has minimal impact on the success of a new product. The way a company structures its new product activities is not the critical issue. Clearly, there are other organization dynamics and key considerations that must be viewed as important to the entire process, but the structure itself is not the key point. What is important is selecting a structure and *sticking* to it. Constantly changing the new product organization is disruptive and counterproductive.

When dedicated resources cannot be found for a free-standing new product structure, a multidisciplinary team that draws upon different functional managers can be effective. The team approach forces interaction of different skilled resources, facilitates decision making, and stimulates commitment by functional departments early in the process.

However, a new product team must receive top-management exposure and credit for new products launched; it needs to be reorganized and rewarded by top management and must be given flexibility within the guidelines of a new product strategy. Moreover, as shown in Exhibit 6-6, the members of the team must be provided the time to spend at least one day a week

EXHIBIT 6-6 New Product Development Organization

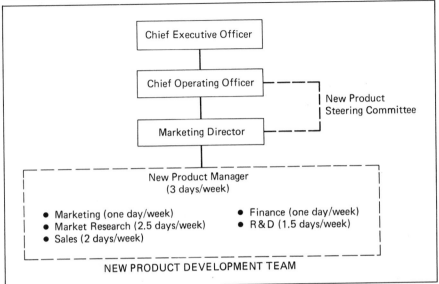

on new products. Without a minimum of 20-to-30 percent time commitment *weekly*, the team concept just won't work. You cannot spend a couple of days each month on new products and expect any results.

Establishing formal and informal communication mechanisms will play an integral role in fusing the process and new product organization together. The new product development team should meet twice each month to review status on each product, set and change priorities, and discuss problems and obstacles with specific products. Status-update reports should be prepared for the marketing director by the new product manager to summarize the stage of development of each new product in the process. Beyond approval of the annual new product plan, the steering committee's responsibilities should include meeting quarterly to monitor progress, establish priorities, and review performance.

Three new product structures, decentralized, centralized, and hybrid, illustrate some common structural alternatives that companies wrestle with in setting up new product organizations. The pros and cons of each are outlined in Exhibits 6-7A-F.

In short, a new product organization structure should accommodate the entire new product effort, including all types of new products that are planned. Usually new-to-the-world and new-to-the company products have a greater chance for success under a free-standing structure, and line extensions, cost reduc-

EXHIBIT 6-7A Decentralized New Product Structure

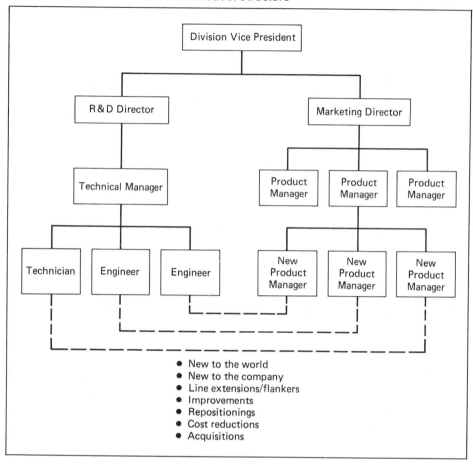

tions, and repositionings are better managed under a functional structure. Working closely with any new product organization should be some type of top-management steering committee that interacts and works with it to set priorities and allocate resources.

ASSIGNING CLEAR ACCOUNTABILITY

A critical factor is the clear assignment of the new product management job to a single executive who has total accountability and is responsible for coordinating new product activities and getting results. This approach provides a focus for top-management attention. It strengthens the stature of new products

EXHIBIT 6-7B Pros and Cons of a Decentralized Structure

Pros

Few organization changes required—basically status quo with additional support and analytical resources.

Ideal structure if primary growth focus is on line extensions and modified products since close to existing business.

Enables product managers to use new products as a strategic tool for defending and growing businesses.

Cons

Diversification into totally new categories and markets is unlikely—constrained by existing business bias.

Acquisitions would be highly unklikely owing to the heavy time commitment required.

Dilutes attention paid to growth opportunities since major focus has to be on existing business.

Without broader diversification, growth objectives will not be met.

EXHIBIT 6-7C Centralized New Product Structure

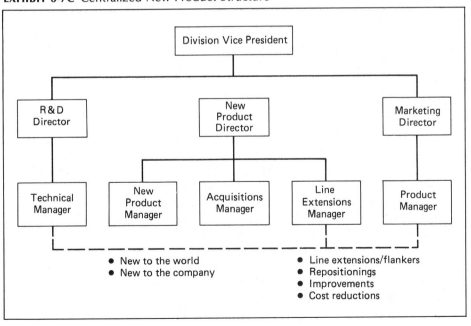

EXHIBIT 6-7D Pros and Cons of a Centralized New Product Structure

---

Pros

Centralized and clear-cut responsibility in one manager.

High visibility and top management exposure.

Fosters greater ability to control overall risk and balances new product portfolio.
   New-to-the-world products
   Line extensions
   Acquisitions

Performance can be measured against clear-cut, isolated objectives.

Technology resources can be focused.

Priority setting for all new product activity can be done at one point—at the top.

Rational resource allocation against growth modes.

Cons

Market efforts may be duplicated by product managers and new product director, particularly with line extensions and product modifications.

Product managers lose some offensive and defensive strategic control over businesses without *any* new product involvement.

Ownership transfer issue could be significantly negative.

New product director will most likely not have the in-depth knowledge of existing product lines as compared to product managers.

---

both for the people involved and the people at the top, and it facilitates the execution of a new product strategy. Finally, it lessens the organizational confusion that can often occur when simultaneous new product efforts take place in various divisions.

The manager's responsibility would encompass development of new product strategy and initial decisions in setting priorities. The focus of a new product manager normally is on higher-risk new products—new to the world, new to the company, and complex line additions and product adaptations. The new-and-improved, flavor, and texture extensions are usually left up to the existing business manager. When the new product manager's time is spent addressing new product development activities without being encumbered by day-to-day operating pressures, the new product function has at least a chance of getting the time it needs.

EXHIBIT 6-7E Hybrid New Product Structure

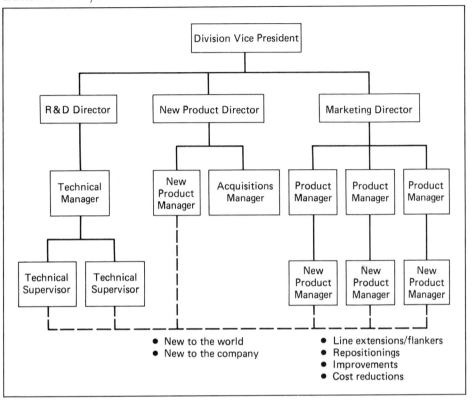

In addition, the new product manager must—absolutely must—report to top management. The span-of-control argument just doesn't cut it. No argument rationalizes any reporting relationship other than one directly to the top of the organization. For a billion-dollar corporation, top management may translate to the divisional or sector president, but it does not mean that the new product manager should report to the marketing director, R&D director, or the head of manufacturing. An organization is not able to place a high degree of importance on the new product function if the new product manager does not report to the top operating decision maker. If that executive cannot afford the time required to add one functional person to his or her supervisory portfolio, it suggests that he or she just doesn't cut the mustard, and "commitment" really means lip service.

The skills required for an effective new product manager rest more on people motivating and leadership abilities than on any specific functional or technical expertise. The key is solid

EXHIBIT 6-7F Pros and Cons of a Hybrid Structure

Pros

> Provides clear accountability and responsibility for division diversification activities through new-to-the-world and -company products, acquisitions, and joint ventures.
>
> Offers focal point for developing single new product and growth strategy.
>
> Places line extensions, cost reductions, repositionings, and product improvements closer to new product director, who knows/understands market best.
>
> High visibility in the organization and top-management support.
>
> Technology resources can be focused and priorities clearly set.
>
> Enables dedicated pool of resources to focus on growth and not fight existing business fires.

Cons

> Conflicts and duplication of effort may arise owing to new product definitions.
>
> Requires heavy dose of top-management support.
>
> Needs cooperative interface and support from operating units.
>
> Mandates that the division work as a team charging collectively against growth objectives.
>
> High-risk position if no new products are introduced or acquisitions made.

---

people-handling skills with experience at working smoothly through various functional departments. Yet at the same time, the new product manager must have an appreciation for the analytical side of new product development, be a risk taker and a product champion, and have entrepreneurial instincts and a sense of vision. Being a persuasive and motivating communicator caps the ingredients.

Thus, the clear assignment of responsibilities provides focus for top-management attention, strengthens stature of new products in the company, and enhances the execution of a new product strategy.

FINDING THE RIGHT PEOPLE

One of the keys to developing successful new products is getting the best people to manage the process. What kind of person is the best type for new products? A renaissance person. A man or woman with leadership qualities—who has a broad and multifaceted mix of skills that provide a base for making associations and juggling numerous people and projects at a time. Most important, he or she is sensitive to other people's needs and can motivate others into action by recognizing them and listening to them. No magic—just personal interaction. That is how the really good new products are developed—by hearing what is being said by distributors, consumers, managers, sales representatives, and buyers and interpreting their needs and ideas into worthwhile products. How can a consumer need, for instance, be addressed if the new product people never hear what the need is?

So many businesspeople just do not listen. They seem to be so preoccupied in "selling" themselves upwards, downwards, and sideways that they can't seem to afford the time to listen to other people. Active listening requires an ability to be comfortable with one's self. The best new product ideas for a company are very often found in the heads of managers in the company. However, they often remain there instead of materializing into a concept or reality because no one is willing to listen to the ideas of "internal" people. Instead, there are many missed opportunities, and a "we need outside creativity" mystique emerges. What often happens is that management people are underutilized and their potential not developed. The main reason is that no one ever listens to them enough to know how capable they really are, and no one ever realizes what great ideas they may have. Consequently, there is a tendency to gravitate to the outside, high-paid "creativity" experts, who have all the answers and new ideas.

The only reason outsiders can infuse a spark of innovative thinking into a company is that, more often than not, because of their high price, management listens to them. Establishing a climate where *everyone* is listened to and individual ideas are respected is the foundation required to generate a productive new product management program.

Cyclical and integrative, rather than linear and deductive thinking is the right approach. Ideas do not flow in a linear progression that starts with identifying a need, eventually leading to a new product that fulfills it. Instead, it takes a core of facts, insights, observations, thoughts, and ideas from other people blended together and churned through a mental association-making process.

Part of getting and keeping a top-notch new product staff is ensuring that management is spending adequate time on the new product effort. That signals that new products are important. Top management, for the most part, should spend 5 to 15 percent of its time each month on new products, and functional departments should be allocating a minimum of 20 percent of their time to new products. Any shorter time commitment stifles the momentum and dilutes the continuity of effort.

REQUIRED SKILLS FOR THE JOB

A consumer durables company had set rather aggressive new product-growth goals. During a five-year period, the company expected new products to generate $125 million in cumulative revenues, which would represent 55 percent of the total growth. Existing products were forecast to increase by only $100 million, thereby accounting for 45 percent of the growth.

From an organization standpoint, the division's new product strategy committee felt that new product responsibility should be split between the new product director and the business-operating managers. The role of the business-operating manager was to be the business leader—in charge of managing a business category. As a result, these managers should be responsible for new products that relate to strategic requirements and roles of the business categories (primarily line extensions, flankers, cost reductions, and repositionings). Structurally, the organization called for shared new product responsibility between business-operating managers and the new product director; development of new products would be assigned according to type.

Process-improvement suggestions focused on the need for heavier doses of business analysis, fewer approval points, and clear-cut accountabilities. The checkpoint approval process needed to be streamlined, driven heavily by business analysis, and tailored by new product type. There were too many approval points—the process was cumbersome, and as a result, frequent delays occurred. Management decided that four major approval points should be established: (1) during new product strategy planning, (2) after business analysis but prior to prototype development, (3) prior to test market, and (4) prior to commercialization.

Moreover, it was felt that the process needed to be managed by separating day-to-day operations from new product responsibilities. People would be able to focus attention on new products rather than fighting fires all the time. Middle management recommended that full-time marketing and research-and-development resources focus on concept generation and business analysis, with multidisciplined task forces taking responsibility for execution through commercialization stages.

A new product director was hired. The job description, which follows, is representative and serves as a model for any new product director.

Job Description of a New Product Director

PRIMARY RESPONSIBILITY

Plan, direct, and coordinate the division's new product process through internal development of new products and businesses, and external development of acquisitions, joint ventures, and the like. Primary focus of the activity should concentrate on new-to-the-world products, new-to-the-company product lines, selected line extensions that require a technological application, and totally new business ventures or acquisitions that would take the division into a new consumer business.

ACCOUNTABILITIES

☐ Assist the division president in establishing and achieving the division's new product strategic and financial goals.

☐ Direct the activities of the new product managers and make sure that resources are allocated appropriately to achieve growth objectives.

☐ Work closely with the marketing and technical directors to ensure that the new product strategy and forecasts are consistent with the division's overall strategic and operating plans.

☐ Develop and recommend to the Management Committee a new product strategy for the division. Establish demanding but achievable long-term growth and profit goals for new products.

☐ Monitor project progress and adherence to the goals and screening criteria.

☐ Supervise the development and implementation of new product and new business ventures and be heavily involved in activities and direct them closely during the first three stages in the development process—idea generation, concept development and screening, and business analysis.

☐ Coordinate the transfer and integration of new products and businesses into the existing business organization at the appropriate times.

Skills a New Product Director Needs

The following mandatory and desired skills are representative of those required in a successful new product director.

MANDATORY SKILLS

☐ Demonstrated leadership qualities; strong people-motivating skills; solid people-handling skills with experience at working effectively with various functional departments.

☐ Analytics-driven risk taker; entrepreneurial instincts and good intuition; exemplifies and encourages product champions; has vision and a positive mental mindset.

☐ Established manager with confidence and respect of peers; has personal credibility with top management—elder statesman status (not a function of age, but more of business maturity and judgment); insightful understanding of, and sensitivity to, the internal culture of the division.

DESIRED SKILLS

☐ Proven track record of getting things done on time while meeting objectives set.

☐ Previous line-management operating experience.

☐ Appreciates the analytical approach to new product development.

☐ Sensitivity to, and previous involvement in, the creativity process.

☐ Superior selling skills—both to internal management and externalities.

☐ Strong communicator—upwards, downwards, and across.

☐ Well organized; strong administrative and detail skills.

☐ Good rapport with the division president and marketing and technical directors.

Skills a New Product Manager Needs

While no one may fill all of these skill criteria, they do provide a good outline of the types of skills that are required to manage new products effectively. The following skills description typifies the strengths needed in a new product manager who would report to the director.

MANDATORY SKILLS

□ Tenacity to serve as a product champion or product sponsor.

□ Creative problem solver; ability to see several alternative solutions to a problem at the same time.

□ Strong project-management skills; can orchestrate several "balls" in the air at once.

□ Exceptional follow-through and execution capabilities; solid project-coordinating abilities.

DESIRED SKILLS

□ Technical and/or marketing experience; demonstrated functional expertise in one of these two areas.

□ Strong skills base in category, market, and competitive analysis.

□ Creative thinker, highly flexible, and adaptive.

□ Good forecasting skills and assumptions-building experience.

□ People motivator and coordinator.

Therefore, setting the stage for innovation calls for establishing the right organization structure, with the right mix of people, rewarded with the right incentives, and managed with the right leadership while supported with the right top-management commitment. Most successful companies are those that do embrace these attributes and somehow make them work together. Rather than going with the flow, the smart companies are trying to change their internal culture. Their goal is to blend structure and discipline with adaptability and flexibility in managing this delicate process of developing and launching new products.

SHARING NEW PRODUCT LEADERSHIP

New product leadership must be shared by senior and functional management. While one person needs to be held accountable for managing and coordinating the development process and also for results, leadership of the new product discipline must be a shared one—not an autocratic one. Effective functional coordination and top-management involvement is needed in order to implement the development process successfully. As shown in Exhibit 6-8, shared participation and leadership are required by multiple managers throughout the process.

EXHIBIT 6-8 How Responsibility for New Products Can Be Shared by Senior and Functional Management

Process Steps	Top Management	Research and Development	Marketing	Market Research	Manufacturing	Sales	Major Decision Points Involving Top Management
1. New Product Strategy	XX	XX	XX	X	X	X	X
2. Focused idea generation	X	XX	XX	XX	X	X	
3. Concept development		XX	XX	XX			
4. Risk assessment/ screening	X	XX	XX	XX			
5. Business analysis	X	X	XX	X	X	X	
6. Prototype development and scale-up		XX	X		XX	X	X
7. Test marketing	X		XX	XX	X	XX	X
8. Commercialization			XX	XX	XX	XX	X

LEGEND: XX   Heavy involvement
X   Moderate involvement

Reprinted with the permission of Dr. Susan Smith Kuczmarski, "Teaching Leadership," 1986.

EXHIBIT 6-9 One Company's Plan for Shared New Product Responsibility

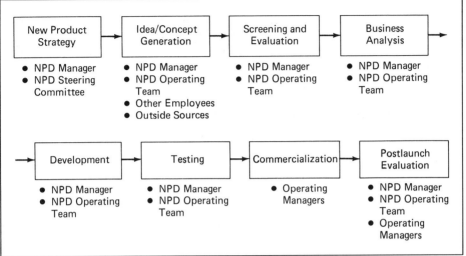

A food company that established a new product operating team also emphasized shared responsibility for moving concepts through the process, as shown in Exhibit 6-9.

Learning to Be a Leader

But how is new product leadership learned and nurtured? Dr. Susan Smith Kuczmarski, who has done extensive research in leadership training, believes that contrary to popular belief, leadership is a learned behavior. (The following material is reprinted with permission from Dr. Susan Smith Kuczmarski, "Teaching Leadership," 1986.) It is not inborn for a select few. She believes that the learning process relevant to leadership hinges on a single requirement: the learner must experience conflict. In the context of new product development, the conflict factor is often prevalent. That may be one reason why new product experience often does enhance managerial leadership skills.

However, Dr. Kuczmarski's research shows that for the learner to profit from the conflict, the experience must occur in a group that has no formal mediator. This implies that corporations with intervening or autocratic managers are not effective for teaching or learning leadership, as they will likely halt group conflict.

Yet it is precisely that conflict which serves as the catalyst or spark that changes a group member into a leader who takes responsibility and resolves the conflict. This process of resolving conflict in a group allows for the development of leadership skills.

Hence, to build and enhance leadership abilities in an organization, it is crucial that corporate enterprises as well as entrepreneurial companies allow some conflict in their organizational settings. This is a particularly difficult pill to swallow; much of our learning experience promotes dissolution, if not resolution, of conflict. Yet to aid in developing leadership in a new product organization, it is useful to nurture and perhaps even instill conflict in a particular organizational setting.

Moreover, all members of an organization need to practice leadership behaviors, even individuals who have always viewed themselves (or have been frequently viewed by others) as leaders. "Once a leader, always a leader" is as untrue as "born leader."

Because leadership skills are acquired when individuals interact in a group, some of the parameters and variables of group dynamics are applicable to the development of those skills. Indeed, it is particularly helpful to describe the group that provides the setting most conducive to learning leadership.

Three group characteristics are central to facilitating leadership development: the group must be participative; it must be supportive; and there must be an informal style with no mediator. Once the initial requirement for conflict is met, the extent to which the group exhibits these characteristics determines the degree to which leadership may be learned in that group.

A *participative* group facilitates a sense of ownership, allows members to demonstrate trust in others, and builds group identity. In general, participation is more easily accomplished in the relatively small group.

A *supportive* group accommodates the process of identification with other group members. This identification process serves a developmental function by enhancing the individual member's self-esteem.

The *informality* in the group structure—absence of a formal mediator—allows members to experience the conflict key to the leadership development process. Accordingly, members engage in or practice leadership behaviors, particularly responsibility taking and decision making, to resolve their own conflicts.

At some point, a group relies for its very existence on each member's desire or need for a harmonious environment. A turbulent organizational structure or a highly disorganized situation intensifies an individual's motivation to resolve the conflict. At the same time, group members act to maintain the group and build a sense of community in the face of that conflict. Group members are motivated to share leadership—not only to ameliorate the conflict but also to maintain and continue the group. Membership brings them a strong sense of shared values, ownership, common goals, identity, self-esteem, and opportunities to pursue a goal.

Successful group-maintenance efforts reward and reinforce the members' actions directed toward the perpetuation of the group. This, in turn, builds the group's potential for continued growth and prosperity. Activities and experiences within the confines of the group work to intensify the sense of community and serve a unifying function, allowing continued practice of leadership behaviors and thereby maintaining the group.

A creative leader can move a step beyond—by arousing expectations and aspirations in the followers. The followers now have altered demands and transformed motives. In this engaging process, a leader must translate his or her own demands, and understand the followers and their needs and expectations.

Further, the leader will act to help the followers satisfy their wants. Additionally, the leader will facilitate the definition of any new needs felt by the group members as well as any new group requirements. The process is iterative and democratic—leaders may become followers and followers, leaders.

As the process evolves, a creative leader not only appeals to the expressed interests of the followers but also encourages a structure for constructively sharing those interests. Thus, effective leaders emerge from settings or organizations closely attentive to the needs of their members.

One Company's Experience in Shared Leadership

To develop a specific new product at Crossland Corporation, the manufacturing, engineering, marketing, and purchasing departments had to work together. Outside competition had already set the clocks ticking, so the new product needed to be launched nationally within four months. With divergent opinions on the critical path, the departmental managers vocally expressed their opinions as to why the other managers' functions had worked to impede the successful introduction of the new product.

The marketing manager asked the other members what they personally wanted to gain by the end of the four-month period—top-management exposure, higher bonus, and so on. Once the desires of each individual were known, the group solidified and began working together cooperatively. The product was launched just over four months later.

Six Action Steps toward Shared Leadership

Here are some action steps that can be used to foster leadership sharing of the new product process:

1. *A leader communicates, both emotionally and professionally, with group members.* A leader who is communicating will display and express emotions or show involvement with the feelings or emotions of others in the group. When a leader communicates excitement, recognition, integrity, and compassion, the followers perceive trust, fair play, and genuine interest in the group.

There are situations where communicating requires a display of professional expertise—knowledge, competency, discipline, and organization. Followers then perceive an understanding of goals, strategies, and relationships, and the ability to handle or manage them.

2. *A leader takes responsibility for selected tasks.* Any activity in the group requires individual members to take responsibility for assigned tasks. For instance, in a planning activity, one member may be responsible for contacting members, another for providing transportation, and a third for finding and organizing the materials to be used in the planning activity.

Once a member takes responsibility for a particular task (e.g., finding materials), then this follower becomes a leader for that need of the group. A leader, specifically, is responsible for delegating tasks to accomplish the need, foreseeing problems and additional needs with respect to the overall activity situation, and coordinating related tasks.

Spontaneous and planned activities such as these pervade the group and provide frequent opportunities for members to practice responsibility-taking behaviors.

3. *A leader nurtures and accepts criticism.* Successful informal communication in the group—learning how to attract and receive support and respect and how to get along with other group members—involves recurring conflict, expressions of hostility, and distance maintenance.

A successful leader nurtures this activity, allowing the conflict to be processed by the members themselves. At the same time, a leader must have adequate confidence in his or her own leadership style and communication skills to be able to accept criticism, not be threatened by it. Leaders with personal security and self-acceptance tend to trust the other members, allowing them to make decisions and take responsibility for their own activities.

4. *A leader teaches others.* Informally, members may instruct others how to handle certain parts of a job or offer help or instruction on how to solve a problem. In the context of a discussion group, informal teaching often occurs when one member makes a point or shares his or her personal thinking on an issue. It is a kind of "teaching" that generally goes unnoticed by other group members. Formal teaching takes place when members with specific competencies are given opportunities to teach others.

5. *A leader shares leadership.* Collaborating on joint enterprises or taking collective responsibility requires working together toward a common goal. This shared leadership activity demands the cooperation of each member, whether follower or leader.

A sense of collective responsibility is crucial to the group; if members do not contribute, the group does not exist. As a result, members must have and must exhibit a strong group-maintenance feeling. Involvement in committee work, for example, contributes directly to the group-maintenance task. Participation through committee channels allows managers to organize and plan, thereby taking collective responsibility for events.

6. *A leader knows and uses the resources of the group.* Because leaders emerge from a group they are cognizant of group members' skills and needs. Leadership effectiveness requires not only knowing the specific skills and resources of each group member but calling upon the members and their skills in appropriate situations or activities.

Furthermore, the leader should have a feel for the developmental needs of each group member—information not easily obtained. Yet the leader must know each group member's needs as well as the individual knows it himself or herself. If that is the case, then the group will most likely satisfy the individual through its activities.

Learning about each group member and his or her needs suggests personal-growth activities; learning about others in the group and their needs suggests activities for the group.

Learning the behaviors that constitute leadership may be best accomplished through a *long-term involvement* in a specific group. This dimension of leadership indicates that learning leadership is the result of experience that is itself the product of a group. The group activities, informal and formal, precipitate certain behaviors, giving members opportunities to practice playing the role of leader. The behaviors are then refined with repeated activity.

Satisfaction comes from recognizing one's own effectiveness as a leader. This sense of satisfaction is a condition that feeds on itself. Leaders feel good about their past performance and are eager to continue the effective behavior. Self-confidence and a feeling of security result.

Insecurity and low self-confidence will result in defensive leadership. Rather than focusing energy on trying to resolve conflict, a defensive leader highlights the conflict by trying to defend himself or herself from existing or anticipated threats.

A confident leader directs one's energies toward goals that are significant—both personally and for the good of the new product group.

FOSTERING TOP-MANAGEMENT COMMITMENT

Consistent top-management commitment, support, and involvement is essential for the success of new products. Top management must communicate the growth objectives throughout the company to ensure that a common understanding exists of the objectives, strategy, process, and organization. Assignment of the best managers to the new product function, along with providing the required functional and analytical support, is the key to managing the growth process effectively. Top management must (1) ensure that a consistent commitment is made to the new-product process, (2) continue to foster an entrepreneurial environment, (3) compensate consistent with new product objectives, and (4) be actively involved in developing the new product strategy and screening criteria.

Typically, companies that are successful in new products just get more and more successful at it. Look at 3M Company, which sets an annual objective across all of its divisions: new products are expected to contribute 25 percent of annual revenues. Interestingly, for the most part, 3M divisions do satisfy this aggressive objective—not because the goal has been set, but because top management has established a belief, commitment, and environment to enable managers to take risks. And that does take guts. At Rubbermaid the new product objective is 30 percent of all revenues, and in 1984 the company launched more than 100 new products.

Accepting failure in new products should not imply that management takes a cavalier or laissez-faire attitude toward the process. The coach of a football team after losing a game does not return to the locker room and say, "Oh well, we lost another one boys. But don't worry, it's OK, let's just try harder in the next game." Likewise, effective top management does not ignore new product failures, and it will make sure that it hears about them. Somehow, news about new product successes has a way of getting to top management far more quickly than news about new product failures—perpetrators of the latter seem to hide out in darkened corporate corridors.

The effective football coach examines with the group the strengths and weaknesses of the team and competition. In this way, there is a cumulative learning effect that, over time, enables a team to recognize its strong points, exploit and capitalize on those strengths, and anticipate how the competition will respond to every move.

Effective new product managers and top executives do the same thing. They recognize the existing given strengths of a company as well as the advantages and vulnerabilities of competition. In turn, the focus of their new product effort becomes how best to apply creatively the existing strengths of the company to new-business opportunities.

Commitment to new products does not mean that only new-to-the-world products are to be pursued. Indeed, the highest-return new products are those that are new to the company or the world. In fact, in examining the new product performance of seventy-five companies in the Fortune 500, we found that new-to-the-company and -world products represented 25 percent of the products launched but accounted for over 55 percent of the companies' most successful new products. However, some very successful new products that generate an extremely attractive return originated from the waste piles in manufacturing plants. For example, in visiting manufacturing plants at the Dole Company, a manager saw piles of pineapple sludge ready to be dumped. He applied this internal "strength" and the obvious market strength of Dole's pineapple leadership role and came up with the idea of Dole Fruit 'n Juice Bars—the category leader in frozen-juice novelties. Anheuser-Busch developed a cheese-flavoring product that originated from the beer spillage. The yeast contained in the beer caused a great enzyme catalyst that produced a more robust cheese flavor.

This is not to suggest that America's most innovative new products come from byproducts and waste heaps. It does suggest that new products may exist right under your nose. The key is to create an environment where managers feel that they can and should be linking pieces of information together to form an idea or concept that will eventually be deemed a new product. Managers need time to make associations, exposure to a variety of resources, and patience to nurture a concept through the internal barriers of a company. Top executives often lack the time, patience, and willingness to look at things in a nonlinear way. For example, Sargento Cheese Company, Inc., looking for other markets, analyzed the cheesecake market only to discover that the category was dominated by one manufacturer—Sara Lee. The typical approach from that point on would have been, "How can we make a cheesecake that is better tasting, has different flavors, comes in a different package (e.g., single-serving cup), and is low in calories?" However, with any one of those product adaptations, the company would have ended up competing with Sara Lee. A variety of other new product activities had led the company's new product operating team to examine the frozen-novelties category.

The result was Montage$_{TM}$, Chocolate Covered Cheesecake-on-a-Stick. This product would not be positioned relative to the leader of the cheesecake category but, rather, would compete in the more fragmented frozen-novelties category as a new-to-the-category product. The key to this example is the process that led the group to make associations from previously collected information, piece them together, and generate a new idea.

This new idea came about primarily because the company president had done four things:

□ Established a new product operating team comprised of marketing, manufacturing, finance, sales, and research and development. He met bimonthly with the team and also with individual members once a month for breakfast or lunch.

□ Hired, from the outside, a full-time new product development manager who reported directly to him.

□ Communicated frequently to the entire company and to the board of directors the role and importance of new products to the company's growth and, therefore, his total commitment to the new product program. Outside consultants had been brought in to help design the new product strategy, and several interactive meetings were held with all levels of management to garner ownership and commitment to the new product process.

□ Developed with the new product manager a strategic charter, financial goals, qualitative and quantitative screening criteria, and strategic roles for new products.

Thus, the president clearly demonstrated a strong commitment to new products. However, he had no choice. During the past five years, the company had introduced more than 125 new products—all line extensions and flankers. Combined in total, they accounted for no more than eight percent of total revenues.

By establishing a separate department with a multidisciplinary team, clearly assigning responsibility for new products, and demonstrating a strong commitment, the company has, not surprisingly, provided itself with the means to generate the returns expected from new products. Wouldn't it be great if more top executives had a strong commitment to new products; if their actions supported their words; if they did recognize that successful new product development requires a blueprint, road map, the best people, time, and commitment?

But most don't. They give eloquent lip service to the importance of new products. They cut new product budgets to boost dividends, staff new product development departments with "creative types," and talk about how the lab technicians are developing some exciting new products. Lab technicians alone, however, do not develop and commercialize successful new products. It takes a team—a team that is properly guided, motivated, and nurtured.

So how can top-management commitment be developed when it doesn't exist? Many managers feel powerless in such a case. But how is gaining commitment behind new products any different from garnering support for a costly advertising campaign on an existing product? It requires the same political acumen and internal sponsorship that is needed when managing upwards.

The point is to find a way to ignite some sparks of commitment from top management. The first step is to identify the "internal coaches"—those who influence decisions of top management. Convince and persuade them that new products are integral to the success of the company, and the groundswell will begin. New product awareness can also be built by having other functional and operating managers become spokespersons who point to the great need for new products in their own areas. Moreover, developing a game plan that top management signs off on is one of the most effective ways for increasing commitment, especially when the plan is reviewed quarterly or even monthly with top management. Such reviews often serve as reminders of the commitment. In addition, a manager who has the guts to call the CEO on the phone and ask him or her out to lunch, establishes an informal setting to begin the "selling" process of new product commitment.

I have seen few CEOs become "born again" new product zealots overnight. However, I have seen top executives gradually increase their comfort with, and understanding of, the new product game and suddenly take a devoted stance on new products. Often a company will not know that the transformation has occurred for many months. A CEO is not going to announce, "Well, I have finally seen the light." A CEO will establish a new product committee, begin allocating funds to functional areas previously underfunded, and begin talking about new product objectives.

Thus, top management must be willing to communicate its new product direction within the company. Then the new product development function can grow and mature in tandem with top management's expectations. The analogy is so obvious but right on target—managing new products is like raising a child. The hardest part in terms of sheer endurance comes in the first few months, when the colic and all-nighters wreak havoc on any sense of normalcy. Some new parents may wonder, "Have we done the right thing?" Then in a year or two, when the child is walking and talking and is the cutest girl or boy in the neighborhood, all of the initial headaches seem forgotten. Just as the mother and father take responsibility for the child's development, the new product manager or committee must establish a well-thought-out new product program. You cannot expect successful results in a few months. However, in a few years, if the setting and people are right, new products will begin to flow.

But what happens if top management is not committed to new products? While they can be gradually turned around over time, there are certain realistic limitations and constraints that must be lived with. However, let's examine a few ways that middle-level managers have been effective in changing top management's perspectives and increasing their level of commitment to new products:

□ Nothing works better than a couple of new product successes. Sometimes it makes more sense to launch a couple of low-risk, me-too-type new products to be able to demonstrate how the process can work. However, simultaneously, top management must be receiving heavy doses of "New products is risky business." Without these constant admonishments, this approach can backfire. Top management becomes accustomed to successes and then is unwilling to accept a failure when it occurs. So, the point of this approach is to build management's comfort with a few successes while "teaching" them about the failures that will ultimately be coming down the road.

□ Another approach is to get top management more involved in the process. Ask members of top management to spend two days each month for the next three months assisting the new product team. If internally developed new products are important to the future earnings and revenue stream of the company, a total of six days a month is not asking too much. Then, ensure that top-management people are exposed to prototype development, concept definition, screening, aspects of business analysis, a team meeting or two, and the like. The objective is to have top management gain a better understanding of the complexity of the process—and an appreciation for the multidisciplinary and multifunctional nature of managing new products.

☐ A third approach is to insist upon monthly-status, update, or review meetings with top management. By establishing a formal two-to-three-hour monthly meeting, top management ends up being exposed to the process and to at least some of the risk elements. However, at these meetings the new product manager needs to solicit thinking from top management and not just spoon feed the accomplishments that have been made during the past month.

More latitude needs to be given to new product people. Yet, as already stressed, a structured process must provide the road map to guide individual turns and twists in the road. There is a need for balance—short- and long-term objectives; individual freedom matched to a systematic approach with clear cut objectives. Management must be willing to bend the rules once in a while; they need to give enough autonomy to new product managers that they build ownership for meeting new product objectives. They need to feel an emotional drive to get new products launched—not just another "management-by-objectives" goal to meet. By providing new product managers with enough time, stability, and consistent funding, top management releases a flare that signals its intentions to support new products.

Innovation and creativity are interactive. They cannot come from a single individual. As a result, top management must be willing to commit the best people to the function. Often, although a full-time new product manager may be assigned to the new product activity, it is supported by a multifunctional team of managers who spend only two half-days a week on new products. The team's bosses see their responsibility as managing the existing businesses—not developing new products. Consequently, working on new products for these team members is not a priority—just one more thing to add to their "to-do" lists. If top management is committed to new product development, it will make sure all managers know that new product participants must have adequate time to be involved in a substantive way. Again, it is not one person who comes up with the new product of the decade—it is a team task and requires a time-committed and dedicated group of players.

IN SUMMARY

The elements involved in structuring and leading an effective new product organization include:

☐ Creating the right environment.

☐ Building new product teams and organizing according to a free-standing or a functionally based structure, determined by the types of new products planned.

☐ Establishing clear accountability, roles, and responsibilities for "who does what" in the process.

☐ Positioning the new product function at the top of the organization so that it reports directly to senior management.

☐ Getting the best people with the right skills to lead, manage, and work on new products.

☐ Sharing leadership for new product management among participants involved in the process.

☐ Fostering top-management commitment.

As rapid growth tapers off, there are fewer new jobs. Workers settle into a routine that implies long-term job security. Suppliers get used to stable relationships with manufacturers.

Most important, the entrepreneur gives way to the manager. An atmosphere slowly builds that places a premium on successful, large-scale production of existing products, not the creation of new ones. This overriding emphasis on production rather than innovation serves as a barrier to the single most important factor in economic rejuvenation, the creation of new businesses.

Eugene Carlson
Reprinted by permission of
The Wall Street Journal,
© *Dow Jones & Company, Inc.*
November 18, 1986
All rights reserved.

7

REWARDING AND MOTIVATING CHAMPIONS

FREE BALLS AND MISSING INCENTIVES

Can you remember what a great feeling it was to get a free ball after making a high enough score playing pinball? You may have even lost the game to another player, but somehow the *real* reward had already come—the free ball. Similarly, companies need to offer more "free balls" to new product participants. An individual manager may not win all the games or always have success with a new product, but if he or she shows enough skill and capability overall, a few free balls are indeed deserving. Free balls can come in the form of pats on the back, recognition from peers, funding for special ideas or projects, financial rewards, promotions, and even a, "Thanks, you really did a great job." Free balls can be fairly inexpensive but can have a high impact value, yet top management often rewards only the highest scorers—those at the very top of the company. Management does not take advantage of the power and motivating potential of free balls.

Most U.S. corporations are living in the Dark Ages in terms of motivating new product people through performance-based compensation and incentive systems. Incentives that motivate are woefully missing. The majority of corporations is often afraid to take *any* risks when it comes to compensating its new product manager in ways other than traditionally accepted pay scales, point systems, and standardized job-description-driven salary increases. Great strides appear to have been made in compensating CEOs through hefty bonus-reward structures that are tied to return on equity, stock appreciation, and other appropriate performance measures. However, top management people apparently believe that they, themselves, are the only ones deserving of incentive systems that are tied to performance. Their bonuses are geared toward high return for high performance, so why can't new-product people also get incentives that are based on actual performance of new products in the marketplace?

The most underdeveloped area of new product management is effective financial rewards and incentive and compensation practices. What is even more concerning, though, is that many corporate executives, compensation consultants, and the like, truly believe that their bonus systems are the *right* ones for new product managers. One cause for this misperception is the fact that many personnel directors have no idea what skills are required to manage new products effectively—nor are they willing to rock the corporate boat by paying new product managers any differently from other "grade 12" people in the company. In their naiveté, they see little difference between the talent and skills required to run a day-to-day business and those required to run a new product program. Furthermore, most outside consultants and top managers fall into the same camp. It's no wonder that nothing has changed for years in the area of new product compensation practices. That's one of the major reasons the small-business entrepreneurial phenomenon has taken off so in recent years. The "serfs" no longer want the security and boring comfort of the "corporatocrasy." They want to take some risks and be rewarded when their performance merits it—rewarded in a way that is commensurate with the result. Compensation programs that enable new product managers to get a "piece of the action," or invest their own equity in a new product, would begin to simulate the entrepreneur's situation. Having your own cash invested in a project can often be a very effective motivator.

And yet, corporate executives and human-resource managers, for the most part, refuse to accept this idea. They are afraid that if you compensate new product personnel differently from operating managers, an imbalance will result. Operating managers will see new product managers getting rewarded for their accomplishments and won't like it. But the inherent riskiness of achieving successful results with new products is usually far greater than the risk of managing an existing, staid business—even when competition is intense. New product managers should be compensated in a way that addresses the risk and, at the same time, offers rewards for market-proven performance.

How is the entrepreneur rewarded? Financially, the rewards are tied directly to the bottom line of the income statement and equity value of the balance sheet. The entrepreneur cannot make a case for why he or she deserves a $25,000 bonus if there is only $5,000 left over in after-tax profit. There is no corporate coffer to run to—entrepreneurs get paid according to how well they perform and what they deliver. Moreover, they are usually investing their own funds. Often, hard-earned money is put into total risk. Nothing motivates a businessperson more than seeing dollars flow out of his or her own wallet. It produces an electrical charge that sparks the entrepreneur into action. Suddenly, the projects that take months to finish in a large corporation are accomplished in weeks. Why can't the same stimulus that works for an entrepreneurial setting be instilled into a bureaucratic corporate setting? The fact is that it can—if top management is enlightened enough to see that different motivating techniques for new product managers can yield a high payout.

One of the problems, though, is that any sound incentive system for new product people should have both a short- and long-term focus to it. Perhaps the payout to the new product team would not occur for three or four years. Well, by that time, in many companies those same people would no longer even be in the new product area. They would have returned to the existing-business operating positions. Thus, a total change of culture is needed before altering the compensation practices of new product personnel. The first change requires an attitude that signals an acknowledgment by top management that new product personnel should be paid differently from operating managers. Next, and even more important, the corporate culture must instill credibility in the new product function, leaving no doubt that it is a career path and that someone who stays in the new product area for five or six years is in a viable and promotable position, not a holding pattern waiting to get back to the "mainstream." Third, new product people will need to make a commitment to work in new products for at least a three-to-five-year time period. Without this type of willingness to hang in for a while, longer-term incentive programs will be meaningless and, therefore, provide no incremental motivation.

THE PRODUCT CHAMPION

Introducing change into an organization is difficult—and new products represent significant change. They upset fixed routines, require the implementation of new procedures and methods, and demand substantial nurturing time and energy. In essence, the new product process goes directly against the set schedules and bureaucracy of traditional organizations. It takes a certain type of person to lead the development of a new product. It takes a "product champion" who can overcome the stifling nature of the corporate organization by infusing entrepreneurial spirit into his or her efforts and the efforts of the group.

Product champions are managers who can integrate diverse skills and focus the creative force of a small group toward the development and launch of a single product idea. They behave like entrepreneurs; they are the idea supporters. Too often a new product concept dies because there was no sponsor behind it—no champion to direct it. The most important characteristic of product champions is that they are obsessed with the success of their product. They encourage experimentation, instill harmony, and build momentum in those who work with them. With their thorough knowledge of the market, the process, and the organization, they foster cooperation throughout the company. Overcoming internal resistance to a new product is one of the jobs of a product champion. Internal selling of an idea is often as important as the external selling effort that comes later in the process.

New champions can appear at any level. Some CEOs who are very committed to new products also serve as an occasional product champion. Consider, for example, Akio Morita, chairman of Sony and a committed proponent of new products and a product champion. No one expected the Walkman to become the sensational best seller that it is—no one except Morita. From the start, Morita saw the tremendous potential in the concept. He created and led a ten-member "Walkman team" to develop and guide the Walkman strategy. He turned the Walkman into a cooperative effort, spreading risk and cost across several Sony divisions. He insisted on a unified international marketing approach and on maintaining what consumers would perceive as a reasonable unit price, even if that meant running a deficit for several months after the launch. Morita's vision and commitment were the driving force behind the Walkman's quick introduction (the first sets were introduced less than one year after the conception of the idea). In its first seven years, the Walkman's success is proven—to the tune of ten million units sold.

The importance of a product champion to the success of new product development cannot be overstated. Almost half of the most successful companies encourage new product champions to promote and shepherd new product concepts through the development process. In fact, many companies count on it. As the vice president of a consumer durables company put it, "The product champion facilitates change by accepting the personal risk and making a personal commitment." His counterpart at an industrial goods company agrees, "The product champion is a key element in our decision-making process. Without a sponsor, a new product concept will die. At least one person has to be enthusiastic about a concept to secure funding."

Analyze your own organization structure relative to the type of new products being developed. The structure, support of top management, compensation practices, and leadership all interact to give companies the insight and the ability to manage innovation. Successful companies understand the true meaning of innovation. They realize the difference between maintenance, which generates today's profits to make tomorrow possible, and innovation, which investigates the source of tomorrow's profits. Successful companies that have created the right environment, right culture, and product champions are willing to accept the risk implicit in managing the new product process. They are willing to experiment, to learn, to change—and to fail. For in accepting the risks that accompany reward, they recognize the possibility of failure.

CAREER RISK IN NEW PRODUCT MANAGEMENT

In most companies, there is minimal career risk in new products. Few managers have ever been fired for a new product failure. At times, the risk is subtle. However, a manager who fails in new products may be moved to a lateral position to reside there for several years without promotion. But for the most part, companies neither reward nor penalize new product managers. No extremes exist—just mediocre, plain vanilla approaches to motivating new product people.

Well, its time to reestablish the death penalty and the millionaire's club in corporations. A balance of rewards and penalties will simulate an entrepreneurial environment more realistically. Entrepreneurs do not receive an annual 10 percent salary increase year after year regardless of their performance. More often they hit it big one year and then make virtually nothing another year when high performance is not maintained. Bringing market reality and actual performance of new products back to new product managers' wallets may sharpen their entrepreneurial acumen.

Yet some companies do not consider new products to be any higher career risk for a manager than responsibility for an operating unit. A new product manager will screw up in the new product area and launch a bunch of failures, then get promoted because he or she has demonstrated a high degree of creativity and an ability to get new products into the marketplace, albeit failures. How stupid! Consider the signals that are sent out to the corporation—new products is an area where screwups are rewarded. So companies need to be careful to "unreward" people in the new product field for bad product performance just as they give high rewards for superior performance.

In actuality, the level of career risk *is* much higher for people involved in new products. A lack of results in new products is far more visible to top management. Unlike the regular business manager who achieves only 12 percent instead of the forecast 15 percent revenue objective, the new product manager who does not launch a new product has nothing to show for his or her efforts. Top management is rarely interested in the number of new product concepts in process—it wants to, and should, see end results. Consequently, the new product manager has a greater "failure exposure."

The chance of a career setback or advancement impediment that new product people take is another risk that must be recognized by top management. However, if managers are encouraged and rewarded in a way that makes it "pay" for them to stay in the new product function for a three-to-five-year period, the "don't stay out of the mainstream" syndrome will dissipate and the function will become one that is perceived as a desirable spot.

While top management should always look for the best managers to fill every position, the reality is that there are usually only a handful of great business managers in any company. The new product area should get some of them if the role of new products in a company is an important one. Finding the best managers must underscore any approach to managing new products successfully. However, to attract the needed risk-taking, creative, and analytical leaders most effective in new products, a greater *financial inducement is required.* The financial incentive needs to come up front as well as later on in the process. You cannot put out one single carrot that will not be attainable for three or four years. Some additional shorter-term carrots are also needed to provide a sustainable motivation to new product personnel.

To build an entrepreneurial environment, reinforce the importance of new products, and ensure that the best managers are attracted and committed to the new product effort, a bonus structure should be in place that recognizes the risks, and rewards successful new product performance.

STIMULATING RISK TAKING

Widespread innovation in new products has been noticeably lacking during the past decade. Managers' aversion to risk is understandable when one looks at the compensation practices of most companies. Most corporations tie compensation of its new product executives to a general performance evaluation—a base-salary increase and a semifixed bonus of some type. These practices lead managers to focus on the "bottom line," concentrating their efforts on performing well in the short term. With the reward systems currently in place, managers have no incentive to step out and take the risks inherent in innovative new products. It simply is not worth the risk. Their potential for reward is higher if they continue to introduce less risky, albeit less profitable, me-too products.

Adequate incentives for new product managers, therefore, will be a cornerstone for developing successful new products in the future. Currently, very few companies tie compensation to actual new product performance. But it is exactly this kind of reward system that will breed success. As one industrial-components president noted, "Compensation for new product managers is one of the key problems within our company. This year, for the first time, we have implemented a bonus system tied to long-term new product objectives."

In a successful consumer nondurables company, each new product manager works with a highly entrepreneurially oriented reward system. At the end of three years, if the new product has achieved its original forecast goals, the managers receive 75 to 150 percent of their base salary as a bonus. If the product falls short of its targets, they get nothing. Obviously, sandbagging has to be guarded against, but the impetus for a successful new product launch far outweighs this potential danger.

Why pay managers in accordance with such irrelevant standards as the number of new products developed? The manager should be held accountable for the success of the new product, not just its introduction. Thus, companies that reward risk taking and provide high upside returns for profitable new products will most likely end up in the winner's circle.

The benefits of rewarding risk taking are twofold. First, companies will be able to achieve the balance of high- and low-risk products needed to attain a portfolio of new product types that will provide some equilibrium to the risk equation. Second, incentive systems that reward success provide an attractive enticement to new product managers to remain in the new product development function. Thus, there is greater continuity in leadership as managers are more likely to see long-term products through to commercialization. Tenured leadership also provides for the accumulation of new product experience, an important asset in the new product game.

Moreover, top-management involvement in new products is required to let employees know that management too is sharing in the new product risks. This means that corporate managers need to leave their corner, glassed-in, ivory-tower offices, and move into the trenches with the people actually doing the work. The successful new product development programs, i.e., the ones with the highest hit rates, belong to those companies that have a high degree of *top-management support*. This suggests a top-management team that fosters an entrepreneurial spirit by compensating employees involved in new products according to market performance. For example, a team of managers who are primarily responsible for the launch of a new product, which by the end of year 3 is generating $100,000 in net pre-tax profit and required only $45,000 in start-up costs, might each receive a $5,000 bonus. *Recognition* of some sort is the key.

New reward and incentive programs need to be designed to support and reinforce new product management. Currently, new product positions are not usually seen as long-term, career-advancing jobs. In order to ensure that strong professionals are attracted and committed to the new product effort, the compensation system must recognize the often high-risk status associated with new product work. Bonus systems, whether individual or group, should be created to reward all associated members with clearly defined new product successes.

NEW PRODUCT COMPENSATION PROGRAMS

The incentive system may be based on a percentage of profits generated from new products or even phantom stock ownership in a new product line, but the key is to tie the reward system to actual market performance. Thus, if all of the new products bomb during a five-year period, then there will be *no* bonuses or rewards for the new product team. Nothing. "That's not fair," whines the risk-averse corporate bureaucrat. Well, tough, that's the downside risk that must accompany an incentive system that is performance based.

On the other hand, when the new products launched during the same period end up dropping $4 million in profits to the corporate bottom line and ten new product people get a $50,000 bonus, the perspective on what's fair and what's not will suddenly change. Obviously, the type of person who is content with a virtually guaranteed 5 percent base salary increase and a bonus based on 15 percent of the base salary, will not be willing to move into a performance-driven compensation plan.

Another problem that is often brought up by naysaying managers when they discuss paying on performance is the lack of control that new product managers have over the success of a new product. Is it really the new product team's fault if the sales force does a rotten job of selling, or if competition reduces the price and substantially cuts demand for the new product just launched? It sure *is* the fault of the new product team. Developing a mock-up prototype is not the only activity involved in managing new products successfully. The process calls for taking an idea from the concept stage all the way to commercialization. This final stage includes motivating the sales force to do the proper sell-in; the business-analysis stage includes examining potential competitive responses, and therefore, a contingency plan should have been developed to counteract the competitor's price decrease. Look, we can develop a list a mile long of all the external and internal factors that are not under the direct control of new product managers. And all of these factors can destroy even the best and most innovative new product. But survival of the fittest reigns. If new product people get rewarded on market performance, then they need to manage the entire process. That means taking the responsibility for ensuring that the launch and support programs are being managed effectively, not just grinding through a bunch of prototypes that are turned over to marketing to do with as they please.

Developing new products is a totally different business function from day-to-day product-line and business management. It calls for different skills, different performance measures, different types of risk-taking individuals, and as a result, different compensation and incentive plans. A Midwest industrial products company, nearly $300 million in sales, paid over $500,000 in bonus money to six new product managers in two years. The managers' bonuses exceeded their base salaries. And what had the company received in return? During the previous three years, this group had launched fifteen new products that by year 3 were generating $60 million in incremental revenues and dropping $4.5 million in incremental profits to the bottom line. So the company paid out $.5 million to the people who had provided the corporation with a net increase of $4 million in profits. Not a bad deal. But the point is that it was a great deal for the company *and* the new product team. Both were rewarded; both were motivated.

Three years ago, blank stares filled the room after I had recommended to the top management of a $5 billion corporation that the new product directors should have a bonus program tied directly to performance of new products in the marketplace. When I described the program in more detail, top management suddenly realized that if new products really succeeded and did extremely well, the new product director's bonuses would be more than the divisional president's bonus rewards. Of course, they said this bonus system just would not work. However, within a few months, they decided to *test* a new incentive system for one division. The system linked bonuses to new product rewards. To date, five new-to-the-company products have been launched, contributing over $40 million in revenues. The "test" is being continued.

Compensation practices are one area, in particular, where large corporations can learn from small entrepreneurial companies. Why are the incentive systems so demonstrably different? Bureaucracy and corporate policies driven by staffers rather than managers are eating away at any remains of entrepreneurship in corporations.

Corporations' incentive systems should embody some of the same characteristics of an entrepreneurial environment, for example:

□ Phantom stock investment—New product managers can buy stock options of a new product prior to commercialization. Up to 10 percent of the "stock" can be purchased. The purchase price might be set by total development, capital, and launch costs. Thus, if $800,000 was the "purchase price," a 2 percent ownership would cost an internal investor $16,000. Therefore, if the new product averages $500,000 in net profits during the next five years, the investor's return during that time would be 2 percent of $2.5 million, or $50,000. On the other hand, if the new product generates a cumulative five-year profit of $300,000, the investor's return will be only $6,000, representing a $10,000 loss.

□ Long-range bonus program—A new product manager would receive a bonus in the third, fourth, and fifth years based on the performance of new products launched during the first two years. The bonus might be based on a percentage of total cumulative profits generated from the new product introductions. Of course, if the manager continued to stay in the new products area beyond the five years, new products launched in Year 3 would be compensated for in year 6.

Any type of reward system that fosters an entrepreneurial, risk-taking environment to motivate managers is the real answer—not size of office and 5 percent annual base-salary increases. The best approach to people management is to find out their unique needs and desires, find a way to match those to the company's goals, and develop a bonus system that will measure and reward performance.

Teams can be rewarded as well as individuals. Is there any reason why a five-person new product team working on three new-to-the-world products should not be able to invest $10,000 each in these new products and buy a small portion of the product's "equity"? The level of motivation, dedication, and perseverance to make those new products succeed will be substantially increased by the new product "investors" involved. Let employees share in the risk and the returns as in a corporation. Again, it's time for U.S. corporations to adopt some of the practices of small entrepreneurial companies, using financial rewards to support managers and motivate them to work toward specific company goals.

For example, one compensation plan that has had strong results in a consumer durables company is an incentive system in which two overlapping bonus programs are in place for the six key managers in the new business development area of their $400 million division. First, there is a long-term bonus that is directly tied to actual external market performance of new products. Second, there is a short-term bonus based on internal performance of successful management of the new products process.

The long-term bonus program is initiated one year after commercialization of the group's first new product. Thus, if the first new product does not get out the door until the end of the second year, it will take a minimum of three years for the long-term bonus to even begin to be activated. Once the program is under way, the bonuses will be paid annually based directly on the performance of the new product in the marketplace, for as long as the people receiving them remain in the new product area. As a result, new product managers have the opportunity to earn as much as 50 percent of their annual base salary in bonus rewards if the new product's market performance matches or exceeds pre-commercialization financial targets. Of course, with this type of program, one that is based on achievement of new product financial targets, you have to beware of underforecasting. New product projections could end up being "sandbagged" in order to meet bonus award targets. However, the checks and balances in this approach are such that if the projections are too low, top management will probably not approve the launch of the project anyway. Moreover, with top management involved in the approval process, the chances are few that the projections will be totally unrealistic.

Let's examine how a long-term bonus payout might work. In years 1 and 2, there would be no bonus payout at all; the first new product was launched at the end of the first year, with the result that the bonus program did not start up until the end of the second year. By year 3 only five new products had been launched, one fewer than the objective of six, and revenues were at $2 million rather than the forecast $3 million. So, no bonus. So close and yet no cigar. Well, that's just the way this bonus system works—you either make it or you don't.

However, in year 4 new product revenues exceeded the goal of $14 million by $2 million. Thus, these $75,000 managers were awarded $37,000 bonuses. In fact, for the next two years, they continued to receive roughly $40,000 bonuses since the new product objectives were being consistently met. By the end of the sixth year, each new product manager had received $115,000 in bonus money. In contrast, a more conservative annual bonus program based on 15 percent of base would have resulted in a cumulative payout during that five-year period of roughly $56,000. However, keep in mind that these new product managers did not receive anything in the first three years. Under the more conservative program, they would have received $33,750 during the first three years.

Clearly, these types of award structures are not tailored to bureaucratic clones. They are intended, rather, to encourage entrepreneurial and risk-taking managers to be motivated and recognized for their performance.

Now, with the above example an additional short-term bonus might represent an upside of 20 percent of base salary annually and would be aimed more toward internal performance in terms of how well the process was managed. It might be based on the number of new products by type that made it to different stages of the development process and adherence to timetables and budgets set for approved projects. So there is a buffer against the three-year wait for a long-term bonus. And there should be. This short-term bonus, if performance meets expectations, should accommodate the inherent riskiness of taking the leap to the new product side of a corporation.

Finally, beyond the six new product managers who participate in this long- and short-term bonus program, the division provides annual cash awards to people who have made significant contributions to the overall success of the new product program or specific contributions to individual new product concepts. A $1,500 bonus is awarded to all team members from all functional areas involved with the development of the top three new products introduced each year. There is an additional reward of $2,000 to the five managers from any function who contribute the most to moving new products through the process effectively.

These awards have had a very positive impact on building a team-oriented environment. The major benefit is that they send a signal throughout the company: New products is important and you can be an active participant in the process, regardless of your functional responsibility. They also recognize the efforts of people who do not have direct responsibility for new products and show that managing new products is indeed a multidisciplinary process that requires the services of numerous functional managers during the development life of the new product concept.

Another example of a longer-term compensation program that is tied to new product performance is illustrated by a smaller $150 million company. There are three key new product people: a new product director, a research-and-development director, and an engineering director. These three people devote 100 percent of their time to new product development. Their compensation program includes a bonus payout that is based on pre-tax operating income generated from each new product. They receive, collectively, up to 10 percent of total annual pre-tax operating income from all of the new products they develop. As a result, these three managers each received zero cash in the first two years, a $6,000 bonus in year 3, a $95,000 bonus in year 4, a $125,000 bonus in year 5, and a $145,000 bonus in year 6. Were they motivated? Yes! By year 5, the new products that had been launched during the five-year time period were generating $45 million in incremental revenue and over $2 million in after-tax profits.

At Iroquois Brands there is a revolving venture-capital fund. Managers can tap into funds to develop new products. Neither short-term earnings nor executive bonuses are penalized when ventures start up. The system encourages managers to look for long-term payoffs. The company pays 75 percent of the development costs of approved projects, and the subsidiary puts up the remaining 25 percent. Repayment plus a 10 percent charge begins one year after the new product goes to market—if it is successful. If not successful, the parent company (Iroquois Brands) takes the loss.

At 3M there are two internal ventures for employees: the Alpha Program and the Genesis Program. Both "venture funds" are aimed at building more innovation and entrepreneurship into the company. These corporate funds are aimed at encouraging individual entrepreneurship to shine through corporate shadows. The Genesis Program is for people who have a technology or process idea they would like to pursue. If funding is provided to the individual, then for a given period of time, he or she is able to spend time developing the idea. While the entire corporation truly instills a sense of urgency and importance on new products, not all good ideas can be pursued at once. Divisions have varying priorities with different timetables. These corporate programs are intended to make people feel that even if their respective division does not currently have the time or resources to support these efforts, the parent company will provide permission to develop it. The Alpha Program is similar in nature but is aimed at innovative ideas throughout the company, for instance, a new idea for information transferring, communication linking, cost savings in the area of word processing, or a new business opportunity.

The real benefit of these two programs is the internal message that is sent out to all 81,800 3M employees: Whoever and wherever you are, we at the corporate level are interested in listening to and possibly funding your own individual ideas. It is a powerful message that may indeed work to further instill an entrepreneurial spirit into the company.

In companies with a great deal of entrepreneurial activity and spirit, one of the most important factors in building an innovative mindset is the green light that managers get for individual projects. The perception becomes, "If top management says that's a good idea, we trust your judgment and respect your intuition on this. Therefore, we'll fund your pursuit of it." It is the free-ball phenomenon. That is, even though you may not win the next game, you're rewarded with a free ball. Wow! is the usual response to this type of corporate communication. The motivating benefit is the recognition that it fosters; employees really begin to believe that it is worth it to be creative and innovative. It is not the bonus nor even the funding. It is the personal recognition. By supporting individual ideas, management can bring an entire culture into focus, centering on the emotional and psychological rewards that come from recognizing individuals as valuable "assets" to the corporation.

While inspiring teamwork is an important part of the success equation, equally paramount is the need to recognize and support the emotional needs of new product players. Yet so often, senior managers see new products as a soft, mushy area that they would prefer not to deal with. Besides, in this still chauvinistic business society, the macho attitude toward managing people continues to dominate the bulk of management styles. Consequently, how can managers justify sensitivity? They think that they may be taken advantage of if they show a "human" side. Stay tough and rough is the motto—the motto for the losers of the future.

The successful new product companies are those that invest in people as well as projects. Demonstrating a desire to invest in human resources suggests the value that management places on the contributions that its people rather than plants, computers, or systems can provide. When employees feel that they are the integral cogs of the development wheel, they tend to act more quickly and consistently.

The overall results when innovation takes hold may be invisible or, at least, immeasurable for many years. Managers have to be rewarded for risk taking. Otherwise, they soon realize that their rewards are based on a predetermined point system that only perpetuates corporate mediocrity and apathy.

Managers should be rewarded based on the performance of a new product in the marketplace—without ceilings and percentage increase maximums. The fact is, however, that instead of receiving $75,000 bonuses for developing a successful $5 million new product that generates 20 percent pre-tax margins by the end of year 2, most managers will get the corporate "golden goose" award, a pat on the back, and another 8- or 10-percent annual salary boost.

Thus, as managers begin to mature in the corporate arena, they see that the only way to escape the imprisoning and inevitable annual salary increase is to get promoted or create a job that will require a new job description, and reclassification of compensation points. Is it any surprise that corporations breed career-mongers who end up focusing the majority of their time on internal politics rather than on identifying external consumer needs and market opportunities? It is because of them that the corporate coffers fill up with a proliferation of line extensions, flankers, and new and improved versions of the same old product.

However, few corporate leaders are willing to get off the merry-go-round that entertains the shareholders with quarterly earnings increases and dividend payouts. "Why risk a new product introduction that could hurt the near-term earnings stream?" Of course, dividends and increases in shareholder wealth are the ultimate objective of any corporation but short- and long-term trade-offs need to be balanced. Successful new products *do* propel stock prices. The corporate engines need fuel—fuel that comes from innovative products that fire up conservative managers by breathing an entrepreneurial spirit into their minds.

SETTING A MANAGEMENT STYLE OF DISCIPLINED FREEDOM

Giving individuals who are involved in the new product function the latitude and room to breathe often breeds a greater degree of innovation. But there must be a balance between structure and flexibility, creativity and analytics, teamwork and individual accomplishment, and discipline and freedom.

That is why I have coined the term *disciplined freedom* to describe the management style or culture that provides a balance whereby individuals have a sense of entrepreneurship and creativity and receive enough direction and control to guide their efforts. Achieving this balance is a very delicate and difficult task for the new product leader who is trying to instill in the people that work with him or her an attitude that embodies flexibility with structure. Creativity requires training, a problem-solving focus, and a blend of feeling and thinking. Visions need to be guided—market information and business analysis provide a reality check on creative vision-making and often help to stimulate creativity further.

Perhaps a good way to think about disciplined freedom is by examining Jean Piaget, a twentieth-century educator, who spent his life studying how children and adults learn. His own observations led him to the belief that children who experience play and learning as *one* were better able to develop. The recall and repetition exercises that were prevalent in most school systems were perceived by Piaget as the totally wrong approach. All that was being accomplished was an ability to remember and recall, not an ability to think independently, creatively, or intuitively. How can creativity or intuition be developed in a child if the only "learning" that takes place is playing back what the teacher has already recited? That is not unlike some companies where managers introduce low-risk new products that play back what top management has recited: "We don't want any new product failures."

Unfortunately, many corporate managers do not nurture creative, independent managers. Instead, they breed mindless nomads who wander the corporate corridors reciting things they know will be well received by peers and superiors. Like the pupil who gets a gold star because she spells and recites all the words correctly, the manager who is typically rewarded in a company is the one who has been a "prudent and pragmatic" business manager. Don't you love those words? What they really mean is that the person who does not rock the boat, take risks, express emotion, or demonstrate any guts is the one who ultimately will rise to the top. Many successful CEOs have indeed been able to achieve commendable results through regimented management styles. But the question is, How much more would their companies have grown if they had been willing to take more risks and instill in their management a feeling that failing is acceptable, that mistakes are okay?

In a corporate culture that embodies the beliefs of Piaget, new product participants enjoy the process of new product development. The more they do it, the more they learn, and the more they learn, the more successes they enjoy. That builds self-confidence and means more active listening, cooperative interplay with other functions, and a willingness to take risks. Managers are encouraged to think and act creatively and individualistically. That spells a productive and usually profitable new product program.

Hearing a CEO for a consumer packaged goods company talk about his attitudes on risk taking suggests an understanding of, and sensitivity to, the inherent risk/return nature of new products. However, listening to his managers he hears a different point of view: John accepts the results of any new product as long as it is not a failure—failure is not part of his vocabulary.

Being truly committed to new products takes guts. It requires a constant blend of tenacity and optimism. It takes a mixture of disciplined freedom, active listening, and sensitivity to the difficulty and riskiness of developing new products. A Piagetian perspective on new product management suggests the ability to allow managers to think for themselves—to expect something other than the pat answer, the one that *should* be made. It suggests an environment that respects the views and ideas of everyone in the group. And collectively, the group fosters a vibrant and dynamic team of intuitive, risk-taking entrepreneurs.

GETTING A SMALL-COMPANY FEEL

One key attribute that needs to be instilled in a new product team is a small-company feel—a climate that makes the individuals feel as if there is some room to move, to try some dead-end paths, and make some mistakes. The small-company feel also involves making managers feel as if they have some stake in the wins and the losses. So reward structures that provide a high upside for the successes, and at the same time, a downside for the failures help to encourage managers to simulate the real world of an entrepreneurial environment and steer away from the risk-free world of endlessly flowing corporate funds.

In innovating companies, a number of aspects of the organization's culture and structure provide new product "power"—power defined as market information, human resources, dedicated time, development funds, and capital investments. A new product manager should not have to be constantly "tin cupping" it through the corporate hallways and management offices to get funding and people to help out with new products. A sign of new product commitment is having these resources in place so that a new product manager can focus time and attention on how best to manage and utilize these resources rather than trying to figure out ways to secure them. Of course, then again, "power" must be pursued in a corporation as well as made available. A certain degree of struggle is usually necessary to get the requisite resources.

An important lesson to be learned from entrepreneurs is that typically they are willing to *apply* what they have learned in the past to new situations—even though the situations may be totally new. Past experiences and performance do not restrain the direction and degree of risk taken in the future. Instead, previous experiences are used as building blocks—cornerstones that are put into place when it's time to erect the next new venture. They quickly learn that their most valuable and trusted resource is themselves. Therefore, a sense of self-worth develops quickly, and performance usually does improve. It is getting some of *these* values back into corporations that is so desperately needed not only for new product management but also for general management.

The environment, more than any one person, makes the biggest difference in building a successful new product team. And that is a job for top management. Top management can make or break a successful new product program. It is as simple as that. Of course, even with top-management commitment, many other variables are needed; but without it, the best strategy, process, organization, and resource base will have an uphill battle, similar to the struggle of Sisyphus, the cruel mythical king who was condemned forever to roll a huge stone up a hill only to have it roll down again upon nearing the top.

Building sponsors or product champions is a key technique of effectively managed new product companies. Most companies recognize that more successful new products get commercialized if someone is personally interested in the new product. The best way to generate product champions is to recognize and reward any that may already exist. Once others in the company understand that sponsorship of a product or products is an accepted and encouraged form of behavior, there is a greater chance that additional champions will pop up. Moreover, the signal should be clearly communicated to new product participants that champions are the lifeblood of any new product program. At the same time, the more subtle, thoughtful, yet effective manager should in no way be misled into believing that he needs to suddenly "beat his chest" before he will be recognized as a productive and effective new product manager. A balance is needed; too often, the person who is overdemonstrative in his or her enthusiasm for a product is perceived as an airhead—and therefore loses ground, decision-making power, and execution effectiveness.

Delegating more responsibility and allowing more individualistic decision making are both catalysts in ferreting out new product champions. As long as a certain degree of freedom is felt, the new product player will be more likely inclined to "stand up for their product," knowing that management will support their future decisions. Again, the attractiveness of having a well-defined new product strategy, process, and screening criteria is that the road map is established, and now there is enough latitude for the driver to take a variety of paths, but eventually he or she will arrive at the scheduled destination.

A mistake that companies sometimes make is to try to balance a sense of urgency and timeliness of new product launches with short-term productivity short cuts. Doing the right amount of homework on a category and spending more time on consumer testing and business analysis for a new concept are essential components of the process. As a result, they are not inefficient time usurpers but rather, in the long-run, time savers. On the other hand, a new product concept can be tested and analyzed to death or remain in a test market for so long that consumer trends shift or competition beats you to the draw. While a sense of urgency is a vital attribute of any new product group, priorities must be set to identify those parts of the process that will remain sacred. It requires a new product manager or coordinator to stay on top of the situation and carefully monitor the progression of each new product's trip down the road to commercialization.

The most frequently cited tools mentioned when new product managers are asked what can have the greatest impact on new product success are time, the right mix of people, top-management support, decision-making autonomy, and information. Interestingly, capital and financial funding are not mentioned as the most common impediments to success.

This implies that the culture—the environment and tone that top managers set for new products—is the underlying key to establishing a committed team of players who are focused and driven to get new products out the corporate doors. Time seems to be the most difficult resource to secure and manage— especially when it is the time of functional managers. The existing business brush fires end up getting the bulk of the attention. Thus, management must communicate to all senior and middle managers the need to allocate time to new products—to plan for it—not just react to deadlines and missed schedules. Resource dilution is a sure-fire way to instill instant mediocrity.

The first rule is constant demonstration of commitment; the second rule is appreciation, understanding, and recognition of good performers. Employees are rarely overthanked for their accomplishments. Usually, management takes the attitude that whatever they achieve is just part of the job: "They get paid to do that." Yet motivating people to great heights produces better results and more effective usefulness of time. Doing enough homework early on often provides greater lead time later in the process. A quick market launch may be all the competitive advantage needed in some cases to preempt a competitive entry and establish your product in the consumer's mind.

Even though executives can verbally support innovation, some, in effect, resist it by setting unrealistic objectives and expectations matched with insufficient resources. It becomes a no-win situation for the new product participants. With minimal resources, there can be only minimal progress and little hope that additional doses of creativity will be appreciated. The worst situation occurs when top management constantly oscillates in its support for new products, and frustration and a lack of understanding result. Priorities shift, and two years later, management does not understand why nothing has been accomplished in the new product area.

IN SUMMARY

Making new connections and new associations and seeing problems and their respective solutions are the skills needed to spark creativity. People have to be encouraged to integrate information, intuition, and instinct. To a great extent, the issue is not to invent new tools and new approaches to developing new products. It is a matter of utilizing the existing resource base and existing internal tools.

A series of small changes by a few people can translate swiftly into a major attitude and cultural change throughout a company. It does not take long for others to follow and adopt the newly accepted behavioral patterns. This suggests that just one or two individuals in a company *can* gradually have a major impact on the environment. It takes the committed entrepreneur's stamina to maintain the improved environment.

Rewarding and motivating product champions must

rest upon recognition and compensation programs that demonstrate to the organization the importance of successes in new products. Stimulating risk taking and balancing short- and long-term incentives will move a company more toward a small-company, entrepreneurial culture. New types of financial rewards need to be developed to motivate individuals and new product teams. "Free balls" and "disciplined freedom" need to become part of a company's new product culture.

Risk, innovation, entrepreneurship, and growth are not liberal or conservative issues. They represent an urgent national priority.

8_____

INNOVATING FOR THE FUTURE

Winning at new products during the 1990s will most likely get tougher—not easier. Three major challenges will further complicate the task of managing new products: (1) global competition will intensify, and foreign barriers to American products may increase; (2) large U.S. corporations may be unable to attract and retain an adequate new product talent pool; and (3) domestic entrepreneurial businesses may make further inroads into territory previously dominated by corporations. Corporations cannot wait three or four more years before aggressively pursuing a new product program. The undertaking must begin today. By the time the blueprint and strategy are developed, the team assembled, ideas generated, and concepts screened, two years may go by before any promising new product sees the light of day.

The ten key success factors presented in the second chapter will most likely become the minimum standards rather than ideal standards for new product success. For even with those factors in place, corporations will be facing the additional challenges of competition from foreign new products and encroaching entrepreneurial niche businesses. Also, properly trained managers may be a scarce commodity. Consequently, corporations must make the commitment now to develop new products and not procrastinate until it's too late.

Moreover, companies will need to think globally in the future when it comes to new products. U.S. corporations need to look beyond domestic borders and design new products that meet foreign consumer needs. Offensively, global new product management offers potential growth opportunities in other countries and also serves as an additional source of ideas and concepts that could be adapted to the U.S. market. Defensively, U.S. corporations need to sharpen their new product tooling to be able to compete with the steadily encroaching foreign manufacturer and distributor—both at home and abroad.

Some companies will continue to hide their heads in the sand and object to taking even further risks by trying to launch new products in foreign markets. But the sand is gradually disappearing, and shortly there may be little left in which to hide. As a result, the need to manage new products globally will rapidly become a critical factor for success.

MANAGING GLOBAL INNOVATION

As economists watch the U.S. balance of payments shift drastically, bankers try to keep pace with the incredible acceleration of foreign investments placed in the U.S. As overseas manufacturers continue to spark head-on competition, U.S. companies will be forced to enter global markets—aggressively. This entry must be accomplished by marketing new products tailored specifically for foreign consumers. Companies can no longer launch products that are just extensions of their U.S. lines nor can they afford the luxury of viewing the world as a dumping ground for their excess products.

With Sony Walkmans wandering our streets and subways, it becomes evident that U.S. companies must revitalize innovation in order to survive over the long haul. Looking at the Japanese successes alone—steel, cameras, copiers, microwave ovens, automobiles, and consumer electronics, to name a few, the U.S. company may be nearly overwhelmed by the speed of foreign product penetration into American households.

Furthermore, products that have reached saturation in the U.S. may represent substantial growth avenues when marketed to appropriate global segments. Indeed, introducing competitively superior new products may garner global market positions. The global innovator of the future will be more of an integrator than inventor—the winners will adopt and nurture a globally sensitive approach to new products that combines standardization with product adaptation.

But whether the product is mostly standard, highly adapted, or totally new, top management must be willing to accept the inherent risks and failures intrinsic in new product development. The traditional emphasis on me-too products and margin maintenance of existing products is counterproductive in a global marketplace. And as foreign competition tightens, the unwillingness to take risks will become a millstone.

Achieving a Global Mindset

For years, the leading United States companies were able to claim that they were not only the largest in the U.S. but also the dominant world actors. During the last two decades, foreign companies have nibbled away at the truth of that statement. In the early 1960s roughly 70 percent (thirty-four) of the world's top fifty companies were U.S. based. By 1987, approximately 40% of the world's top fifty industrial corporations were U.S. based.

This shift in the location of industrial giants can be attributed to any number of factors: explosion of imports, spread of technology, scale economies, government support, and global thinking. Perhaps the most significant factor in foreign-competitor growth is their view of the marketplace—their feeling that the entire world is an acceptable market. One can find Japanese cameras in Paris, France, and Paris, Illinois; German cars in Athens, Greece, and Athens, Georgia.

Meanwhile, many U.S. companies remain confined to our national borders. They assume that the domestic market continues to offer growth potential for their products. They do not foresee the rapid influx of foreign goods. Nor does their long-range planning consider the impact of market saturation—just how many cars can an urban family of four own?

To succeed in tomorrow's marketplace, U.S. companies need to change their thinking—radically. Domestic provincialism is hampering their recognition of worldwide growth opportunities. U.S. companies need to develop a globally aware mindset, to think as their foreign counterparts do, in terms of global markets. For instance, a U.S. major appliance company may have a 30 percent market share at home but a worldwide share of only 5 percent. In contrast, a Japanese major appliance company might have a home market share of 10 percent and a global market share of about 8 percent.

Assuredly, there are U.S. companies who have competed in the global marketplace for years. Yet, symptomatically, many of these companies persist in tracking market share only in the U.S. They have little or no information on what their share of the worldwide market is. Seasoned multinationals are moving toward a globally aware and internationally sensitive orientation. This is slowly replacing the historically dominant home-country view. Regional marketing and new product development geared toward specific foreign markets are taking on increased importance.

Yet how many times have successful U.S. managers who were transferred overseas returned to the U.S. as outcasts. "Out of the mainstream" is commonly cited as the rationale for home-country bias. Further, CEOs who maintain a domestically-oriented mindset except at annual-report or financial-analysts time block any global mindset in their managers. Even a move as elemental as developing product packaging with international graphics—enabling the same new product to cross cultural borders—is a step in the right direction.

Terms for Barter/Medium of Exchange

Second, once a global mentality is achieved, U.S. companies might consider a reevaluation of their "terms for barter." Too often, companies have marketed cars, soup, or tractors only to well-developed Western countries—those countries with a standard of living comparable to that of the U.S. After all, they would be the only countries whose customers could afford these products.

It is time for U.S. firms to realize that less-developed countries (LDCs) offer a vast untapped marketplace. While the ultimate consumer in these countries may have little to spend on U.S.-made goods, the gains to a U.S. manufacturer may be enormous in terms of negotiations for essential resources. For example, H. J. Heinz's entry into Zimbabwe illustrates the kind of reciprocity that can become commonplace in dealing with LDCs. Heinz entered into a joint venture with the host country. The company will provide information and expertise in farming techniques and crop utilization to be applied to commercial agricultural products grown in Zimbabwe. In return, the government gave the company the right to market products in Zimbabwe. Heinz has set aggressive growth targets for Third World countries. In 1984 the company had roughly a $100 million LDC revenue base. By 1990 they expect over $1 billion in sales revenues to be generated by LDCs. The company's acknowledgment of reciprocity—give and take—in these countries will aid in the establishment of a long-term relationship and the attainment of the aggressive financial goals Heinz has set.

Manufacturing on a World Scale

Third, companies might consider working within world-scale manufacturing economies, as many large manufacturers already do. With fixed overhead and the economic burden spread over larger volumes, unit costs decline. Money, then, can be infused into new product and process research and development. Instead of reinvesting, U.S. companies have a tendency to drop the cost savings to the bottom line and reinvest only after quarterly dividends have been distributed.

World-scale manufacturing, managed wisely, can provide product-quality reliability and consistency. Quality can be more easily monitored and maintained if the bulk of manufacturing is done in a few centralized locations. This does not imply that housing manufacturing under one global roof is the attractive way to go. Freight costs, entry tariff barriers, and political risk must influence that decision. Worldwide sourcing builds flexibility and provides cost-effective ways of serving global markets. As a defense against severe price competition, worldwide sourcing can be utilized to decrease labor costs and improve import logistics. Less obvious, however, is the possibility that global sourcing can offer an entry into a foreign market.

One of the most expedient modes of accomplishing global manufacturing or global sourcing is through joint venturing. Joint ventures offer a more attractive entry mode than direct investment. Working with a local partner greatly reduces the venture's risk by hedging against political uncertainty; the relationship enhances the opportunity for local funding and provides a source of information on cultural sensitivities.

Traditionally, foreign joint ventures have a reputation clouded by risk and a lack of control; multicountry sourcing takes considerable time to establish and manage. Creeping expropriation is always a threat—a government slowly usurps the business by tariffs, regulations demanding that profits not leave the country, and the like. However, a sound understanding of the country's goals and objectives will provide guidance to a company in determining which countries to choose and how best to serve the new market.

In all, there is much to be gained by viewing the world as your oyster. Nevertheless, the pearls do not come easy. It takes time, patience, and strategy to develop a company that is truly multinationally oriented in new product management.

Your Company's Position in the Global New Product Life Cycle

In order to determine where your own company lies in the global new product life cycle, consider three stages that a company usually passes through before becoming a full-fledged global participant.

1. *Cave Dweller*—The company believes that overseas operations are always second to the domestic market. The primary motivation behind launching new products internationally is to dispose of excess production or increase plant-capacity utilization.

2. *Naive Nationalist*—The company recognizes there are growth opportunities outside the domestic market. The company sees that cultural and market differences exist on a country-by-country basis and, as a result, sees product adaptation as the only possible alternative. Product standardization is not considered for new products. Moreover, duplication of management talent occurs

and no cross-synergies among new products accrue since the company views each country as totally distinct from others.

3. *Globally Sensitive*—The company views regions or the entire world as the competitive marketplace. New product opportunities are evaluated across countries, with some standardization planned as well as some differentiation to accommodate cultural variances. New product planning processes and control systems are reasonably standardized, and there is cross-fertilization between management know-how and technical expertise. The focus is on integration of global activities and is not segmented by country.

Organizationally, a company will most likely restructure as it passes through each of these phases. During each phase, changes in structure, decision making, product sourcing, marketing approach, location of management, and pricing policy move the company closer to effective global new product management.

Determining where a company currently falls in the global new product life cycle is critical for determining the type of approach to take to new product development. In particular, the role assumed by top management in global innovation will be driven by the stage of the life cycle that the company is in.

New product risk decreases as a company moves from one stage to the next. The third phase capitalizes on all of the internal strengths that a company has on a worldwide basis. Thus, there are more competitive levers and internal "assets" upon which to build a successful new product strategy. The objective of any company that currently competes or will soon compete in the global marketplace should be to move through the life-cycle phases as quickly as possible so that it will be well positioned to take on foreign innovation.

Standardization Versus Adaption

While some U.S. companies are well acquainted with the opportunities and benefits of launching new products beyond domestic borders, many continue to be plagued by the inherent risks associated with developing new products for culturally different markets. As the chairman of a consumer nondurables company remarked, "With all of the difficulties involved in developing new products for the U.S. market, how can I afford to swallow the risks of worldwide new product development?"

Manufacturers routinely identify different purchase dynamics, psychographics, and motivation-to-buy characteristics for segments of U.S. consumers. Adding an international dimension may complicate the process of launching new products successfully, but the cornerstone of success is viewing the world as a cohesive singular marketplace, which consists of a variety of consumer segments. All the benefits of standardization notwithstanding, no product is universally accepted without either product or communication adaption. No exceptions.

Even in the U.S., a car shipped to California has different optional and standard equipment from one destined for New York. Coffee served in a Boston restaurant chain is different from coffee in the same chain in Phoenix. In the U.S. there are a myriad of so-called standard products that are adapted to different market segments, e.g., blacks, working women, childless couples, and the elderly.

To accommodate cultural differences, even McDonald's, the epitome of standardization, has made adaptations in foreign countries. McDonald's International serves beer in Germany and wine in France and offers a delivery service in Brazil.

The number of new product failures that didn't take into account cultural differences abound—from Campbell soups in Brazil to major appliances in Japan. These failures can be traced to improper segmentation or poor identification of consumer tastes and perceptions. Thus, successful new product development always requires consumer tailoring to the specific buying characteristics of a market. This consumer tailoring applies not only to the product itself but to the communicated message as well. The degree of adaptation or change is driven by the degree of difference in the product's use. This raises the question of brand-name transferability; does the Kraft name really generate a worldwide brand franchise? Can the communications message to consumers be the same? The answer really lies in the degree to which consumer behavioral patterns differ from one country to another.

Old Products for New Markets

Global new product innovation can be easier than it first appears. For instance, a company may move an existing product from one country to another by making only a few modest changes. New territory may offer a ready market for several existing products. French-made Job rolling papers had served cigaret smokers in France for years. Job brought the same product to the U.S.; they changed the communication message concerning the papers' end use. The result provided a new growth market. In the same way, Perrier positioned European bottled drinking water in the U.S. as a civilized alternative to alcohol—drinking water never sounded so classy.

It is also possible to commercialize a new product "back in time." Treadle sewing machines from Singer and crank cash registers from NCR no longer have wide appeal in sophisticated U.S. markets. Yet some LDCs, as they progress, find these products not only suitable but desirable. An existing product can be a genuinely new product for the LDC markets.

As a company approaches a new market segment, even one in a foreign country, there are options available in the way the company may choose to develop a new product. A company may be totally innovative and introduce a new-to-the-world product, or it may simply, but effectively, modify an existing product. The degree of product adaptation or innovation is influenced by the behavioral shift required of the consumer.

For some products there are no major changes in consumption patterns—gasoline/petrol, for instance, is used for the same purposes around the world. Occasionally, the local market may require changes in octane or lead content, but the product is essentially unchanged; the innovation here is flat. In some instances, slight innovation can alter the perceived benefits of a product. Additions or enhancements to a product, such as the addition of fluoride to toothpaste or menthol to cigarets reflect minor end-use benefit shifts. Nevertheless, the products' purposes remain basically unchanged, and the innovation is not extensive.

Some changes in marketing, rather than changes to the product per se, lead to a perceived change in value. Frozen entrees, boilable pouches, and aseptic packaging reflect increased convenience and shelf stability. This type of product innovation can open vast new markets for a company's familiar products.

Finally, some products—computers, microwave ovens, video recorders, and such—are the result of intense innovation; they provide new consumption and use patterns previously unknown to the market. No matter which approach a company takes to global new product innovation, the requirements of product adaptation must be matched with the benefits of standardization to succeed in the global marketplace. Local tailoring will remain a key component of successful global innovation, but utilizing standardization, whenever appropriate, will ultimately drive down product and marketing costs.

Putting the Pieces Together

The first ingredient for developing a global new product strategy is identification of the role that new products will fill to satisfy the strategic as well as financial objectives of the company—on a worldwide and country-by-country basis.

The global role of new products must first be determined. Will they serve as a wedge to maintain competitive leadership? A vehicle to gain access to a new market? Defend a competitive entry? Should the company's new products build or maintain the reputation of the company as a technology leader? The answer depends on the overall blueprint the company has developed.

Next, screening criteria must be developed that are appropriate to each strategic role for new products. The global marketer cannot afford to set across-the-board hurdle rates. The degree of risk for each new product concept must be assessed on a country or regional basis.

An integrated system for identifying global new products is as essential to global success as basic market research is to domestic success. The networking may be accomplished by information exchanges between the advertising agencies and the sales force, or country marketing managers. Companies such as S. C. Johnson in Racine, Wisconsin, have developed a systematic approach that capitalizes on available sources of new product activity. S. C. Johnson has a worldwide reporting system, which reports monthly any new products introduced into the foreign markets in which it competes. Furthermore, the research-and-development activities throughout the world are also reported to management. This system helps build a worldwide awareness of new product development activities and allows reproduction of suitable ideas with little duplication of effort.

The ultimate key to successful global new product management is establishing a more extensive communications system. And a formalized procedure will help ensure that a constant flow of worldwide new product activities crosses boundaries—cultural, geographic, and functional. Yet only with internationally aware and globally geared top management can U.S. companies realistically preempt the foreign invaders.

The analytical process in managing new products globally is far more complex than for domestic markets. While examining product categories for potential attractiveness is still a key part of the execution process, two added layers of analysis are needed—country and culture evaluations. As shown in Exhibit 8-1, even after some potentially sound categories have been identified, country analysis needs to be conducted that looks at political stability, trade relationships, tariffs, lending sources, risks in the economy, policies on direct investment and repatriation of funds, and the like. Moreover, even if a country passes the acceptability test, far more extensive consumer research is needed, even before idea generation begins to gain a perspective on the cultural nuances and differences that may influence consumer problems and potential need areas. All in all, doing enough homework usually calls for a bit more work when dealing with new products in countries that may be new to a company.

Thus, establishing a global new product blueprint, strategy, development process, organization structure, intelligence network, and so on, will be critical if innovation is to be managed on a worldwide basis.

ATTRACTING AND KEEPING A MOTIVATED, TALENTED STAFF PERSON

The right people to attract to the new product management function are those who get psyched about risky business: people who demonstrate an ability to stand up for what they be-

EXHIBIT 8-1 Global Innovation Requires Country and Culture Analysis

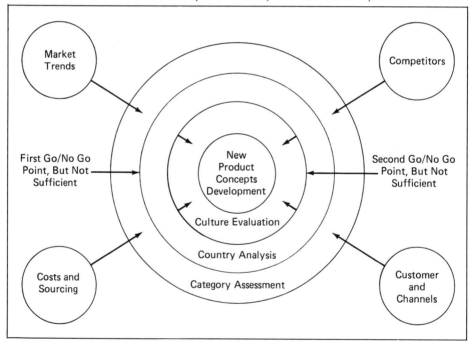

lieve; people who have the gumption to support a new product concept about which management appears neutral; people who are tenacious in follow-through and have risk taking in their blood as well as perseverance and an ability to motivate others.

Nurturing new products along the development process requires skilled product champions. Since new products do not evolve by themselves, special care and cultivation are needed. Sound analysis and adequate homework are part of the success formula, but the right team of new product and functional managers is the other part of the equation.

What kind of person is best for managing the new product process? A renaissance person.

Not necessarily a scientist, engineer, or financial specialist but a seasoned, well-rounded, mature manager with demonstrated leadership skills. The characteristics of the best type of person include:

☐ Has a broad and multifaceted mix of business skills.

☐ Has the ability to make associations from pieces of information.

☐ Juggles numerous people and projects at the same time.

☐ Is sensitive to what other people say; has active listening skills.

☐ Motivates others to action.

A new product manager often has working with him or her functional staff people who typically report to someone else. As a result, the new product manager's primary role is to lead, motivate, cajole, coordinate, and stroke the new product participants. Thus, it is mandatory that the renaissance person (1) has demonstrated people-management and motivation skills—the ability to deal with a variety of functional skills; (2) is an analytics-driven risk taker, has entrepreneurial instincts and comfort with intuition but makes decisions based on sound analysis; and (3) is sensitive to the creative process of idea generation and concept development.

Keeping product champions motivated and new product managers committed to the new product function will be a major challenge for large corporations. Unless an environment can be created that offers something of the same sense of freedom and feeling of accomplishment that are often found in an entrepreneurial setting, large companies will not be able to retain the talent pool needed for new product management.

New product people *should* be treated differently. The level of risk involved in their job is usually greater than in existing-business management. Consequently, companies need to reward and recognize performance differently. Rewards can come in the form of bonuses, financial incentives, investment opportunities, career advancement, exposure to top management, or even status in the company. The key is for top management to demonstrate visibly that new product performance is an integral part of the company's future, and consequently, when successes are achieved, those who were responsible for it are recognized.

THE ENTREPRENEURIAL COMPETITOR

Large corporations need to learn from small start-up businesses. They need to learn that an entrepreneur's optimism, drive, commitment, and dedication all stem from an intense desire to succeed. A sense of urgency prevails; an aggressiveness and attitude reign that have few boundaries (other than the usual obstacle of cash flow). Therefore, the small entrepreneurial business is often highly focused on a single product line or category. It is like a laser beam, with an intensity and power that cuts through competition. The charge for large corporations is to create a culture internally, somewhere in the organization, that replicates this type of environment.

Innovation has become very difficult in a traditionally bureaucratic corporate environment. Hierarchical management structures, reward systems geared toward year-end earnings, and near-term profitability pressures foster a setting that makes managers risk averse.

Innovation is not an act in and of itself but rather a process that integrates management actions with strategic goals. Consequently, rigid organizational barriers that tend to stifle innovation must be broken down and a supportive culture built to reinforce measured risk taking. How will your own company build innovation into the fabric of the company in the future?

A final note on innovating for the future. While no easy answers exist, companies must be willing to commit their best managers to new products if they want the effort to succeed. In the end, it is the people managing the blueprint, strategy, and process who ultimately create the successes and the winning new product companies.

INDEX